The Right Moves

A Girl's Guide to Getting Fit and Feeling Good

By Tina Schwager, P.T.A., A.T.,C.
and Michele Schuerger

Edited by Elizabeth Verdick

free spirit
PUBLiSHiNG®

Works
for kids™

Library of Congress Cataloging-in-Publication Data

Schwager, Tina, 1964–
     The right moves : a girl's guide to getting fit and feeling good / Tina Schwager, Michele Schuerger ; edited by Elizabeth Verdick.
              p.   cm.
     Includes index.
   Summary: Explains how girls can achieve total fitness by focusing on three broad areas: developing a positive self-image, choosing nutritious foods, and exercising regularly.
     ISBN 1-57542-035-X (pbk.)
     1. Teenage girls—Health and hygiene—Juvenile literature.   2. Exercise for women—Juvenile literature. 3. Physical fitness for women—Juvenile literature. 4. Sports for women—Juvenile literature. 5. Teenage girls—Nutrition—Juvenile literature. [1. Teenage girls—Health and hygiene. 2. Exercise. 3. Physical fitness. 4. Sports for women. 5. Teenage girls—Nutrition.]
    I. Schuerger, Michele, 1961– . II. Verdick, Elizabeth. III. Title.
    RA777.25.S39 1998
    613.7'043—dc21   98-9851
                                              CIP
                                              AC

Cover illustration by Mike Gordon
Book design by Marieka Heinlen
Illustrations by Mike Gordon and Marieka Heinlen
Index prepared by Eileen Quam and Theresa Wolner
Author photos by Vicki Sears

This book contains many recommendations for Web sites. Because Web sites change often and without notice, we can't promise every address listed will still be accurate when you read it. When in doubt, use a search engine.

10 9 8 7 6 5 4 3 2 1

Printed in the United States of America

Free Spirit Publishing Inc.
400 First Avenue North, Suite 616
Minneapolis, MN 55401-1724
(612) 338-2068
help4kids@freespirit.com
www.freespirit.com

Dedication

The Right Moves is dedicated to each and every girl who has ever felt uncertain about who she is or where she's going. It was written from our hearts to yours to help you realize the unlimited potential that lies within you. This book is also a special gift to our nieces—Jessica, Rachel, and Kaitlin—for the unique and wonderful girls you are, and for the amazing women you will become.

Acknowledgments

The completion of this book has been a true journey. And now that we've reached our destination, it's nice to reflect on all we have experienced along the way. Words can't begin to describe the gratitude we have for our teacher, mentor, and friend, Joan Jones. Fate put us in your hands, and you helped guide us on the path to this glorious place. We love you! To the members of our weekly writers' workshop—Barbara, Carl, Bev, and Gail: Week after week, you cheerfully took our quizzes and listened to endless details about everything from the Food Guide Pyramid to cheerleading. Thank you for your comments, suggestions, and laughter, and for sharing in our joy when we received our good news (being published!). We look forward to celebrating similar triumphs with each of you. We extend a heartfelt thank you to Laurie Powell, Psy.D., whose contribution to this book goes far beyond the expert information she provided on these pages. You helped inspire us to not only visualize our dream but to go for it with all our heart and soul to make it a reality. Many thanks, angel girl! We would also like to acknowledge the valuable input of Shirley Nelson, R.D., in the completion of the nutrition section of this book. Your suggestions, knowledge, and most of all, enthusiasm, helped us immeasurably in finishing a difficult task. To our friends and family, especially Shannon, David, Todd, and Tom: Finishing this project has been a long process for us, and the patience, understanding, and encouragement extended by each of you helped us stay focused on our dream. Thanks for being such an important and loving part of our lives. And finally, to the power above, around, and within: Thank you for placing this wonderful task in our hands and showing us that we had the strength to see it through. When we came up with the idea for *The Right Moves*, our goal was to create a resource for girls of all ages that would help them feel good about themselves from the inside out and encourage a lifestyle of total fitness. We wanted to provide young women with the necessary tools to build an empowered attitude, recognize the limitless potential that shines within them, and know that anything is possible. We hope and pray the finished product is a gift whose words speak like those of a trusted friend. Faith is a victory.

Table of Contents

Introduction

"To lose confidence in one's body is
to lose confidence in oneself."

Simone de Beauvoir, author

Imagine this: You're lounging on your bed day-dreaming about having a perfect body and perfect looks. You think:

> Wouldn't it be cool to have a fairy godmother who could wave her magic wand and turn me into an oh-so-perfect-looking princess? Then Prince Charming would carry me off to his castle where I'd live in perfect happiness for the rest of my perfect life!

What's wrong with this picture? Well, most of us don't have fairy godmothers. More importantly, daydreaming about the "perfect" body isn't a healthy thing to do. Wishing you looked like someone else (a celebrity, a friend of yours, a model, even a princess) can make you feel terrible about yourself. You begin to think that you don't measure up, which destroys your confidence. Your self-esteem nose-dives and crashes to the ground in a heap. The result? You feel worse than ever, and when this happens, it's harder to pursue your goals, enjoy life, and live the dreams that *really* matter.

P.S. You don't need Prince Charming to sweep you off your feet. Your own two feet can get you exactly where you want to go.

Too many girls struggle each day with their body image and self-esteem. Many see their body as the enemy, obsessing over small flaws and the never-ending "What ifs":

What if I'm too fat?   What if I'm too skinny?   What if I don't fit in?   What if I don't measure up?   What if people think I'm ugly?   What if I fail?

1

Instead of concentrating on developing their inner qualities of character, confidence, and intelligence, many girls worry endlessly about their outward appearance. They judge and scorn their bodies, instead of feeling
good about all of the wonderful things their bodies allow them to do
(dance, swim, run, play, hug). Many young women strive for the "perfect"
body and are very self-critical. They look at themselves in the mirror, convinced that their legs aren't long enough, they're not thin enough, their hips
are too wide, or their breasts aren't the right size. According to Naomi Wolf,
author of *The Beauty Myth:*

- By age 13, 53% of American girls are unhappy with their bodies.

- By age 17, 78% of American girls are unhappy with their bodies.[1]

If you're overly critical of your body and insecure about your looks, you're not alone. As we prepared to write this book, we developed a survey to get in touch with girls and get information on their body image, self-esteem, and knowledge of fitness. We sent the survey to 300 girls ages 12–17. Many of the young women who responded had negative things to say about themselves, especially their weight and appearance. They said they were unhappy with specific body parts (legs, stomach, thighs) or were generally dissatisfied with their looks. When asked to define what fitness meant to them, the girls who took part in the survey focused on the pursuit of the "ideal" body.

---

[1] Wolf, Naomi, *The Beauty Myth: How Images of Beauty Are Used Against Women* (NY: William Morrow and Company, Inc., 1991).

Here's what some of them said fitness is:

"Having a perfect body."

"Being at a weight that makes you feel happy."

They hoped our book on getting fit would offer information on:

"What diets work for losing weight in specific areas."

"Weight loss."

"How to get rid of cellulite."

While our survey was small, the results had a big impact on us. We realized how hard teenage girls could be on themselves; looks and body size are often the primary measure of their self-worth.

For many teenage girls striving for thinness, eating becomes a source of guilt—even for those who don't have an eating disorder.[2] They see exercise as an activity that helps burn fat, rather than something that makes them feel good and improves their health. Many young women spend their adolescence poring over fashion magazines, reading about diets and comparing themselves to models and celebrities. In their quest to lose weight, some girls experiment with diet aids (pills, drinks, etc.), take laxatives, or learn to throw up their food. According to a 1995 survey conducted by the Centers for Disease Control and Prevention (CDC),[3] girls are significantly more likely than boys to:

1. think they're overweight

2. try to lose weight

3. take laxatives, vomit, or try diet pills to lose weight

4. exercise to lose weight

---

[2] See Chapter 13, "Battling Eating Disorders."

[3] CDC "Youth Risk Behavior Surveillance System" (a representative sample of 10,904 high school students in the United States), 1995. For more information on nutrition studies by the CDC, contact: Centers for Disease Control and Prevention, National Center for Chronic Disease Prevention and Health Promotion, Division of Nutrition and Physical Activity, 4770 Buford Hwy., NE, Atlanta, GA 30341; 1-888-232-4674; *www.cdc.gov*

Although many young women focus their attention on their weight and on dieting, they don't necessarily have a good understanding of nutrition, what a balanced diet is, and *what* or *how much* they should really be eating each day. In other studies, the CDC found that:

- Only 1 in 4 girls eats more than one vegetable a day, not counting French fries.

- 9 out of 10 teen girls get insufficient amounts of calcium.

Poor dietary habits can affect a girl's physical development and increase the danger of future health problems. For example, bone growth peaks during the teen years. According to the U.S. Department of Agriculture,[4] girls who don't consume enough calcium, a mineral that promotes strong bones, may not reach their "optimal peak bone mass," putting them at a higher risk of getting osteoporosis (loss of bone mass) when they're older.

Many young people today simply aren't getting accurate information about nutrition and the benefits of healthy eating. New research has revealed that teen obesity is more widespread than ever before. In fact, an estimated 22% of U.S. teens are obese.

Obesity not only causes low self-esteem for many young people but is linked to health problems later in life, including heart disease, high blood pressure, and diabetes. Data from the National Institutes of Health (NIH)[5] has shown that obesity in teens: 1) is the result of a lack of physical activity, and 2) may lead to obesity in adulthood. Teens who develop good eating and exercise habits early on have a better chance of keeping weight off and growing up into healthy adults.

A 1996 report by the Surgeon General[6] shows that teen girls are less physically active than teen boys. Girls who once enjoyed running around outdoors, climbing trees, skating, shooting hoops, doing cartwheels in the grass, and all sorts of other activities become so self-conscious that they no longer exercise, and they may avoid getting involved in organized sports. Girls who do exercise and participate in athletics tend to have higher self-esteem and are more emotionally healthy. They also get the benefits of regular physical activity and develop their strength, endurance, and agility.

---

[4] USDA "Continuing Survey of Food Intakes by Individuals," 1994–95.
[5] NIH "Consensus Development Conference Statement, Physical Activity and Cardiovascular Health," 1995.
[6] You can receive a copy of the report, "Physical Activity and Health, At-a-Glance," by calling 1-888-232-4674.

There's more good news about being involved in athletics—it encourages girls to:

- handle pressure
- be part of a team
- work toward goals
- learn how to win and lose
- be more independent and self-reliant

All these tools can help you now and later in life—in college, on the job, or in many other situations. If you've been hesitant to join a team or get involved in athletics, take a risk and try out for a sport that you think you might enjoy. It's worth it!

When you look in the mirror, what do you see? We hope you see a healthy, active, confident young woman who's excited about life. If this description fits you, terrific! If it doesn't, you can take steps to improve your health, self-esteem, and outlook, and this book can help.

Know what? You don't need a fairy godmother to turn you into the confident young woman you're striving to be—all you need is yourself. Those fairy-tale heroines who supposedly did the happily-ever-after thing didn't have to face some of the stresses that you deal with every day: peer pressure, diet and fashion fads, and pictures of skinny models with the "perfect" body. Images of thin bodies hit you wherever you look: from TV and fashion magazines to music videos and movies. Even when you were very young, you probably had to cope with the images—think "Barbie." This doll represents a totally unrealistic ideal (tall, blonde, long-legged, thin, large breasts). No wonder so many young women today think their bodies don't measure up!

Becoming obsessed about your body and looks threatens your health (both physical and mental). Here's why:

1. **You can't live up to unrealistic expectations.** Young women aren't Barbie dolls, and most girls can't become mega-models. The celebrity "look" is often the result of hours spent with personal trainers, makeup artists, hairstylists, lighting

experts, and—in some cases—plastic surgeons. Photos of models and TV stars are almost always touched up and altered by computer, so you don't see any natural flaws. Trying to be "perfect" like these images is a waste of time. Perfection doesn't exist. *Nobody's* perfect, so why do you think you should be?

2. **Your success in life isn't determined by your weight, breast size, or other physical traits.** You are more than your body parts—you have a mind and a heart, too. Having the figure of a fashion model, a flawless complexion, or a new wardrobe isn't the key to happiness. If you were to wake up tomorrow looking like the perfect girl you're wishing to be, you wouldn't necessarily live happily ever after. Life presents a lot of different pressures (school, grades, parents, boys, jobs, the social scene, just to name a few), and looking good doesn't guarantee that you're equipped to handle every challenge that comes your way.

3. **You might make choices that harm your body.** If your goal is to look skinny or muscular at all costs, you could end up dieting, overeating to combat stress, starving yourself, or exercising too hard. Or you might find that your anxieties about your body weigh you down so much that you're unable to move at all—you become inert and "veg out" on the couch all day, figuring there's no point to joining a sports team or trying any physical activity. All these behaviors can take a toll on your body, your health, and your self-esteem.

What Are the "Right Moves"?

We wrote this book because we believe that you can more successfully face the challenges of growing up into a healthy, self-confident woman if you have a strong body, mind, and spirit.

- A *strong body* means your muscles are toned, you have endurance and flexibility, and you have enough energy for work and play.

- A *strong mind* means you have a positive attitude, can make healthy decisions, are clearheaded and open to challenges, and are willing to think for yourself.

- A *strong spirit* means you have faith in yourself, are in tune with your inner voice, and can bounce back when things don't go your way.

We also believe that you can take some basic steps (i.e., the "Right Moves") to get fit and feel good inside and out. Here are a few of the steps you'll learn about in this book:

- Eat a variety of nutritious foods each day.
- Say no to dieting.
- Choose physical activities for a healthy body.
- Exercise because it's fun.
- Have a positive attitude.

Getting fit and feeling good isn't about striving for perfection (that's unhealthy), obsessing over what you eat, or being able to bench-press 200 pounds. It's about taking control of your own well-being by choosing a lifestyle that includes having a positive self-image, learning about the benefits of good nutrition, and exercising because it makes you feel good.

If you're wondering why it's important to eat right and get fit, here are just a few reasons:

1. **Exercise and nutrition help your physical development.** Your immune system is strengthened (you can fight sickness better) and you build stronger bones. Plus your heart, lungs, and vital organs will be healthier.

2. **Your grades might improve.** Exercise sharpens your mind, so you'll be more alert and may have a better memory. Your concentration will improve, too.

3. **You'll sleep more soundly.** People who are physically active during the day rest better at night. You'll wake up feeling more refreshed and energized.

4. **You can better cope with stress.** Too much stress makes you anxious and restless. Because exercise releases these feelings, you'll be more relaxed and ready to face your problems. Healthy eating can be a stress-buster, too. When you eat a nutritious snack, you'll realize that you're doing something good for yourself, which can improve your outlook.

5. **The benefits of exercising regularly and eating healthy foods can last a lifetime.** If you start taking care of yourself now and keep up the healthy habits into adulthood, you'll probably have fewer health problems later in life. You might even add two to ten years to your life expectancy.

How to Use This Book

You can use *The Right Moves* in a variety of ways. Read it cover to cover and practice what you learn a little at a time; then go back and skim various sections whenever you need a refresher. Or use the book as a resource, turning to a specific chapter or section when you have questions about nutrition or exercise, or simply need a self-esteem boost.

The book is divided into three parts. *Pump Yourself Up* includes ideas to help you develop your self-esteem, learn to accept your body and feel good about who you are, discover ways to pamper yourself when you need a lift, and visualize the future you desire. Use a journal or notebook to do the suggested activities or to keep a written record of the positive changes going on inside you. *Food Is Your Fuel* is all about the benefits of eating healthy foods. Eating right isn't about being rigid or counting calories—it's about learning how to make healthy choices. You'll learn the basics of good nutrition, how to read food labels, how to choose healthy snacks, how to recognize an eating disorder (and get help), and why "diet" is a four-letter word. Just in case you find yourself in a fast-food restaurant or ice-cream place, you'll also learn how to make the best food selections in these and other going-out situations.

The operative word in the *Bodies in Motion* section is FUN—as in having a good time while you improve your health, increase your energy level, and maintain a fit, toned body through exercise. You'll find information on gearing up to exercise, why sweating is cool, what cross-training means, how to handle sports injuries, and more. You'll learn about fun workout ideas (like in-line skating, kick boxing, and yoga), as well as the pros and cons, body benefits, and equipment needed for each activity.

You can choose to get fit. You can choose to eat right. You can choose to look, feel, and act confident. It's up to you. If you have any questions or comments about this book, we're here for you! Write to us care of:

Free Spirit Publishing Inc.
400 First Avenue North • Suite 616 • Minneapolis, MN 55401-1724
help4kids@freespirit.com • *www.freespirit.com*

Pump Yourself Up

"You've got to believe in yourself first.
Take risks and don't be afraid to fall."

Mary Lou Retton, 1984 Olympic gold medalist, women's gymnastics

Quiz

Why Eat Right and Exercise?

This quiz can help you find out how much you know about the benefits of eating right and working out. Write your responses on a separate sheet of paper, then check out the answers on pp. 11–12 and decide if it's worth giving good health and fitness a try.

1. **FACT** or **fiction?**
Girls who play sports do better in school.

2. **FACT** or **fiction?**
Physical activity improves your mood.

3. **FACT** or **fiction?**
A diet low in fat and high in vitamins and minerals, combined with regular physical activity, can keep you healthier.

4. **FACT** or **fiction?**
Physically active girls are less likely to be sexually active at a young age.

5. **FACT** or **fiction?**
Girls who are involved in athletics are less likely to use drugs.

6. **FACT** or **fiction?**
Exercising while you're a teen may decrease your risk of getting breast cancer as an adult.

7. **FACT** or **fiction?**
Girls who play sports are less likely to tolerate an abusive relationship.

8. **FACT** or **fiction?**
Participating in gym class has positive benefits.

9. **FACT** or **fiction?**
Physical activity doesn't have to be strenuous to be effective.

10. **FACT** or **fiction?**
Eating right and exercising now (and for the rest of your life) may mean a brighter future for you.

Answers

1. **FACT.** Female athletes tend to do better academically, receive higher grades, and score higher on standardized tests, according to the President's Council on Physical Fitness and Sports' 1996 report called "Activity in the Lives of Girls."[1] The Women's Sports Foundation[2] reports that girls who are involved in sports have a lower drop-out rate and are three times more likely to graduate from college.

2. **FACT.** In 1996, the President's Council on Physical Fitness and Sports found that regular exercise (three times a week or more) can make you healthier, not only physically, but mentally, too. That's because physical activity can boost your self-esteem, increase your self-confidence, and generally make you feel more positive about your body. Exercise may also help relieve the painful feelings associated with depression and anxiety.

3. **FACT.** Many health organizations (including the Centers for Disease Control, the President's Council on Physical Fitness and Sports, and the National Institutes of Health) have found ample evidence that eating right and exercising can reduce your risk of heart disease, obesity, high blood pressure, some forms of cancer, and other health problems.

4. **FACT.** The Centers for Disease Control's 1995 survey "Youth Risk Behavior Surveillance System" found that the more often a teen girl exercised each week, the more likely she was to postpone her first sexual encounter. In 1994, the Women's Sports Foundation reported an 80% decrease in unwanted pregnancies among girls who play sports.

5. **FACT.** The Women's Sports Foundation has reported that girls who play sports are 92% less likely to use drugs than girls who are inactive during their teens.

---

[1] For more on the President's Council on Physical Fitness and Sports, see p. 260.
[2] For more on the Women's Sports Foundation, see pp. 260–261.

6. **FACT.** According to Nike's PLAY (Participating in the Lives of America's Youth) Foundation,[3] girls who are physically active during their teens decrease their risk of getting breast cancer when they're adults. Exercising just two hours a week may reduce the risk of getting this disease by 60%. Many medical experts agree that a diet that's high in fiber and vitamins, and low in saturated fat, may also help reduce your risk of breast cancer.

7. **FACT.** Nike's PLAY Foundation has found that girls who play sports may be less likely to stand for an abusive relationship, perhaps as a result of the inner strength and self-respect that athletics can help develop.

8. **FACT.** You may hate changing into your gym outfit or having to shower at school, but taking part in physical education classes *does* have its rewards. Gym class allows you to be more active, relieve stress through physical exercise, develop your muscles and athletic skills, and even gain a better body image. But according to the Surgeon General, daily enrollment in physical education classes dropped from 42% to 25% from 1991 to 1995.

9. **FACT.** You don't have to do long, intense workouts at the gym or run marathons to get the benefits of exercise. Moderate physical activity each day—taking a brisk walk for a half hour or dancing like crazy around your bedroom for 15 minutes—can bring rewards. According to the Surgeon General, these kinds of regular physical activities can help teens build strong bones, muscles, and joints; reduce body fat; and increase lean muscle mass.

10. **FACT.** There are so many good reasons to eat right and exercise: 1) a lower risk of disease or chronic health problems, 2) a decreased risk of depression, drug abuse, and sexual activity at a young age, 3) a stronger body and sharper mind, and 4) a more positive attitude about yourself and about life. All of this can add up to a brighter future.

Now that you've got the facts, you can see that nutrition and exercise have benefits far beyond the ones you may see when looking in the mirror. Eating right and working out is great for your mental, emotional, and physical health. So if you're still wondering what's in it for you, the answer is *everything*.

---

[3] For more on the Nike PLAY Foundation, see p. 260.

1
Building Self-Esteem

"No one can make you feel inferior without your consent."

Eleanor Roosevelt, former first lady

Self-esteem (noun): a confidence and satisfaction in oneself; self-respect. Although self-esteem may be easy to define, it's not easy to develop. Why? Because studies have shown that girls start to lose their self-esteem around the time they hit puberty—call it the Mystery of the Shrinking Self-Esteem. Girls begin to worry about their looks, their bodies, what they say and do, who likes them and doesn't like them, whether they're popular or not, and lots of other things. All this worrying takes a lot of time and energy. As a result, many girls become more quiet in class or in social situations—it's harder for them to speak their minds.

In fact, studies done by the American Association of University Women (AAUW)[1] showed that 45% of elementary school girls thought they were "good at a lot of things." That's a sign of high self-esteem. Guess what happened when the girls got to middle school—only 29% of them felt that they were good at a lot of things. And by high school, the number dropped to 23%. Does this mean the girls suddenly forgot how to do all the things they were once good at? Of course not. What happened was they lost their self-esteem. Once teen girls reach high school, their self-confidence may be at an all-time low. Your self-esteem can plummet for a lot of reasons. As you mature, the people around you may begin to treat you differently. Do the following situations sound familiar?

- Boys make comments (positive or negative) about your looks and body. You begin to base *your* self-worth on *their* opinions.

- At at time in life when you're starting to grow and change, form new opinions, and carve out your identity, you may feel pressure from adults to "behave" and "act more mature." Translation: "Be a good girl."

---

[1] AAUW "Shortchanging Girls, Shortchanging America, Executive Summary," 1994.

- Your friends and other girls at school—who are probably going through puberty, too—begin to focus on their looks (hair, makeup, weight, and clothes). It's hard not to get caught up in this new emphasis on appearance.

Suddenly you feel uncomfortable in your own skin. You wonder if you measure up in everyone else's eyes. On top of all that, you're surrounded by media images of beauty and "perfection." TV shows, movies, music videos, magazines, and other media bombard you with their versions of how an ideal young woman should look.

> "I have a very strong opinion that it's important who you are on the inside. It's really sad that girls feel like they have to be this perfect person with a perfect body."
>
> **Alicia Silverstone, actress**

The Role of the Media

Media images of the ideal woman have changed a lot in recent years, depending on the current trend. Today's trend is that young women should look super thin *and* muscular. Runway models have perfected the "waif" look (tall, thin, small breasts). Statistics show, however, that fashion models are approximately 9% taller and 23% thinner than the average woman. In other words, most models are *underweight,* which just isn't healthy. When you see photos of fashion models, remember that computers can do amazing touch-ups and erase any so-called "flaws"—freckles, wrinkles, uneven skin tone, sags, or a hair out of place.

Many female celebrities work out intensively with personal trainers to sculpt their bodies to look more muscular than usual. (Working out *is* good for your body, but many actresses will train for more than three hours a day to achieve the results they want for a part in a movie or TV show. That's overkill.) Some celebrities get breast implants to appear full-figured, and when this "look" becomes the norm, other women want to get the surgery themselves—including teen girls. (Just so you know, cosmetic surgery can be *very* painful. If you get a nose job, your face will be bruised for weeks. Breast implants take a long time to heal as well, and the implants have been linked to health problems. Liposuction means the doctor takes a vacuum and sucks fat out of your body—ouch!).

Teen girls often diet and work out in an effort to look like the images of women on television. Girls Incorporated,[2] an organization dedicated to promoting self-confidence in girls and women, conducted a survey of 2,000 teen girls in 1995 to measure the influence of television viewing. According to their study, about 15% of teen girls are dieting and exercising to look the way TV stars do. With such unrealistic standards of beauty, it's hard NOT to want to change your appearance to match the popular ideal. But take a closer look. The women on TV have a team of makeup artists, hairstylists, clothing consultants, and lighting experts to make them appear beautiful. (Would you really want all those people following you around all day?) Ask yourself if the female characters you're watching on television are strong role models for you, or if they're stereotypes—the sex object, the beauty queen, etc. If you decide that you don't like what you see, turn the TV off. Go outside and look at the beauty of nature instead.

What Is Beauty?

Everyone feels insecure about their looks at one time or another. Even celebrities have had bouts of self-doubt:

Cindy Crawford, model: "When I was young, I had a very crooked smile. I also had a mole on my face, which was not considered beautiful at all. My sisters called me Moleface, and I was very self-conscious about it."

Mariah Carey, singer: "I always thought I was ugly. My best friend was this perfect-looking blond, and I had all this frizzy hair and these bushy eyebrows."

Jacinda Barrett, model: "I was really ugly in school. I had these stick legs and big kneecaps like Olive Oyl. I wanted a bra so bad, but I didn't have anything to put in it."

Bette Midler, singer: "If only I'd known that one day my differentness would be an asset, then my early life would have been much easier."

---

[2] You can find out more about this organization by contacting: Girls Incorporated, 30 East 33rd Street, 7th Floor, New York, NY 10016; 1-800-221-2606; *www.girlsinc.org*

You've heard it before, but it's worth repeating:

Genuine beauty comes from the heart and radiates outward.

This means that every woman, no matter what age, can be beautiful as long as she feels beautiful within her own heart. It doesn't matter if your eyes are brown or green, if you're tall or small, or what your skin color is. The outside is a shell that holds the real you: your essence, your spirit. In order to truly shine, you need to feel good on the inside.

If you doubt this fact even for a moment, look up the word "beauty" in the dictionary. You'll find a definition like this one: **beauty** (noun) a combination of qualities that give pleasure to the sight or other senses, or to the mind. Beauty is a package deal—it's an accumulation of everything from your sense of self to your sense of humor . . . from how you present yourself to the world to how well you treat others. You may not love every single one of your features (few people actually do), but if you work on viewing yourself as a complete person who has strengths, dreams, and goals, you'll begin to feel more comfortable with who you are. Your enthusiasm for life will radiate outward, and other people will notice.

If you're still not convinced, take a moment to think about someone you greatly admire and deeply respect—a family member, friend, teacher, mentor, or role model. The person could even be an accomplished athlete or other public figure. Now look at the following traits and think about the ones that best describe the person you have in mind:

artistic ❧ friendly ❧ kind ❧ silly ❧ helpful ❧ light-hearted ❧ honest noble ❧ warm ❧ caring ❧ athletic ❧ enthusiastic ❧ thoughtful creative ❧ generous ❧ witty ❧ loving ❧ curious ❧ imaginative ❧ clever compassionate ❧ original ❧ open-minded ❧ accepting ❧ independent energetic ❧ courageous ❧ patient ❧ cheerful ❧ trustworthy ❧ forgiving funny ❧ inspiring ❧ supportive ❧ encouraging ❧ optimistic ❧ playful

Blend any combination of words above and what do you get? Bona fide beauty. Look at the words you selected to describe your special person, and you'll realize that the things you admire most about her (or him) have more to do with inner qualities than physical appearance. When your inner qualities shine, people are drawn to you. They like who you are and how you make them feel.

When you're surrounded by images of women who represent the media's ideal of perfection, it can be a challenge to remember that beauty is really all about what's on the inside. Don't measure yourself by the media's unrealistic ideals. Comparing yourself to other girls you know isn't a great idea, either—it can be very self-defeating. You can't compare an apple to an orange, right? Both have unique features and qualities. It's not worth your time and energy to constantly wonder how you measure up to others because you are who you are. You'll never be someone else, and that's a good thing! Besides, Mother Nature didn't intend for everyone to look the same. We live in a world of diversity, and that's what makes it great. Each and every person has unique gifts to share, so instead of trying to fit in by conforming, why not celebrate what makes you different?

To discover your inner beauty, think about what makes you special. Is it your smile? Your songwriting talent? Your way with children or animals? Your determination? As you recognize your strengths, you'll become more comfortable with who you are. You'll find within yourself a beautiful young woman who has the power to be anything she desires.

Raising Your Self-Esteem

Experts agree that you can do some things every day to build a stronger self-image. Try some of the following ideas:

1. **Take good care of yourself.** When you eat right, exercise, get enough sleep, and make time to pamper yourself, you'll feel better on the inside and look better on the outside.

2. **Stick up for yourself.** Don't expect other people (parents, teachers, friends, etc.) to take a stand for you or come to your rescue. If someone or something is bothering you, say so. You'll feel better about yourself and stronger inside.

3. **Set goals and take steps to reach them.** When you have a plan for what you want out of life, you can work toward your own success. Your goals can be big or small, short-term or long-term.[3]

---

[3] To learn more about goal-setting, see pp. 29–33.

4. Relax and have fun! Life shouldn't be all work and no play. Although school, a part-time job, homework, and other commitments will keep you busy, you need to make some time for fun, too. Go out with your friends, rent a funny video, buy a joke book, play around outside, and laugh a lot. You'll feel better and happier. (According to scientists, laughter increases your breathing rate, muscular activity, heart rate, and other body functions. In other words, giggling is good for you.)

If you're feeling really down about your looks, your body, or any other part of you, take a moment to think about why.

- Are you setting impossible standards for yourself? (*Quit it!*)

- Do you expect to be "perfect"? (*There's no such thing.*)

- Are other people making you feel bad about yourself? (*If they are, talk to them about how they make you feel. Be honest. Maybe they aren't even aware of how their actions affect you. If talking it out doesn't help, you're better off staying away from these people.*)

- Are you being influenced by the media? (*Avoid TV shows that make you wish you looked like someone else. If you buy fashion magazines, don't let yourself fall into the trap of comparing yourself to the images on the pages.*)

Above all, keep in mind that you're more than your looks. You have your own dreams and ambitions, special qualities, unique gifts, and one-of-a-kind ideas. Make the most of them!

Some days you may feel like your self-esteem is going down the drain (or maybe you feel this way most days). If you're having a self-esteem "leak," you can do lots of things to help yourself. Here are a few ideas:

- Get a piece of paper and make a list of all of your positive attributes. What are your talents? What special things do you do for others? What makes you unique? If writing this kind of list seems impossible, ask a family member or trusted friend to help you. You may be surprised at all of the wonderful things they have to say about you! Keep the list in a handy place so you can reach for it whenever you need a pick-me-up.

- Practice saying positive things about yourself. Instead of saying "I hate my looks," "I'm such a loser," or "I look terrible today," use statements that will boost your self-esteem: "This outfit looks nice on me," "I'm good at soccer," "My friends really care about me."

- Store good feelings in a self-esteem bank.[4] Here's how: 1) Write down five things you did today that make you feel proud. 2) Do this every day and store the list in a special place. 3) Read through your lists any time you need a self-esteem boost.

- Find a female mentor or role model—an adult relative, a teacher or someone else at your school, or a family friend. This person can give you advice and be a friendly ear when you need one. Or get a big sister (an adult volunteer with the Big Brothers/Big Sisters program). You can contact this organization at Big Brothers/Big Sisters of America, National Office, 230 North 13th Street, Philadelphia, PA 19107; (215) 567-7000.

- If you're really feeling down, turn to an expert for help. You can find a Teen Clinic in the Yellow Pages, or talk to your school counselor or school social worker. For further help, get a referral for a therapist who specializes in helping teen girls.

---

[4] From *Stick Up for Yourself! Every Kid's Guide to Personal Power and Positive Self-Esteem* by Gershen Kaufman and Lev Raphael (Minneapolis: Free Spirit Publishing Inc., 1990).

Self-Esteem Resources

You can find lots of books and Web sites that are specially designed for girls. Many of these resources discuss self-image problems and offer information on how to improve your self-esteem.

Books

The Body Project: An Intimate History of American Girls by Joan Jacobs Brumberg (NY: Random House, 1997). This book was published mainly for adults, but it's got tons of information that will help you realize why so many teen girls today are having a self-image crisis. The author puts a historical perspective on girls' body images and their unhealthy attitudes toward their appearance.

Brave New Girls: Creative Ideas to Help Girls Be Confident, Healthy, & Happy by Jeanette Gadeberg (Minneapolis: Fairview Press, 1997). Tons of activities, tips, ideas, and advice will help you learn how to look in the mirror each day and say "I like myself a lot, thank you very much!"

The Girls' Guide to Life: How to Take Charge of the Issues That Affect You by Catherine Dee (Boston: Little, Brown and Company, 1997). This girl-friendly guide to figuring out life is filled with tips on looking out for #1 (you!), feeling great about being female, and growing up to be confident, self-assured, and successful. It includes sections on developing a winning attitude about athletics and on how NOT to be influenced by how women are portrayed in the media.

Reviving Ophelia: Saving the Selves of Adolescent Girls by Mary Pipher, Ph.D. (NY: Ballantine Books, 1994). This landmark book by a clinical psychologist explores the reasons why so many girls today are dealing with depression, eating disorders, addictions, and other problems—all of which spring from a loss of self-esteem and self-worth (as the result of a "girl-poisoning" culture). The book is filled with fascinating stories of real girls.

Web sites

A Girl's World Online Clubhouse
www.agirlsworld.com/
Here you'll meet Amy, Geri, Rachel, and Tessa—different girls with different personalities. You can visit their rooms, find out about their likes and dislikes, and learn what they think about various issues. You'll also find career ideas, advice columns, cool quizzes, a chat room, fun and informative articles, links, and more.

Club Girl Tech

www.girltech.com

Founded in 1995 by a woman who develops software, Girl Tech's mission is to encourage girls in the area of technology by creating products and services just for them. Girl Tech is devoted to raising girls' awareness of and confidence in using technology. Visit this site to find information about inventors, athletes, and adventurers—all girls and women. Check out their chat room, book and movie reviews, celebrity interviews, games, "girl-powered" search engine, and other fun stuff—and then let them know what you think!

!Girl Power! Campaign Homepage

www.health.org/gpower/

This is the homepage for Girl Power!, the national campaign sponsored by the U.S. Department of Health and Human Services to help encourage and empower girls to make positive choices and make the most of their lives. Here you'll find lots of helpful tips: ways to increase your Girl Power!, ways to feel better about yourself (great for when you're having a self-esteem crisis), health and safety tips, and much more. They're always adding more fun stuff, so keep checking in to see what's new.

The Just For Girls Web Site

www.girlscouts.org/girls/

Sponsored by the Girl Scouts of the U.S.A., this site offers tons of tips, strategies, stories, answers, games, and ideas to inspire and entertain you. You'll find information about their new initiative GirlSports,® as well as fitness tips, book reviews, a pen-pal network, an advice column (with helpful suggestions from a mother/daughter team), science and technology Q & A's, self-help information, suggestions for staying healthy in body and mind, links to other sites for girls, and much more.

New Moon Magazine/HUES

www.newmoon.org

This is the online version of *New Moon: The Magazine for Girls and Their Dreams.* Written by, for, and about girls, it includes poetry, artwork, an advice column, news stories, essays, links to other sites, and more. Check out the "Girl Guidelines" page to find out how you can get involved. You can also get information about *HUES* (Hear Us Emerging Sisters), a magazine for high school and college women, published by the people who bring you *New Moon.*

The T-Room

www.troom.com/

Sponsored by Tampax, this site features interviews with inspiring athletes (all girls and women), a Q&A page where you can get answers to the important (and sometimes embarrassing) questions on your mind, health information especially for girls, an advice column, a pen-pal club, quizzes and trivia questions, links to other sites for girls, and much more.

2
Staying Positive

"The courage to soar to great heights is inside all of us."

Kerri Strug, 1996 Olympic gold medalist, women's gymnastics

A positive attitude works like magic. As long as you believe in yourself, you can make changes, accomplish your goals, and feel good about who you are. You've got to think like a winner because attitude is everything.

When you're coping with puberty, it can be difficult to stay positive. Your body is developing in new ways, and your emotions are more intense. Peer pressure, parents, school, and a part-time job can add to the stress you're already handling. You may be feeling confused, uncertain, and inadequate, but you're definitely not alone. It's normal to feel insecure about all the changes taking place in your life. The fact is, the transition from teenager to woman can be scary and confusing.

Why Think Positive?

Thinking positive elevates your mood and can help you feel better. Have you ever been around someone who constantly puts herself down or complains about everything from bad grades to her wardrobe? What a drain! It's much easier to be around a person who has a positive attitude than someone who's negative all the time.

Are you an optimist or a pessimist? An *optimist* tends to look on the bright side of things, finding the good in almost any situation. *Pessimists,* on the other hand, see potential problems in almost every situation. Some experts say that the world needs both kinds of people—optimists offer encouragement, while pessimists are more cautious. But if you're *always* pessimistic, you may not be very happy. You might decide not to take many risks because you've predicted your own failure from the start. Your inner critic may be making you think these kinds of things:

- I'm not sure I can do it well enough, so why try?

- It will never happen anyway.

- It's too much work.

- I could never do that!

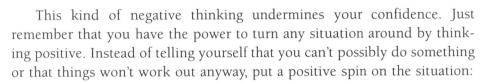

This kind of negative thinking undermines your confidence. Just remember that you have the power to turn any situation around by thinking positive. Instead of telling yourself that you can't possibly do something or that things won't work out anyway, put a positive spin on the situation:

Change This:

"I'm no good at sports."

"It's not worth the risk."

"What if people think I'm a failure?"

Into This:

"Sports are fun, and I can find one I'm good at."

"I'll give it my best shot and see what happens!"

"It's what I think of myself that really counts."

In other words, tell yourself that you'll score a basket in the next game or pass the big history test, and you create the chance to make it happen. When you have confidence in your abilities, you'll be more likely to work harder and achieve results you can be proud of. This is called the power of positive thinking.

> "Just as you can strengthen muscles by using them, you can strengthen positive thoughts by thinking them. Positive thoughts are sometimes called affirmations. Create a positive statement about yourself, then write it down, read it, and say it out loud. Soon your positive thoughts will be strong enough to compete with your negative ones."
>
> **Dr. Laurie Powell, psychologist**

Following are some examples of self-defeating put-downs and ways to turn your thinking around. See what a difference positive thinking can make!

Old Attitude	New Outlook
I'll never have a good body.	I'm excited to exercise and eat right so I can look and feel my best.
My life is so boring.	My life can be as exciting as I want it to be. It's up to me.
I can't believe I did something so stupid. I can never show my face again.	Making mistakes is part of being human. I'll learn from what happened and move on.
It's too hard to get in shape.	Choosing fun physical activities takes the "work" out of working out.
I'll never get straight A's, so what's the point in trying?	I'll give good grades my best shot.
I'm not pretty enough.	My inner beauty is a mixture of many unique qualities and talents.
I'm so unpopular.	Having good friends who care about me is more important than being popular.
I won't be cool if I don't do what everyone else is doing.	I won't be afraid to believe in myself and to just be me.
There's nothing about me that says I'm special.	I love it that there's no one else in the world exactly like me.

Embracing change is exciting, but new options can seem scary and uncomfortable at first. You may not be #1 at everything you try. If you're a total goof at first, so what? Keep trying and give yourself the same support and understanding that you'd offer your friends if they were trying something new. As you begin to take your enthusiasm for exploration to the limit, you may make some wonderful discoveries about yourself, such as:

• hidden talents

• new interests

• skills you'd like to improve

• things that make you happy

You've got nothing to lose by thinking like an optimist. The trick is to make positive thinking feel natural. For some people, changing old ways of thinking takes a long time, so don't expect yourself to change overnight. As you try new ways of thinking, keep the following do's and don'ts in mind:

DON'T focus on what other people might think of you.
DO concentrate on deciding what *you* think of *them*.

DON'T try to be someone you're not.
DO remember that you're only trying to change old ways of thinking—not become someone else altogether.

DON'T blame yourself when something goes wrong.
DO realize that people make mistakes and that life doesn't always turn out exactly as planned. Learn from your mistakes.

DON'T expect perfection.
DO realize perfection isn't possible. (Give yourself permission to make mistakes and *not* be good at everything.)

DON'T question your worth as a human being.
DO remember that you're a unique and special person who has a lot to offer the world.

1ST

For
Being
My
Best

Handling Puberty

When you're going through puberty, it can sometimes seem impossible to be positive and to have high self-esteem. That's because your body is undergoing major physical changes, and your emotions may go up and down like crazy—also known as "mood swings."

The physical changes you may be experiencing are a normal part of life, and they'll probably take place over a period of several years—not all at once. Maybe your body hasn't started to go through the changes of puberty and you're feeling like you're the only girl among your friends or classmates who isn't developing. You may be stressed out and anxious about when you'll catch up to everyone else. Don't worry. Some girls don't get their period until later in their teens, and there's nothing wrong with that. Your turn will come.

If you're having trouble dealing with the ups and downs of puberty, keep the following things in mind:

1. **The changes are natural.** When you go through puberty, your body shape changes dramatically. Your breasts get bigger, you gain more weight around your hips and stomach, you grow taller, and your percentage of body fat increases. These are the normal body changes of puberty, which prepare you for menstruation, pregnancy, and childbirth. You aren't "getting fat"—you're becoming a woman.

2. **Girls everywhere go through this.** You don't have to feel like you're the only one who's insecure about the physical and emotional changes of puberty. Most girls get their first period at around age 12 or 13, but many start as early as 10 or in their late teens (there's no absolute "right time"). All around the world, other girls of all ages are experiencing or will experience the same things as you.

3. **You don't have to go through puberty all alone.** You can talk about the changes with a friend or an adult you trust (your mom, an aunt, a big sister, or your mentor). You can also find some great books about getting your period and dealing with puberty. You'll find some suggestions on p. 27.

Books

The Information Please Girls' Almanac by Alice Siegel and Margo McLoone (Boston: Houghton Mifflin Company, 1995). This book covers all you need to know about what happens during puberty and ways to take care of your body.

Our Bodies, Ourselves: A Book by and for Women by the Boston Women's Health Book Collective (NY: Simon & Schuster, 1996). A classic! Revised and updated for the 1990s, this guide features some of the most up-to-date information you can find on women's bodies and health.

The Period Book: Everything You Don't Want to Ask (But Need to Know) by Karen Gravelle and Jennifer Gravelle (NY: Walker, 1996). Karen and her teenage niece, Jennifer, explore the physical, emotional, and social aspects of getting your period. Sensitive and practical, this guide offers answers to the questions that you might be too embarrassed to ask.

What's Happening to My Body? Book for Girls: A Growing Up Guide for Parents and Daughters by Lynda Madaras (NY: Newmarket Press, 1987). An oldie-but-goodie packed with tons of information about the physical and emotional changes of growing up.

At puberty, the hormones (chemicals in your brain and bloodstream) in your body increase, and the chemical reactions may cause mood shifts and intense emotions. Have you experienced any of the following feelings recently?

- a crying spell that came out of nowhere

- an overwhelming crush on someone

- a sudden flash of anger

- worries about the future

- anxiety about everything from grades to boys to the environment

- intense happiness about something good that happened to you

27

These emotions are completely normal (you might even experience *all* of them in one day, especially during the week before your period). During the week before your period, you may get symptoms of PMS—or premenstrual syndrome—which include cramping, irritability, fatigue, and sadness. The emotional changes can be a wild roller-coaster ride.

You can take steps to balance your emotions. Experts agree that regular exercise[1] is an excellent way to improve your outlook and elevate your mood. When you exercise, your brain produces a chemical called serotonin, which influences your mood and the amount of energy you have. If your levels of serotonin are too low, you're likely to feel tired and cranky. To raise your serotonin level, you need to work out moderately three or more times a week. (TIP: You'll feel happier and more energetic if you exercise consistently—not just once a week or a few times a month—because your serotonin level will stay constant.)

A diet that includes lots of fresh, wholesome foods[2] raises your energy level and helps stabilize mood swings. But sometimes it's hard to think about eating a healthy salad when your taste buds are crying out for an extra large pizza and a chocolate shake. What causes these cravings? Sometimes food cravings are a result of stress, anger, and other feelings. Food has a deep emotional connection for most people. Sometimes you eat not to satisfy hunger but to block out painful emotions. Because food *tastes* good, you temporarily *feel* good while eating it. So if you have a sudden and unexplained need to eat macaroni and cheese ("comfort food"), ask yourself whether you're truly hungry or if something might be bothering you.

Although puberty might cause uncomfortable physical and emotional changes, you can still practice positive thinking. Decide that you want to be happy, and you're taking a step toward achieving this goal. Following are a few tips for feeling good:

1. **Believe that you deserve to be happy.** Don't feel guilty about feeling good. Happiness is a choice that's yours to make.

2. **Don't be afraid to feel good.** Just because something good happens to you doesn't mean something bad will naturally follow.

---

[1] You'll learn more about exercise in Part Three, "Bodies in Motion."

[2] You'll learn more about nutrition in Part Two, "Food Is Your Fuel."

3.   **Enjoy each moment.** If you make yourself wait until certain conditions are met (for example, "I won't be happy until I can lose some weight" or "I'll finally be happy once I get a boyfriend"), you're postponing your own happiness. Why wait for something you can have right now?

4.   **Accept the bad things that happen and move on.** Why beat yourself up over a mistake you made? Why tell yourself that the bad thing that happened will make you unhappy forever? Get your painful feelings out in the open instead of bottling them up, then *move on.* Recognizing and acknowledging your feelings is good for you; dwelling on them isn't. If you're sad, cry. If you're mad, punch your pillows and scream (not *at* someone, though) until you start to feel a little better. Talking to someone about your emotions helps, too.

 ## Book

Your Emotions, Yourself: A Guide to Your Changing Emotions by Doreen Virtue, Ph.D. (Los Angeles: Lowell House Juvenile, 1996). This reassuring guide explains mood swings, stress, emotions, and why all of these things can make you feel crazy. You'll learn how to understand your emotions, express them, and feel good about yourself, too.

> "Once you get over that peak of puberty, you hit a nice stride."
>
> **Claire Danes, actress**

Setting Goals

Your future is before you, a blank canvas ready for you to start painting. So much awaits just over the horizon . . . promising opportunities and things you've always wanted to do but have been too scared to try. Sometimes envisioning what the future holds can be overwhelming, especially if all you see is the big picture and you can't figure out how to get there. In order to take your vision of what lies ahead and shape it into a form you can live with, it's important to:

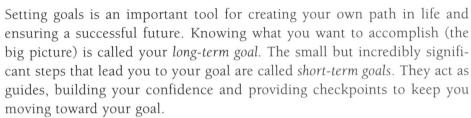

1. Define your goals.

2. Put your dreams into action.

Setting goals is an important tool for creating your own path in life and ensuring a successful future. Knowing what you want to accomplish (the big picture) is called your *long-term goal*. The small but incredibly significant steps that lead you to your goal are called *short-term goals*. They act as guides, building your confidence and providing checkpoints to keep you moving toward your goal.

You'll need to figure out the best way to fit any new steps into your day-to-day life (whether you're changing old habits, starting an exercise program, learning to eat healthy, or any other goal). Making changes is a slow, gradual process—it's not like working on a computer where you type in some stuff and *voilà,* input complete. After all, you're human, not a machine. Changing your eating and exercise habits and gaining a good sense of self-esteem is more like breaking in a new pair of shoes—things feel a little uncomfortable at first, but the more your wear them, the more they begin to take on the shape of your foot. Eventually, you'll feel so comfortable with the positive changes in your life that you'll stop thinking about how "new" they really are.

Planning and patience are two things that will help you reach your goals. If all you think about is what you *ultimately* want, you may never get there, so break your long-term goal into realistic, smaller steps (short-term goals). You may want to keep a Goals Notebook so you can track your progress. This notebook can be a place for writing down each goal, the steps you plan to take, your target dates for reaching your goals, and anything else that will help you. If you want, you can put other inspiring things in your notebook—quotes by famous risk-takers, daydreams about your future, encouraging messages from your family and friends, and tips on how to stay motivated and succeed.

When setting goals, you can use the following ideas to jump-start your own. Record the steps you need to take and your target dates, and soon you'll be on your way to reaching your goals.

1. My goal . . .

2. My target date for reaching it . . .

3. The first step I need to take . . .

4. My target date for taking the first step . . .

5. The second step I need to take . . .

6. My target date for taking the second step . . .

7. The third step I need to take . . .

8. My target date for taking the third step . . .

9. Other steps might include . . .

10. My target dates for taking these steps . . .

11. My ideas for staying on track . . .

12. Potential roadblocks . . .

13. How to deal with the roadblocks . . .

14. People who can help me along the way . . .

These five tips can help you plan your goal-setting/goal-reaching strategy:

1. Set realistic goals.

Say you make it your goal to run a marathon, but you consider jogging about as fun as a trip to the orthodontist. Your goal isn't realistic because you won't enjoy taking the steps to reach it. Not sure what excites you? Take some time to think about your options. Join a new club, take an exercise class at your local YWCA, find a hobby, or volunteer to pitch in for a worthy cause. You might uncover a hidden interest or talent.

Drastic adjustments in your lifestyle will lead to frustration if you can't stick to your plan; changes that occur gradually are more likely to be lasting. What you strive for should be something that you would truly like to attain—something that not only interests you but also inspires you and makes your spirit race. It's okay to shoot for the moon, just keep one foot on planet Earth.

2. Re-evaluate your goals regularly.

Nothing is set in stone when it comes to pursuing a dream. Halfway to achieving your goal, you may look at where you are and decide that you're headed in the wrong direction. It's okay to change your mind. For example, say you've always wanted to become a ballerina. You take dance classes, only to discover that performing pliés is a pain in the patella, and twirling on your toes is an impossible feat. Don't give up your dream. Take some other dance classes like tap or hip hop. You may rediscover your love of dance and music, but to a different rhythm.

Be willing to bend. Adjust your long-term goal so it still resembles what you've always wanted but fits you to a "T." Setting short-term goals will really help you out. They give you a reason to pause along the way to evaluate things, catch your breath, redirect your energy, or change your mind altogether. Successfully accomplishing small steps toward your long-term goal keeps you motivated to continue. And if your path takes a detour, go with it! The ultimate destination may be better than you ever imagined.

3. Be aware of potential pitfalls.

Roadblocks are natural on the path to accomplishing your goals. These obstacles can come in all shapes, sizes, and severities (a sports injury, doing poorly on an exam, or a major fight with your parents). How would you help a friend who's having trouble dealing with the challenges that life is throwing her way? Probably with an understanding hug and some words of encouragement. When unforeseen circumstances slow you down on your path to success, don't give up. You may discover that an obstacle is really a gift in disguise.

Another way to deal with roadblocks is to ask for help. Asking a friend, relative, teacher, mentor, or clergy member for advice or encouragement when you get stuck is NOT a sign of failure. It actually takes a strong person to reach out for a helping hand. Someone may offer you a new perspective or provide the boost you need to keep on going. The path to your goal may not always be smooth, but every pothole, speed bump, and detour provides a valuable learning experience.

4. Listen to your body.

Ever heard the phrase "gut feeling"? Your body responds physically to what you think and feel. As you pursue your dreams, you may experience physical sensations such as sweaty palms, a racing heart, or a nervous stomach. These feelings are your body's way of talking to you. Your body could be saying "Whoa! This is more than I can handle . . . back off," or maybe "Yikes! Pretty scary . . . but exciting, too." Learn to listen to what your body is telling you. If something doesn't feel right, a change of plans may be in order. Then again, an adrenaline rush may help recharge you and give you the needed push to see things through.

5. Stay positive.

Never give up! Everyone stumbles and falls along life's way. Reaching your goal may end up taking much longer than you expected. But no matter what, keep on going. Tell yourself that one way or another, you're going to do what you set out to do. If a fear of failure or a negative attitude is interfering with your momentum, brush up on your self-confidence strategies. Surround yourself with positive, motivating messages—magazine clippings that lift your spirits, little notes with empowering reminders, favorable comments from teachers, a list of your strengths. Keep inspirational items like these handy so you can see them every day. Tape them to your mirror, on the refrigerator, or inside your locker.

3
Be Good to Yourself

*"I just love the peace and quiet when I can
be alone with my thoughts."*

Amy Grant, singer

When you feel sad, lonely, worn out, stressed, or fed up, you've got to work extra hard to hold on to a positive attitude. Even the most confident, strong, and upbeat person can have a down day. But taking comfort in a huge slab of chocolate cake isn't the answer; nor is "vegging out" on the couch for a week.

Instead of getting bogged down in gloomy, negative feelings, direct your energy toward solving the problem. Knowing that you're taking action to change things for the better is very empowering. To boost your spirits in the meantime, take a few moments to pamper yourself, using the ideas below or creating some of your own. Indulging yourself can be totally uplifting.

A Dozen Ways to Pamper Yourself

1. Have a "spa" slumber party.

Getting a healthy glow from head to toe may be the perfect antidote to your dreary mood. Invite a friend or two for a sleepover and spend time giving each other manicures, pedicures, or facials. Be as extravagant as your mood demands and your budget allows. Products for your skin, hair, and nails come in every fragrance, formula, and price range. While you're basking in your homemade spa, snack on some healthy treats like fresh fruit, air-popped popcorn (skip the butter), and herbal tea or mineral water.

If you'd rather spend time alone, take a warm bubble bath and send your bad mood down the drain. Follow up with a foot massage. Pampering your body makes you feel good inside and out.

2. Write on.

Transfer all that clutter—negative thoughts, worry, self-doubt, whatever—from your head to paper. Writing down your personal feelings is a healthy way to acknowledge and release them. Start a journal and make a list of your accomplishments, hopes, dreams, and fears. Journal writing helps you get in touch with your feelings. It also enables you to look back on your thoughts at a later date and say, "Hey! I didn't think I could overcome that obstacle, but I did—and I can do it again."

3. Plant herbs or a garden.

Tending to nature's greenery is a very calming experience. Try growing houseplants or herbs in a small pot or window box, or plant a vegetable garden. Homegrown herbs are flavorful additions to salads and sauces, and fresh-picked veggies make great snacks. Plant some flowers in a small garden plot and watch them blossom. As you celebrate nature's creations, remember that one of them is you.

4. Splurge on a little special something.

Buy yourself an inexpensive present to brighten your day—a cool pen, a funky pair of socks, a hair clip, whatever you want. You don't need to spend a lot to lift your spirits. Or use your imagination to come up with something special that's totally free. Why not pick a flower from your garden and put it in a vase in your room? Tear out scented perfume ads from a magazine and use them as sachets in your dresser drawers. Or update your picture frames with recent photos of your family and friends and, for a personal touch, add clever captions to each one.

5. Awaken your senses.

Aromatic scents from candles, incense, oils, bath beads, or lotion can be a delightful way to improve your mood. Many people believe that "aromatherapy" can alter your emotional state by stimulating certain responses in your brain. Choose fragrances intended to calm you or energize you, and bask in their soothing benefits.

6. Read for pleasure.

Allow your imagination to explore new horizons with a piece of classic literature, the latest bestseller, or a fun and entertaining magazine. Find a relaxing place to read—under a tree, in a big comfy chair, or in front of the fire—and lose yourself in the pages.

7. Let your inner artist loose.

Expressing yourself through color, brush strokes, lines, and textures is a great way to clear your mind and focus your energy. Don't worry if you don't have much artistic talent. Grab some paintbrushes, markers, crayons, or clay and go wild! Your masterpiece doesn't have to be museum-worthy to make you feel good.

Making a collage is another cool creative outlet. Take photos of people in your life who make you feel good and arrange them on a big piece of paper or cardboard. Cut out inspiring words from a magazine and glue them onto the paper along with the photos.

8. Make a tape of your favorite songs.

Song lyrics can be like the encouraging words of a friend. They say just the things you need to hear, when you need to hear them. Compile a list of songs that speak to you in a special way and record them on tape. Listen to your homemade "power mix" any time you need a boost.

9. Bake a treat.

Get out the oven mitts and bake a treat. Cookbooks and magazines on cooking the light and healthy way are loaded with nutritious, low-fat recipes for baked goods that taste great.[1] Fill your kitchen with the aroma of fresh-baked pumpkin bread or blueberry muffins. Wrap up some of the goodies, add a bow, and you've got a tasty gift sure to warm a friend's spirit.

10. Stargaze.

Studying the constellations on a clear night is a great way to put things in perspective. Gazing at millions of stars above can make your problems seem very small in comparison. Allow your mind to wander and imagine your hopes and dreams coming true. Wish upon a star.

11. Perform an act of kindness.

When you're feeling down, helping someone else can make you feel a lot better. Help an elderly neighbor with his errands, offer to babysit for free for a working mom, or do some extra chores around your own house—without being asked. Doing something thoughtful and unexpected is a sure way to put a smile on someone else's face and helps you forget your own troubles for a while.

12. Move your body.

If you're feeling stressed out, there's no better relief than the high that comes from exercise. Put on your favorite tape or CD, pump up the volume, and dance like a maniac, or hop on your bike and go for a long ride. Elevate your heart rate and your outlook at the same time.

"To be true to one's self is the ultimate test in life."

Flo Hyman, volleyball player

---

[1] For cookbook and magazine ideas, see pp. 110–111.

Visualize It

"If one is lucky, a solitary fantasy can totally transform one million realities."

Maya Angelou, poet

Seeing is believing! When you believe in yourself and what you want to achieve, you've taken the first step toward making your dream a reality. Step two is developing a clear image of what you desire. Add to that a strong sense of self-confidence, and your goal comes even closer.

Having a vivid picture of the things you'd like to accomplish keeps you focused on the end result. A fun way to do this is to create a "collage of dreams." Clip pictures and words (from magazines, catalogs, or other publications) of things you'd like to be or do, paste the images onto a piece of cardboard, and hang the collage in your bedroom or school locker. Or read some success stories of people who have accomplished their goals. You'll be inspired by their achievements, and you'll learn about the steps and the risks that they took.

Another effective way to reach your goals is through *visualization,* or mental imagery. Athletes have used this technique for years; research into the connection between mental practice and sports performance dates all the way back to the 1930s. Competitors use visualization to clear their heads, calm their nerves, and plan their winning strategy.

If you could look inside the mind of an athlete skilled in visualization, you'd see a "movie" playing over and over in her head. Take a figure skater, for instance: Before a competition, she mentally rehearses her program, visualizing her body gliding across the ice in perfect sync with the music. She sees herself achieving every jump with ease. She feels her body rotating through the air, shoulders square, landing on one foot, knee bent, sinking into a deep edge. (Whew! Feels like the real thing.)

What's great about visualization is that it's a tool anyone can use to become a champion. Imagine yourself acing a test, shaving time off your last sprint, expressing yourself with confidence, or successfully meeting *any* of life's challenges.

How to Relax and Visualize

Visualization can:

- relax both your mind and body
- organize your thoughts
- help you stay calm, cool, and collected
- increase your self-confidence
- help you get ready for success

If you're ready to give it a try, here's how:

1. Get comfortable.

Pick a spot where you won't be disturbed, and get comfy. Lie on your back. If you feel like you're going to nod off, sit up so you don't become *too* relaxed.

2. Relax your body and breathe easy.

Become aware of your breathing. Feel your breath moving in and out of your body. Get a sense of where one breath ends and another begins. With just a few minutes of focused breathing, you can calm your body and start creating positive mental images.

Next, pay attention to any unwanted tension in your body. Sometimes you don't even realize that the tension is there until you're lying still. Common hiding places for excess muscle tension include your forehead and facial muscles, neck and shoulders, chest, lower back, and your hands and feet.

To help yourself relax, perform the following sequence. Begin at your head and slowly work your way down your body:

1.   **Tense your forehead, jaw, and cheek muscles.** Hold for a count of five. Take a deep breath, and as you exhale, let those muscles relax. Envision all your stress draining away.

2.   **Squeeze your shoulder blades together and tighten your chest.** Count to five, take a deep breath, and as you exhale, relax your muscles and release the tension within them.

3.   **Lock your elbows, clench your fists, and push your arms against the ground.** Hold for a count of five. Take a deep breath, exhale, and let your arms go limp.

4.   **Now tighten your rear end and your stomach muscles.** Hold, count to five, inhale, and as you exhale, slowly relax your muscles.

5.   **Move the focus to your legs.** Flex your thighs, push your knees down, pull your toes back toward your shins, and dig your heels into the floor. Keep tightening these muscles. Hold for a count of five. Take a deep breath, and as you exhale, let go of all the tension in your muscles.

6.   **Lie still and notice any remaining tension you may feel in any part of your body.** Take a deep breath, and as you exhale, imagine the rest of your tension pouring out of your body, into the floor, through the earth, and disappearing forever.

3. Visualize

Picture yourself confident and strong, handling a new situation with finesse or succeeding at whatever feat you choose: presenting an oral report in front of your classmates, approaching your parents about a subject you've been too nervous to bring up, excelling at a new sport, or handling any other type of situation. Let your mind wander, exploring possibilities you normally wouldn't consider. Be creative and guide yourself with vivid, detailed images of each scene unfolding in a positive way.

On pp. 41–42 is a script for a visualization exercise. Read it a few times for reference, then relax and let the images play back in your mind. A tape or CD of nature sounds or soothing music in the background can add to the experience. You may want to record the words to the script and play the tape while you visualize. If the sound of your own voice doesn't comfort you, ask a family member or a friend to read the script for you to tape-record. Make sure the person speaks slowly, taking long pauses so you have time to get lost in the visions you create. Allow the voice and empowering words to help you form the mental pictures that will inspire you to succeed. Or do the visualization exercise with a friend, taking turns reading the script aloud while the other visualizes. It's fun, and talking about the exercise afterward can make you both feel even more committed to accomplishing your goals.

One final thought before starting: If the idea of a visualization exercise doesn't rock your world, there are other ways to help you focus on the mind/body connection. You can try meditation, t'ai chi[1] (an ancient Chinese discipline of meditative movements practiced as a system of exercises), deep breathing, or even prayer—whatever works for you.

Visualization Script

Imagine yourself in an ideal place. It can be any place—the beach, the mountains, or a beautifully decorated room. The place can be somewhere you've been or only dreamed of. This is *your* place . . . the spot where you feel safe, comfortable, and totally content.

As you breathe deeply, allow the peace you feel to fill your body. Each breath adds to your sense of relaxation and tranquillity. Become aware of all your senses and how they respond to everything around you. Notice how the air feels and how your body feels. See the colors and details of your surroundings. Hear the sounds and enjoy their soothing rhythm. Are there any special fragrances or tastes that you're aware of? Experience each of these as well. Feel how inviting it is here, how relaxed you are. Always remember that this is your place, and by simply taking a few deep breaths, letting go of the tension in your body, and visualizing, you can return here any time you choose.

Without letting go of the peace you feel, allow the image of your special place to gently fade. Slowly replace it with a new vision—one of you facing one of the many challenges you've been preparing for. Whatever is on your mind—right here, right now—let this thought develop into a vivid picture. Immerse yourself in the details of this image.

---

[1] For more on t'ai chi, see p. 225.

Feel the warmth and happiness you've brought with you from your special place. Feel your body, mind, and spirit working together to help you reach your goal. Tell yourself that your body is strong, refreshed, and ready to take on any challenge. You're confident. You're ready. You're in control. Every move you make is effortless. Each step of this journey brings you closer to achieving your goals.

When you're ready, allow the image to softly fade away. Gently begin moving your hands, your feet, and then your arms and legs. Become aware of your body. Slowly open your eyes. Take your time getting used to your surroundings again. Give yourself a few moments before getting up. Inhale deeply and enjoy your relaxed body and your empowered state of mind.

• •

Speaking of relaxing, it's important to get enough rest each night. Most people need to sleep an average of eight hours per night, but as a teenager, you may need up to ten hours. When you get enough sleep, you're more energized and better able to concentrate. You'll simply feel a lot better in the morning and all day.

Try to go to bed at roughly the same time each night, so your body gets used to the routine. If you need to take a short nap during the day, that's fine. (NOTE: If you're sleeping more than ten hours every night and taking frequent naps during the day, there may be an underlying problem. See your doctor to make sure there's nothing physically wrong with you. If you're healthy, the oversleeping may be a sign that something's troubling you. Ask yourself what's happening in your life and how you can fix the problem.) For times when you just need to wind down, do step #2 on pp. 39–40, "Relax your body and breathe easy."

• •

Food Is Your Fuel

"There are three things I commit to on a daily basis:
Exercising for an hour a day, tops.
Never skipping meals. And accepting the
size and shape I was born with."

Paula Abdul, singer/dancer

Quiz

Nutrition 101

Sink your teeth into this quiz to rate your nutrition expertise. Decide if each statement in the quiz is "fact" or "fiction." Write your answers on a separate sheet and add up your score at the end. (TIP: Don't worry if you're not a nutrition expert yet—that's part of what this book is for!)

1. **FACT** or *fiction?*
Fruit-flavored carbonated waters have fewer calories than regular sodas.

2. **FACT** or *fiction?*
When you're at the movies and in the mood to munch, popcorn is always a low-fat snack.

3. **FACT** or *fiction?*
Being a vegetarian means your diet consists only of vegetables.

4. **FACT** or *fiction?*
In general, foods that come from animals (like milk, cheese, meat, poultry, and fish) are naturally higher in fat than foods that come from plants (like pasta, rice, carrots, corn, etc.).

5. **FACT** or *fiction?*
If you're trying to cut back on fat, ordering a salad when dining out is a guaranteed healthy choice.

6. **FACT** or *fiction?*
If you're trying to lose weight, skip the bread.

7. **FACT** or *fiction?*
Drinking lots of water helps you burn extra calories.

8. **FACT** or *fiction?*
Snacks at a health food store are automatically low in fat.

9. **FACT** or *fiction?*
Monounsaturated fats are better for you than saturated fats.

10. **FACT** or *fiction?*
It's possible to overdose on vitamins.

11. **FACT** or *fiction?*
Tofu is an excellent protein-rich alternative to meat.

12. **FACT** or *fiction?*
Frozen yogurt makes a healthy, low-fat lunch.

13. **FACT** or *fiction?*
When it comes to pizza toppings, Canadian bacon has less fat than pepperoni.

14. **FACT** or *fiction?*
As long as they're fat free, snacks like muffins, cookies, and ice cream won't make you gain weight.

15. **FACT** or *fiction?*
Ounce per ounce, potato chips and pretzels have about the same amount of fat.

16. **FACT** or *fiction?*
Strawberry jam is better for you than light cream cheese.

17. **FACT** or *fiction?*
Brown sugar is better for you than white sugar.

18. **FACT** or *fiction?*
One cup of cooked broccoli (you know, that funny-looking green stuff in the produce section, sometimes found next to the dip at parties) contains more vitamin C than one cup of orange juice.

19. **FACT** or *fiction?*
It's more fattening to pig out on a hot fudge sundae at midnight than right after lunch.

20. **FACT** or *fiction?*
Skim milk has less calcium than whole milk.

Answers

Give yourself one point for each correct answer, then see "Your Score" on p. 49 to find out how you did.

1. **fiction.** Many fruit-flavored carbonated waters contain high amounts of fructose and corn syrup (otherwise known as sugar), which means you may be drinking up to 150 calories per serving. (Gulp!) Bottled waters with no added sweeteners are a better choice. Or, if you prefer, try making your own seltzer by adding a splash of your favorite 100% fruit juice to a glass of soda water.

2. **fiction.** In the summer of 1995, the Center for Science in the Public Interest (CSPI)[1] found that a medium tub of buttered movie popcorn can have as much saturated fat as six Big Macs! Some theaters offer the air-popped variety of popcorn, which is nearly fat free and low in calories, too. Other fat-free munchies at the movies include Dots, Good & Plenty, Red Vines, Gummi Bears, Sweet Tarts, and Hot Tamales.

3. **fiction.** Vegetarians choose from a variety of foods, including vegetables, fruits, grains, dry beans and peas, sweets, and more. Some vegetarians do include animal products such as milk or eggs in their diet, while others don't. There are different degrees of vegetarianism, depending on a person's preferences.

4. **FACT.** Foods that come from animals not only are higher in fat than plant foods but also contain cholesterol (a white, crystalline substance found in certain foods and in your body tissue). Too much fat and cholesterol in your diet may cause health problems like heart disease. To keep your diet lean, choose animal products that are lower in fat, such as skim milk, low-fat yogurt, reduced-fat cheese, skinless poultry, fish, and lean meats.

5. **fiction.** Salads are frequently topped with high-fat foods like cheese, nuts, and bacon bits or other processed meats. Watch out for fatty salad dressings, too. If the dressing isn't low calorie, you could be adding a whopping amount of fat to your meal. For example, some salad dressings such as ranch, Caesar, and blue cheese contain up to 17 grams of fat per

---

[1] The CSPI is a nonprofit education organization dedicated to teaching the public about the nutritional content and quality of food. For more information, contact them at CSPI, 1875 Connecticut Avenue, NW, Suite 300, Washington, DC 20009; (202) 332-9110; *www.cspi@cspinet.org/*

serving. If you're concerned about the amount of fat in your diet, choose a low-fat dressing or order your salad dressing of choice on the side. Add just enough for taste, or dip each bite of salad in a little dressing. (TIP: Beware of hidden calories and fat lurking in salad bars. Many offer pre-made salads like potato or pasta salads, which may contain high-fat products like oil or

mayonnaise. Pile your plate with lots of fresh veggies and fruit instead.)

6. **fiction.** Low-fat grain products such as bagels, English muffins, pita bread, and whole grain breads are healthy, quick-energy foods, not to mention good sources of fiber and carbohydrates. But be careful—not all bread products are created equal. Doughnuts, croissants, muffins, focaccia, scones, and those incredibly sweet-smelling, warm and gooey cinnamon buns at the mall are loaded with fat and high in calories, too.

7. **fiction.** While it's true that water is vital to good health, it won't magically burn extra calories. The only way you're going to burn those is by working out.

8. **fiction.** Some health foods, such as nuts, granola, and carob- or yogurt-covered raisins, are actually high in fat. Play it safe by reading the food labels[2] so you know exactly what you're eating.

9. **Fact.** Both are pure fat, but monounsaturated fats can help lower your blood cholesterol level. Examples of foods with monounsaturated fats include cashews, peanut butter, avocados, and certain types of oil (canola, olive, and peanut). Saturated fats tend to raise your cholesterol level. Examples of foods that contain saturated fats include butter, chocolate, egg yolks, and coconut oil. Try to eat these foods sparingly.

10. **Fact.** Believe it or not, some vitamins can be toxic if you consume large quantities of them, so don't fall into the "If one is good, then more are better" mindset. A good example of a vitamin that should be taken with care

---

[2] See Chapter 8, "Ready to Read Labels?"

is vitamin A. While vitamin A promotes good vision and helps your body resist disease, produce energy, and maintain your tissues and nervous system, too much vitamin A can be toxic. Excess vitamin A stored in the body may lead to vomiting, headaches, hair loss, a dry mouth and nose, and damage to the liver. Because it's difficult to get too much of this vitamin just from food, megadoses of supplements are usually the culprit when it comes to the symptoms described. Before you begin taking any vitamins, talk to your doctor and always follow recommended dosages.

11. **FACT.** Soybean-based products (such as tofu) are not only rich in protein but are loaded with calcium, zinc, B vitamins, and iron. Because these foods are also low in saturated fat and cholesterol free, they're a healthy alternative to meat.

12. **fiction.** While it's true that frozen yogurt can be low in fat, it's usually full of sugar, too. Also, frozen yogurt doesn't contain the calcium and protein (which you need for good health) often found in regular yogurt. Frozen yogurt for dessert or a snack is fine, but not as a meal.

13. **FACT.** An ounce of Canadian bacon has about 2 grams of fat, while an ounce of pepperoni has about 11 grams of fat. (TIP: Healthier pizza toppings include veggies and/or pineapple.)

14. **fiction.** Fat free or not, snacks that have too many calories can pack on the pounds. Instead, try healthy snacks like fresh vegetables or fruit, which give your body the vitamins and minerals it needs. An added benefit is that fruits and veggies contain fiber, which fills you up and may keep you from overeating at mealtime.

15. **fiction.** An ounce of potato chips has about 10 grams of fat, while an ounce of pretzels has about 1 gram of fat.

16. **FACT.** Strawberry jam has less than 1 gram of fat per serving, and light cream cheese has about 5 grams of fat per serving; if you're trying to watch your fat intake, strawberry jam is a better choice. However, jams (and jellies, too) are often full of sugar. You may want to try a 100% fruit spread instead.

17. **fiction.** Surprise! Brown sugar is actually white sugar with added molasses. Both are still sugar, which you should avoid when you can.

18. **Fact.** Although both are excellent sources of this vitamin, one cup of cooked broccoli has about 140 milligrams (mg) of vitamin C, and one cup of orange juice has about 125 mg of vitamin C.

19. **fiction.** Food doesn't become more fattening just because you eat it at night. What counts is the total amount of fat and calories you consume overall. Most people feel and sleep better if they don't eat just before they go to bed, so you may want to avoid late-night snacking.

20. **fiction.** The great thing about skim milk is that it contains about the same amount of vitamins and minerals—including calcium—as whole milk. The only thing missing is the fat.

Your Score

12 points or less

Okay, you didn't score so hot, but that's no reason to think of yourself as a nutrition catastrophe. You can improve your nutrition know-how, and this book can help. Becoming nutrition savvy is definitely worth the effort if you're into improving your health, having more energy, and looking your best.

13–16 points

You're nutrition conscious and have a basic grasp of nutrition—but there's room for improvement. Good nutrition isn't all that complicated if you follow the basics. The U.S. Department of Agriculture's Dietary Guidelines for Americans[3] make choosing healthy foods much easier.

17–20 points

Can't fool you—you're a nutrition expert. You know about the important role that good nutrition plays when it comes to your overall health and fitness. Now all you have to do is make sure to put all that knowledge into practice and eat right each day.

---

[3] See Chapter 6, "How to Eat Right."

5
Food for Thought

"My body is a temple, and I want to take the best care of it that I can."

Jennie Garth, actress

What exactly does "eating right" mean? It depends on the source. A book on dieting, for example, might give you the idea that eating right is about counting calories and depriving yourself of many of the foods you enjoy. Ads and commercials for packaged "healthy" foods might tell you that consuming these products means that you're eating right. Your parents or other adults may tell you to clean your plate or to eat certain foods because they're "good for you." Is that what eating right means? With so many different messages, it's easy to get confused about what a nutritious diet really is.

When doing the research for *The Right Moves*, we read other books, looked at health magazines, talked to nutrition experts, and relied on our own expertise. We also gathered informational materials from government sources, in particular the U.S. Department of Agriculture (USDA) and the U.S. Department of Health and Human Services (USDHHS). These organizations offer solid nutrition information in easy-to-read publications. Throughout Part Two, you'll learn about these materials, discover some nutrition basics, and find out how to make good choices about the foods you eat—now and for the rest of your life.

We define "eating right" as making food choices that fuel your body, mind, and spirit. This means you:

1. eat foods that build a healthy body from head to toe

2. have a healthy attitude about food

Starting good eating habits while you're young ensures that your body has all the vitamins and minerals it needs each day to grow and develop. If you know about nutrition and what your body requires for good health, you might be less likely to overeat, consume lots of fast food and/or junk food, or experiment with crash diets—all of which can harm your body.

Eating right starts in your head. When you tell yourself that you want to practice good eating habits—not go on a diet—you're developing a healthy attitude about food and eating. It's easy for people of all ages to form unhealthy relationships with food, but especially for teen girls. That's because you receive so many conflicting messages each day about how you should look, what you should weigh, and how to go about getting the "perfect" body. If you're dealing with low self-esteem (and many teen girls are), it's even more difficult to sort through all the different messages and figure out what's best for you. Just remember that food is your fuel. It gives your body the energy to get through the day and to meet all of life's challenges (physical and mental). With the right fuel, you'll be on your way to a stronger you.

Ten Reasons to Eat Right

Developing a healthy body, and a healthy attitude about food, takes some time and effort on your part—but it's well worth it. Consider these ten reasons for eating right:

1. Eating right shows you care about your body.

Just like recycling shows you care about the environment, choosing to eat healthy foods makes a positive statement, too. Eating right proves that you respect your body and want to treat it well.

2. Eating right enhances your natural beauty.

When you eat lots of fresh fruits and vegetables, plus foods rich in fiber and vitamins, you're taking care of yourself—and it shows. Shiny hair, good skin tone, strong teeth and nails, fresher breath, and a healthy glow are just some of the rewards of a healthy diet.

3. Eating right can be enjoyable.

Eating is meant to be a pleasant experience. Whether you're in a restaurant, at a picnic, in the school lunchroom, or at home, savor every delicious morsel. Good company, easy conversation, and nutritious food add up to a great time.

4. Eating right helps keep you healthy.

Eating right is an excellent way to ward off obesity, a heart attack, and some forms of cancer. Getting enough calories and nutrients each day is also important for building strong bones and muscles, developing healthy organs, and strengthening your immune system. You've got an entire lifetime ahead of you, so why not eat right to feel your best?

5. Eating right helps maintain your weight.

Eating right means paying attention to nutrition as well as to *how much* you eat. If you regularly overeat or eat too little,[1] you'll have a hard time maintaining a weight that's right for your body. It's not healthy to have lots of extra fat or to be underweight—nor is it healthy to be *obsessed* about your weight. The trick is to find the right balance in your diet.

6. Eating right boosts your brain power.

When you're feeling tired and run-down from a lack of nutrients, it's easy to space out in class or while studying. Fuel your body with the vitamins and minerals needed for good health, and your concentration will improve. Schoolwork, part-time jobs, sports, and extracurricular activities all depend on an alert mind.

7. Eating right can prevent you from getting obsessed about food.

Nourishing your body with nutritious meals and snacks makes you less likely to obsess over food or try fad diets that can negatively affect your health.[2] Give yourself a break—eating is meant to bring pleasure, not pain.

8. Eating right TASTES GOOD.

If you're used to eating canned veggies or satisfying your fruit requirement with a bowl of sugary fruit-flavored cereal, you don't know what you're missing! Foods packaged in a factory just can't compare to all the flavorful foods that nature gives us, from sweet strawberries to fresh corn on the cob.

---

[1] See p. 58 for more information on obesity; see Chapter 12, "Diet Is a Four-Letter Word."
[2] See chapter 13, "Battling Eating Disorders," for more on food obsessions.

9. Eating right gives you energy and makes you feel good.

Fueling your body with healthy foods gives you the get-up-and-go to walk farther, run faster, and dance longer. You'll have more energy to make the most of each day.

10. Eating right keeps you feeling more positive.

A well-nourished body feels stronger and healthier, which can improve your whole outlook. Taking care of yourself—inside and out—is the key to higher self-esteem and greater self-confidence.

> "Healthful eating is one of your best personal investments!"
>
> **Roberta L. Duyff, Registered Dietitian, author**

6

How to Eat Right

*"It's not just about keeping weight down or looking good.
It's about feeling good, being healthy."*

Crystal Bernard, actress

You might be wondering what you should eat to nourish your body and feel great, too. The good news is, learning to eat right is easy. The U.S. Department of Agriculture and the U.S. Department of Health and Human Services have devised basic dietary guidelines to help you develop healthy eating habits.[1] In this chapter, you'll learn all about these simple guidelines, which you can follow for better health today and every day of your life.

Why Eat?

The human body needs food to survive and function. If you didn't eat at all, you wouldn't be able to stand up, walk around, smile, or do much of anything. Normal body functions like cell renewal, digestion, breathing, and muscle contractions all depend on energy from

the proteins, carbohydrates, and fats you consume. In fact, you use 70% of your energy just to keep your body working. Where do you get the energy? From food.

---

[1] The "Dietary Guidelines for Americans," developed by the USDA and USDHHS, contain seven basic steps to a healthy eating plan for people two years and older. To receive your own copy of the guidelines, write or call: The Center for Nutrition Policy and Promotion, 1120 20th Street NW, Suite 200, North Lobby, Washington, DC 20036; (202) 418-2312. If you're online, you'll find the guidelines at the National Agricultural Library Web site—go to *www.nal.usda.gov/*

During digestion, the food you eat is broken down into nutrients that are absorbed into your bloodstream; then they're converted into glucose, or blood sugar, and delivered to your cells. The human body needs more than 40 different nutrients for good health, and each nutrient has a specific function. Take a look at what some of the main nutrients do:

1. *Carbohydrates* are a source of energy for your body. They're divided into two groups: complex carbohydrates, also known as starches, and sugars.

2. *Fats*, which are made up of fatty acids, give you energy and help your body absorb vitamins such as A, D, E, and K.

3. *Proteins* supply amino acids, which keep your body tissues healthy. Like carbohydrates and fats, proteins can supply energy, too (but then they can't do their main job of maintaining your body tissue).

4. *Vitamins and minerals*[2] spark chemical reactions in your cells and have other specific functions in your body. Vitamins (like A and C) and minerals (like calcium and iron) all work together to help carbohydrates, fats, and proteins supply the energy your body needs.

5. *Water* makes up about 50% to 75% of your body weight. Water regulates your body temperature, carries nutrients to your cells, and helps eliminate wastes.

Food contains calories (or a measure of how much energy the food gives your body), which are calculated based on the make-up of certain foods. For example:

- 1 gram of protein = 4 calories
- 1 gram of carbohydrate = 4 calories
- 1 gram of alcohol = 7 calories
- 1 gram of fat = 9 calories

Some people (children and pregnant women, for example) need more calories per day for proper body functioning, and others (such as the elderly) need less. Experts say that teen girls should eat about 2,200 calories each day. If you're a really active teen, you may need to consume more.

---

[2] For more information about the vitamins and minerals needed for good health, see p. 89.

Eating a healthy diet and getting enough calories each day is essential for your body. If you diet and restrict your calorie intake, your body will have trouble functioning normally, and you'll feel sluggish and cranky (hungry, too).

Seven Steps to Eating Right

The Dietary Guidelines have been created to encourage everyone to:

- meet their nutritional requirements
- promote good health
- be physically active
- reduce their risk of chronic health problems such as heart disease, diabetes, stroke, some forms of cancer, and osteoporosis

The Dietary Guidelines aren't a complicated eating plan—they're basic steps that, once learned, can easily become a good habit.

1. Eat a variety of foods.

No single food source can supply all the nutrients that your body needs every day. For instance, oranges are healthy because they're loaded with vitamin C, but they lack protein. Peanut butter, on the other hand, is full of protein but lacks vitamin C. To nourish your body properly, you need to eat lots of different foods each day.[3] With so many delicious foods to choose from, who'd want to eat the same thing day in and day out anyway?

2. Maintain a healthy weight, and balance the foods you eat with physical activities.

Medical experts say that being too heavy or too thin may increase your chance of developing health problems. If you're heavy, you may be at risk for high blood pressure, heart disease, diabetes, arthritis, breathing difficulties, and certain forms of cancer. If you're underweight, you may be at risk for amenorrhea (the absence of the menstrual cycle), infertility, or osteoporosis.

---

[3] In Chapter 7, "Your Road Map to Healthy Eating," you'll learn about the Food Guide Pyramid, which explains how to choose a variety of foods from the five major food groups.

How much you should weigh depends on many factors, including:

- your age
- your height
- heredity
- your frame size
- your body composition
- how physically active you are

If you're not sure what a healthy weight for you should be, ask your doctor or school nurse to show you a weight chart and help you figure out if your weight is within a healthy range. But keep in mind that weight charts don't always tell the whole story; they can't tell the difference between a body with lean muscle tissue and one with fatty tissue. In other words, the chart doesn't know if you have strong muscles from working out or lots of flab from an inactive lifestyle. It's possible to weigh within the range for your height on a weight chart but still have too much body fat. It's also possible to be a muscular athlete and weigh more than the recommended weight but have little body fat. When it comes to weight charts, remember these facts and use your own best judgment.

Everyone needs a layer of body fat under their skin to buffer their body from the cold (like insulation) and to protect their internal organs. Girls and women are supposed to have a certain minimum percentage of body fat (about 17%) to be able to menstruate; you need approximately 22% body fat to have *regular* monthly periods. (Anywhere from 18% to 25% body fat is considered acceptable for women.) Most of your fat will probably be around your buttocks, hips, stomach, and thighs, where the extra padding can protect your uterus. This is normal, so don't think that gaining weight in those areas means you're "getting fat." (P.S. It's normal if you're heavier in other places on your body, too.)

Exercise is just as important as body-fat ratios and weight charts, if you want a healthy body. As long as you're active, eat sensibly, and feel good, you probably don't need a calorie-restrictive diet. If exercise and good nutrition *aren't* currently part of your lifestyle, now's the time to learn how to eat right and exercise more often. According to the Dietary Guidelines, you should try to do about 30 minutes of moderate physical activity on most days of the week. These physical activities can include anything from walking around your neighborhood to cleaning up your room; you can also be more active by limiting the amount of time you spend watching TV or working at a computer.

Many health experts simply recommend exercising at least three times a week for one half hour or more. You could choose a dance class, biking, in-line skating, or just about any other physical activity that gets your blood pumping. Whether you work out three times a week or more, be sure you *enjoy* the activities so you're more likely to stick with them.[4]

Are Overweight and Obese the Same?

Many health experts agree that there's a difference between being overweight and being obese. Obesity is defined as being 20% or more above your ideal weight range, putting you at a higher risk for diabetes, high blood pressure, heart disease, and other health problems. Obesity is rising among children and teens in America. Why? Because many young people are eating more high-fat foods but are less physically active than ever before. Obesity can lead to even more inactivity because it's tiring to carry around extra body weight while exercising or doing everyday activities. Being overweight isn't considered to be as serious of a health risk as obesity, but can cause health problems. However, extra weight *isn't* a problem when the weight comes from added muscle instead of extra body fat; added muscle makes your body stronger.

Maintaining a healthy body weight is good for you. If you're overweight or obese, your weight can be managed through long-term changes that include decreasing the amount of fat in your diet and incorporating more physical activities into your life. Going on a crash diet isn't the answer, especially since you're still growing and need extra calories and nutrients during your teen years.[5] Before starting a weight-reduction program, talk to your doctor or school nurse to get information on losing weight safely and effectively. If you lose weight slowly and steadily, you'll have a better chance of keeping it off.

Are you healthy and of average weight for your age and size, but convinced that life would be better if you could just drop a couple pounds? It's

---

[4] See Chapter 15, "A Fitness Plan That Fits You," and Chapter 22, "Pros and Cons of Your Workout Options," for ideas on finding activities that suit you and are enjoyable.

[5] See Chapter 12, "Diet Is a Four-Letter Word," and Chapter 13, "Battling Eating Disorders," for more on the dangers of dieting.

time to put your preoccupation with your weight into perspective. Losing weight isn't going to guarantee invitations to parties, attract "Mr. Right," or make your friends care about you any more than they already do. Life doesn't change just because you're a smaller jeans size.

Too many girls and young women in this country suffer from distorted perceptions about their "ideal" weight. According to Anorexia Nervosa and Related Eating Disorders Inc. (ANRED),[6] 50% of girls in the fourth grade think they're fat and are dieting, and 90% of eleventh and twelfth grade girls are on diets. These statistics are alarming because many of these girls are not only obsessed with their weight but also base their entire self-image on a number on the bathroom scale. If you're convinced that dieting is your ticket to a happier life, be aware that an obsession with food and weight can do a lot of harm to your body and self-esteem.

How do you know if you're really the right size and shape? If you eat right based on the Dietary Guidelines (plus indulge yourself every once in a while when you feel like it) and exercise at least three times a week for a half hour or more, you're the right size and shape for you.

3. Eat plenty of vegetables, fruits, and grain products.

The Dietary Guidelines recommend that you eat lots of fruits, vegetables, and whole grains each day.[7] All these foods are considered nutrient dense. They provide the vitamins, minerals, and complex carbohydrates your body needs for energy and good health, plus fiber, which moves food through your digestive system and helps you feel fuller.

Fruits, vegetables, and whole grains are not only loaded with vitamins and minerals but also taste great and are generally low in fat. Adding more of these foods to your diet is no problem—just follow these simple tips:

- Drink 100% fruit juices instead of sodas or fruit-flavored drinks.

- Use fruits and vegetables as a garnish on fish and poultry.

- Top unsweetened cereal or yogurt with fresh fruit.

- Top whole grain pancakes or waffles with strawberries or peaches.

- Freeze sliced bananas and grapes for refreshing snacks on hot days.

---

[6] You can read more about ANRED on p. 132.
[7] For daily serving recommendations, see Chapter 7, "Your Road Map to Healthy Eating."

- Make popsicles from frozen pureed fruit and water. Just pop the fruit in a blender, push the puree button, and mix in some water. Freeze your popsicles in popsicle holders or just fill up an ice tray and put a toothpick in each one.

- Spoon fresh fruit toppings over low-fat frozen yogurt.

- Add extra vegetables like lettuce, tomatoes, red onions, cucumbers, bell peppers, and sprouts to sandwiches.

- Mix chopped celery and scallions in egg and tuna salad.

- Toss veggies like tomatoes, onions, broccoli, or carrots into casseroles, stews, soups, or stir-fry dishes.

- Stir chopped tomatoes, green peppers, and onions into pasta sauces.

- Keep cut up, raw veggies in the refrigerator for snacking.

4. Choose foods that are low in fats, saturated fats, and cholesterol.

Everyone needs to have some fat in their diet to maintain good health. That's a fact. Fats support the work of other nutrients in your body, as well as help your body to grow. However, part of eating right is consuming less *total* fat, saturated fat, and cholesterol.

You've probably heard something about cholesterol, a fat-like substance in your body and in animal products like dairy. You may know that it's important to have a low blood cholesterol level—maybe you've even had your cholesterol tested at the doctor's office. Your body makes the cholesterol it requires, but you also get cholesterol from some of the foods you eat (egg yolks, meat, poultry, and cheese). A diet high in fat and cholesterol may increase your blood cholesterol level and your risk of heart disease, obesity, and some forms of cancer.

Fats contain *saturated* and *unsaturated* (monounsaturated and polyunsaturated) fatty acids. Saturated fat is the kind that raises your blood cholesterol level. You find saturated fat in meat, milk, and dairy products like cheese and ice cream, as well as in bakery treats like doughnuts and cakes. Butter, margarine, and mayonnaise also contain some saturated fat. Unsaturated fats (found in olive oil, corn oil, and many kinds of seafood) can reduce your blood cholesterol when they replace saturated fats in your diet.

The USDA and the USDHHS recommend that you get no more than 30% of your calories from fat. To help you calculate the number of fat grams you should have each day, the USDA and USDHHS provide two easy formulas (below). Both are based on a daily intake of 2,200 calories. If you train extra hard or don't exercise at all, you'll have to adjust the daily calories up or down to fit your needs.

Fat-Gram Formulas

Watching your fat intake doesn't mean calculating every gram of fat that you put into your mouth; these fat-gram formulas are provided only as a general reference. If you consume extra fat on any given day, it's not the end of the world. Just be sure to take it easy on the fats for the next couple of meals, and eat a few extra fruits and veggies for balance.

A. Multiply your total day's calories by 0.30 to get your recommended calories from fat per day. Example:

$$2,200 \text{ calories} \times 0.30 = 660 \text{ calories from fat}$$

B. Divide the calories from fat per day by 9 (each gram of fat has 9 calories) to get grams of fat per day. Example:

$$660 \text{ calories from fat} \div 9 = 73 \text{ grams of fat per day}$$

NOTE: This guideline refers to what you eat over the course of a day, not per meal.

You don't have to carry a calculator around for the rest of your life to figure out fat grams—reading food labels[8] is an excellent way to keep an eye on your fat intake. In most cases, you don't even have to bother figuring out the math since the food manufacturer does it for you. On the label under the words "Nutrition Facts," you'll see the percentage of calories from fat right next to the total number of calories per serving. If the percentage is high, you know the food contains a lot of fat.

---

[8] See Chapter 8, "Ready to Read Labels?"

To help reduce the amount of fat and cholesterol in your diet, try these simple fat fixes:

- Remove the skin from chicken and turkey, and trim the fat off other meats.

- Choose lean meats, fish, and poultry. Opt for meats that are roasted, grilled, or broiled instead of fried in oil.

- Choose skim or low-fat milk over whole milk. Select reduced-fat cheese and low-fat yogurt. These lower-fat options help you get the calcium you need without adding extra fat to your diet.

- Limit eggs to three or four per week. If you eat more than four eggs, skip the egg yolks. Many recipes provide "no-cholesterol" alternatives, which call for egg whites only.

- Go easy on fatty toppings like salad dressings, butter, margarine, gravy sour cream, and mayonnaise.

- Cook with nonstick sprays instead of butter, margarine, or oil.

- Use oils sparingly and choose corn, safflower, canola, olive, peanut, or sunflower oil over coconut oil.

- Eat more whole foods like fruits and vegetables and fewer processed foods like ready-to-heat frozen entrees and meals that come in a box.

- Cut down on snacks like potato chips, cheese puffs, and high-fat crackers.

- Limit your intake of high-fat sweets (muffins, pastries, ice cream, etc.). To satisfy a sweet tooth, try frozen fruit bars, low-fat frozen yogurt, or angel food cake topped with fresh strawberries for dessert.

- Go easy on nuts and seeds—they're a great source of protein, but they're also loaded with fat.

5. Use sugars in moderation.

Sugars are carbohydrates, which your body needs for energy. But there's a difference between eating *natural* sugars—those found in fruits, grains, milk, and some vegetables—and *added* sugars, which sweeten or preserve food. Foods with natural sugars provide your body with nutrients (if you eat an orange, you're consuming some natural sugar, but your body is getting lots of vitamin C, for example). Eating a sugary treat, on the other hand, supplies your body with calories from sugar, but won't give you many nutrients.

Does the following scenario sound familiar? It's 10:30 A.M., and you didn't eat breakfast before school. Now your stomach is growling like crazy in the middle of class, and you buy a cinnamon bun at the cafeteria to tide you over until lunch. You feel full and energized, but a short time later, you're tired and craving another sweet snack. Why does this happen? Because the sugar only satisfies your body temporarily, giving you a sudden burst of energy and a feeling of being full. But when the extra sugar enters your bloodstream, your pancreas releases a hormone called insulin, which carries the sugar to your liver; your liver goes into overdrive to get rid of the extra blood sugar, and this process zaps your energy. You end up crashing, which can make you tired and cranky.

Are You Eating Too Much Sugar?

To find out if you're consuming too much sugar, ask yourself the following questions. Which answer best describes your eating habits? How often do you:

1. eat pre-sweetened cereal?

☐ never   ☐ 1 or 2 times a week   ☐ once a day   ☐ several times a day

2. drink sodas, punch, lemonade, chocolate milk, or fruit drinks?

☐ never   ☐ 1 or 2 times a week   ☐ once a day   ☐ several times a day

3. eat candy or chew gum with sugar in it?

☐ never   ☐ 1 or 2 times a week   ☐ once a day   ☐ several times a day

4. add sugar to iced tea or coffee?

☐ never   ☐ 1 or 2 times a week   ☐ once a day   ☐ several times a day

5. eat sugary snacks and desserts like cookies, cake, or brownies?

☐ never   ☐ 1 or 2 times a week   ☐ once a day   ☐ several times a day

Did you check "once a day" for most of the questions? Or did you answer "several times a day" for a few of the questions? If so, you can probably see how all of that sugar adds up each day. It may be time to cut down your sugar intake. As you lower the amount of sugar you eat, you just might find that you don't crave it as much, either.

A big reason to cut down on sweets is to prevent tooth decay. Snacking on sugary foods is terrible for your dental hygiene because the sugar ends up sitting on your teeth, causing plaque build-up and cavities. When you do eat sugary foods, brush and floss as soon as you can. Consuming too much sugar poses another problem, too. When you fill up on foods that contain loads of sugar, you may be less likely to eat wholesome foods like fruits and veggies. Substituting sweets for nutritious foods robs your body of the essential vitamins and minerals it would get otherwise.

Even if you don't eat lots of candy bars, cookies, and other sweets, you may be consuming added sugar every day because so much sugar is hidden in foods. Food manufacturers use sugar as a preservative and flavor enhancer, so processed foods are loaded with it. In fact, sugar is our nation's most popular food additive, but you might not know this unless you read food labels.[9]

Once you begin reading the labels on food packages, you'll find sugar lurking in surprising places. It's frequently added to spaghetti sauces, salad dressings, peanut butter, ketchup, mayonnaise, crackers, bread, canned goods, frozen meals, cold cuts, jelly, jam, dried fruit rolls, yogurt, gelatin, packaged mixes (like macaroni and cheese, rice and noodle dishes, and boxed dinners where all you add is the hamburger or tuna), and fruit drinks. Some of the biggest culprits are soft drinks. A 12-ounce (oz.) can of soda may contain as many as 9 teaspoons of sugar. If you can't imagine a day without a cola, maybe now is a good time to switch to 100% fruit juice or carbonated water instead.

One way to cut down your sugar intake is to pay attention to the ingredients list on food packages. The list will include sugars already present naturally in the food, as well as those that have been added during processing. The next time you scan the ingredient list for a product's sugar content, don't overlook hidden sugars disguised as:

* brown sugar

* corn syrup

* dextrose

---

[9] See Chapter 8, "Ready to Read Labels?"

- fructose (fruit sugar, which occurs naturally in foods)

- glucose

- honey

- lactose (milk sugar, which occurs naturally in foods)

- maltose

- molasses

- raw sugar

- sorbitol, Manitol, Malitol, and/or Xylitol

- sucrose (table sugar)

- syrup

- turbinado

If any of the above names are mentioned several times or listed first or second on the ingredient list of the product you're considering, it's probably very high in sugar.

If you'd like to decrease the amount of sugar you eat each day, do it gradually to make the process easier. Here are a few tips:

- Ask the family member who does the grocery shopping not to buy sweet snacks (you won't eat them if you don't have them).

- Choose brands with less added sugar, or none at all.

- Eliminate soft drinks from your diet. If you crave something fizzy, try carbonated water; flavor it by squeezing in the juice of fresh fruits like lemons or limes.

- Beware of fruit-flavored beverages, punches, or lemonade—they're usually loaded with sugar. Drink 100% fruit juice instead. You'll quench your thirst and add vitamins to your diet at the same time.

- Have lots of naturally sugar-free snacks handy for between-meal grazing.

- Fresh fruit, sliced veggies, and air-popped popcorn (unbuttered) are satisfying alternatives to sweets and junk food.

• •

Artificial sweeteners such as Aspartame (NutraSweet, Equal) and saccharin (Sweet 'n' Low) replace sugar in food, eliminating the calories but retaining the sweetness. Experts are still investigating the potential health hazards of artificial sweeteners, so you might find a warning on food labels containing them. For example, products made with saccharin usually have a label saying that saccharin has been linked to cancer in laboratory rats. Because they're tested extensively to meet the standards of the Food and Drug Administration (FDA), artificial sweeteners are generally considered safe to consume. However, some people have reported side effects, including dizziness, headaches, mood swings, nausea, breathing difficulties, and menstrual problems.

• •

6. Use salt and sodium only in moderation.

Are salt and sodium the same thing? Many people think they are. But salt, the common name for sodium chloride, is made up of sodium (60%) and chloride (40%). Sodium, a mineral found in many foods, helps regulate fluids and your blood pressure. Studies have proven that too much sodium in your diet can increase your risk of high blood pressure, stroke, or heart or kidney disease. A high salt intake may also increase the amount of calcium that leaves your body when you urinate (increasing your need for the mineral) or cause water retention, which means you'll end up feeling bloated.

The USDA recommends that you consume about 2,400 mg of sodium per day (that's about equal to one level teaspoon of salt). Most Americans consume much more than this—without even realizing it. Food manufacturers frequently use sodium as a flavor enhancer or a preservative so food can sit on the grocer's shelves longer before spoiling. If you eat a lot of packaged foods (frozen dinners or potato chips, for example), you're probably consuming more sodium than you need each day. Fast food is loaded with sodium, too. Here are some other high-sodium products:

• butter, margarine, and cheese

• cereal

• frozen pizza

- pancake and baking mixes
- bottled pasta sauces
- seasoned salts
- soup mixes and bouillon
- condiments (relish, pickles, ketchup, mustard, and soy sauce)
- pre-seasoned, packaged mixes (such as flavored rice and seasoning mixes)
- processed meats (packaged lunch meats, hot dogs, bacon, and sausage)
- canned foods (chili, tomato sauce, vegetables, olives, and especially soups—they can have as much as 1,600 mg of sodium in a single serving)

These tips can help you reduce the amount of sodium in your diet:

- Try leaving the salt shaker off the table so it's less convenient to use. You can also use salt substitutes found in the spice aisles at the grocery store.
- Don't salt foods before you taste them—you may discover that they're better without it.
- If you're eating fast food, skip the processed meats on pizza and take the pickles off burgers.
- Have fun with low-salt recipes. Use spices like fresh ground pepper and cumin, experiment with fresh garlic and onion, and try fresh herbs like parsley, basil, chives, and cilantro to flavor your food.
- Don't sprinkle extra salt on already salty foods like French fries or popcorn.
- Suggest that the cook in your house reduce the amount of salt called for in recipes by one half, or ditch the salt altogether.
- Squeeze fresh lemon over steamed vegetables and fish to wake up their natural flavors.

7. If you ever drink alcoholic beverages, do so only in moderation.

The USDA and the USDHHS set this particular guideline for adults. If you're under the legal drinking age, you shouldn't be drinking alcoholic beverages at all, *especially* if you'll be driving or if you're pregnant. According to the Dietary Guidelines, alcoholic beverages provide calories but no nutrients, and should be consumed only in moderation. The suggested amounts differ for women and men—women should consume no more than one drink per day and men should consume no more than two drinks per day (a "drink" refers to one 12 oz. beer or 5 oz. of wine).

Research has indicated that moderate drinking may lower the risk of coronary heart disease in some people; but drinking lots of alcohol can cause health problems, including cirrhosis of the liver, inflammation of the pancreas, high blood pressure, damage to the brain and heart, stroke, and an increased risk of some cancers. If you've experimented with alcohol or if you drink on a fairly regular basis, be aware that alcohol use can lead to health problems, especially when you begin drinking at a young age.

For Your Information

According to the 1995 Youth Fatal Crash and Alcohol Facts from the National Highway Traffic Safety Administration:

- For every 100,000 young licensed drivers, 14 drivers under the influence of alcohol were involved in fatal crashes—that's twice the rate for drivers ages 21 or older.

- 35.5% of youth fatalities were alcohol-related.

From the 1995–1996 PRIDE (The National Parents' Resource Institute for Drug Education) survey of more than 60,000 girls nationwide in grades 6–12:

- Depression and suicide are often linked to use of alcohol. Of the girls suveyed, more than 4,800 said they thought about committing suicide, and of those, over 3,000 reported using alcohol.

- Not "everyone" is doing it (drinking): 50% to 75% of girls are NOT drinking.

If you think you need help with a drinking problem or just want to learn more about the effects of alcohol, check out a copy of the following book: *Taking Charge of My Mind and Body: A Girls' Guide to Outsmarting Alcohol, Drug, Smoking, and Eating Problems* by Gladys Folkers, M.A., and Jeanne Engelmann (Minneapolis: Free Spirit Publishing Inc., 1997).

The more you know about the Dietary Guidelines for Americans, the better prepared you'll be to make the right choices for your body. To learn more about nutrition, you can get in touch with the USDA. For current publications, call or write the U.S. Department of Agriculture, Washington, DC 20250; (202) 720-2791. If you're online, go to: *www.usda.gov/*

The benefits of following the Dietary Guidelines can last for the rest of your life. You'll feel better and look better, guaranteed. Why not give it a try?

Old Attitude	New Outlook
It's too much work to eat right.	The benefits of eating right will last a lifetime.

7

Your Road Map to Healthy Eating

*"Once you've learned how to stay confident
in yourself, no one can take that away."*

Rebecca Lobo, 1996 Olympic gold medalist, women's basketball

The U.S. Department of Agriculture developed the Food Guide Pyramid to help you create a well-balanced eating plan based on the Dietary Guidelines for Americans. Think of the Pyramid as a road map whose main purpose is to make the path to good nutrition less complicated. The Food Guide Pyramid places more emphasis on foods packed with nutrients and less importance on foods high in fat, sodium, and sugar. If you follow the Pyramid, you shouldn't have a problem getting the vitamins and minerals your body needs. (BONUS: Making nutritious selections from the major food groups listed in this chapter will help you maintain your weight naturally. Take a look at the Pyramid for help in choosing what and how much to eat.)

The Food Guide Pyramid is made up of six different food groups. You've probably heard of the five major food groups—they're included in the Pyramid, along with an additional sixth group (fats, oils, and sweets). The USDA recommends that you choose a variety of foods from the five major groups each day. When it comes to the sixth group, eat less of these foods because they provide little nutritional value.

From the bottom up, the six groups listed on the Pyramid are:

1. Bread, cereal, rice, and pasta

2. Vegetables

3. Fruits

4. Milk, yogurt, and cheese

5. Meat, poultry, fish, dry beans, eggs, and nuts

6. Fats, oils, and sweets

When you look at the Pyramid below, you can see that the groups are contained within four levels. These levels are explained on pp. 72–74.

The Food Guide Pyramid

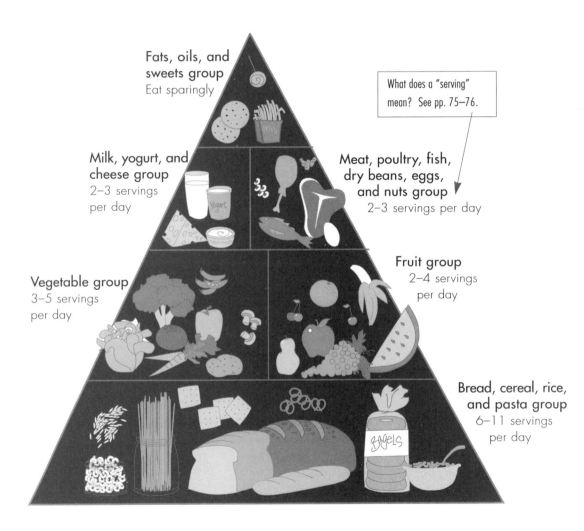

Fats, oils, and sweets group
Eat sparingly

What does a "serving" mean? See pp. 75–76.

Milk, yogurt, and cheese group
2–3 servings per day

Meat, poultry, fish, dry beans, eggs, and nuts group
2–3 servings per day

Vegetable group
3–5 servings per day

Fruit group
2–4 servings per day

Bread, cereal, rice, and pasta group
6–11 servings per day

SOURCE: Adapted from the Food Guide Pyramid of the USDA.

Level 1: bread, cereal, rice, and pasta group

You'll find this level at the base of the Pyramid: it's made up of bread, cereal, rice, and pasta—all foods from grains. These foods are a major source of carbohydrates, and it's recommended that you eat 6–11 servings per day. Choose from:

bagels ⊕ brown rice ⊕ corn tortillas ⊕ English muffins ⊕ flour tortillas ⊕ French bread ⊕ graham crackers ⊕ granola ⊕ grits ⊕ hamburger buns ⊕ hot dog buns ⊕ Italian bread ⊕ oatmeal ⊕ pancakes ⊕ pastas ⊕ popcorn ⊕ pretzels ⊕ pumpernickel bread ⊕ rice ⊕ rye bread ⊕ rye crackers ⊕ sourdough bread ⊕ waffles ⊕ wheat bread ⊕ whole grain bread ⊕ whole grain cereals ⊕ whole grain crackers

Level 2: vegetable group and fruit group

The second level of the Pyramid is made up of foods that come from plants (fruits and vegetables). These foods are an important source of vitamins, minerals, carbohydrates, and fiber, and it's recommended that you eat at least five servings a day. Choose from:

Vegetables

alfalfa sprouts ⊕ artichokes ⊕ asparagus ⊕ bean sprouts ⊕ beets ⊕ broccoli ⊕ brussels sprouts ⊕ cabbage ⊕ carrots ⊕ cauliflower ⊕ celery ⊕ collard greens ⊕ corn ⊕ cucumber ⊕ eggplant ⊕ endive lettuce ⊕ escarole lettuce ⊕ green beans ⊕ green pepper ⊕ hominy ⊕ iceberg lettuce ⊕ kale ⊕ lima beans ⊕ mushrooms ⊕ mustard greens ⊕ okra ⊕ onions ⊕ peas ⊕ potatoes ⊕ pumpkin ⊕ radishes ⊕ romaine lettuce ⊕ rutabagas ⊕ spinach ⊕ squash ⊕ sweet potatoes ⊕ tomatoes ⊕ turnip greens ⊕ turnips ⊕ vegetable juices ⊕ watercress ⊕ zucchini

Fruits

apples ⊕ apricots ⊕ bananas ⊕ blueberries ⊕ cantaloupe ⊕ cherries ⊕ cranberries ⊕ dates ⊕ figs ⊕ grapefruit ⊕ grapes ⊕ guava ⊕ honeydew melon ⊕ kiwifruit ⊕ lemons ⊕ mangoes ⊕ nectarines ⊕ 100% fruit juices ⊕ oranges ⊕ papayas ⊕ passion fruit ⊕ peaches ⊕ pears ⊕ pineapples ⊕ plums ⊕ raisins ⊕ raspberries

Are You Eating Enough Fruits and Veggies?

Many people don't eat enough foods from Level 2. Do you? Think about what you ate yesterday and what you've eaten today. How many fruits and vegetables have you consumed? On a separate sheet of paper, write down the type of fruit or vegetable and how many servings were eaten. See if each column adds up to five or more servings.

	Number of Servings Today	Number of Servings Yesterday
Breakfast	_____	_____
Lunch	_____	_____
Dinner	_____	_____
Snacks	_____	_____
Daily Total	_____	_____

If you're eating at least five servings of fruits and veggies each day, you deserve applause! If not, you aren't getting your 5-a-day, which is the minimum to aim for. Make a conscious effort to add more of these foods to your diet. Topping your breakfast cereal or yogurt with fresh fruit, putting tomatoes and lettuce on your sandwiches, and snacking on raw veggies are good ways to start.

Level 3: milk group and meat group

Level three of the Pyramid contains the milk, yogurt, and cheese group and the meat, poultry, dry beans, eggs, and nuts group. The foods in these two groups come mostly from animals and are important sources of protein, calcium, iron, and zinc. You should try to eat 2–3 servings from each of these food groups per day.[1]

---

[1] Unless you're a vegetarian. See pp. 77–82 for more on vegetarianism.

Chapter 7

Choose from:

Low-fat milk products

low-fat cottage cheese ⊚ low-fat milk (1%) ⊚ low-fat/nonfat yogurt ⊚ skim milk

Milk products with higher fat or sugar

cheese ⊚ chocolate milk ⊚ frozen yogurt ⊚ fruited yogurt ⊚ ice cream ice milk ⊚ pudding ⊚ reduced-fat milk (2%) ⊚ whole milk

Meat, poultry, fish

beef ⊚ chicken ⊚ ham ⊚ hamburger ⊚ lamb ⊚ luncheon meats ⊚ pork salmon ⊚ shellfish ⊚ trout ⊚ turkey ⊚ veal

Dry beans

black beans ⊚ garbanzo beans ⊚ kidney beans ⊚ lentils ⊚ lima beans mung beans ⊚ navy beans ⊚ pinto beans

Eggs

eggs ⊚ egg substitutes

Nuts (and seeds)

almonds ⊚ cashews ⊚ macadamia nuts ⊚ peanut butter ⊚ peanuts pistachios ⊚ pumpkin seeds ⊚ sesame seeds ⊚ sunflower seeds ⊚ walnuts

Level 4: Fats, Oils, and Sweets

The tip of the Pyramid is made up of fats, oils, and sweets, and it includes products that are high in fat and cholesterol. Most of these items provide calories but not many nutrients. Small indulgences from this group are perfectly fine. Just make sure that eating too many fats and sweets doesn't become a habit. Choose from:

butter ⊚ cake ⊚ candy ⊚ cheesecake ⊚ chocolate ⊚ cinnamon buns cookies ⊚ cream ⊚ cream cheese ⊚ croissants ⊚ Danish rolls ⊚ doughnuts éclairs ⊚ fast food ⊚ fried foods ⊚ fruit-flavored drinks ⊚ fudge ⊚ gravy jam ⊚ jelly ⊚ margarine ⊚ marshmallows ⊚ mayonnaise ⊚ muffins ⊚ oil pastries ⊚ pie ⊚ potato chips ⊚ salad dressings ⊚ shortening ⊚ soda sour cream ⊚ sugars ⊚ whipped cream

How Many Servings?

The Pyramid suggests a range of servings for each major food group. How many servings you need depends on your age, sex, and activity level. Most people should consume *at least* the minimum number of servings from the five major food groups. The more active you are, the more servings you'll need. For example, a teenage girl who works out 3–4 times per week, plays on a soccer team, and walks to and from school needs more than the minimum amount of servings suggested.

It isn't necessary to measure *everything* you eat. As long as you can estimate a serving size, you should be able to maneuver your way around the Pyramid with confidence. Use the following guidelines to help determine what constitutes a "serving size" for common foods included within the groups listed below. You'll notice that the serving sizes are much smaller than what you might eat during a meal, so it's a lot easier than you might think to eat the recommended amounts each day.

One serving equals:

Bread, cereal, rice, and pasta

- 1 slice of bread
- ½ bagel or English muffin
- 1 oz. of cold cereal
- ½ cup cooked cereal
- ½ cup pasta
- ½ cup cooked rice

Vegetables

- 1 cup raw leafy greens such as spinach or lettuce
- ½ cup cooked vegetables or chopped raw vegetables
- ½ cup cooked dry beans
- ¾ cup of vegetable juice

Fruits

- 1 medium orange, apple, or banana
- ½ cup diced, canned, or cooked fruit
- ¾ cup of 100% fruit juice
- ¼ melon
- ½ grapefruit
- ¼ cup dried fruit
- ½ cup small fruit such as berries or grapes

Milk, yogurt, and cheese

- 1 cup milk
- 1 cup yogurt
- 1½ oz. of natural cheese
- 2 oz. of processed cheese

Meat, poultry, fish, dry beans, eggs, and nuts

- 2–3 oz. of cooked lean meat, such as poultry without the skin, or fish
- 1 egg/2 egg whites
- ½ cup cooked dry beans
- 2 tablespoons of peanut butter
- ⅓ cup of nuts

Fats, oils, and sweets

Serving sizes are not listed for fats, oils, and sweets because the idea is to eat these foods sparingly.

> Some foods belong in more than one food group (they're known as cross-over foods). For example, some types of dry beans, such as lima beans, could be counted as servings in either the Meat/dry beans group or in the Vegetable group; same goes for lentils and dry peas. However, you can't count *one* serving of a cross-over food as a serving from *both* groups in one day.

If the food you're eating is from a package or can (crackers, soup, a frozen meal, etc.), read the label[2] to determine the serving size. Near the top of the label, you'll see a heading called "Servings Per Container." *These serving sizes differ from serving sizes recommended in the Food Guide Pyramid.* Food manufacturers base *their* portions on amounts that people usually consume. If you eat more than the standard serving size on the label, you're taking in more than the listed amount of fat and calories.

When you make food at home or eat out at a restaurant, do the best you can to estimate the food group servings of the main ingredients. For example, if you're eating a cheeseburger, the ingredients may count toward several food groups:

1. Bread, cereal, rice, and pasta group *(bun)*
2. Vegetable group *(lettuce, tomatoes, onion)*
3. Milk, yogurt, and cheese group *(cheese)*
4. Meat, poultry, fish, dry beans, eggs, and nuts group *(ground beef or ground turkey)*
5. Fats, oils, and sweets *(condiments)*

---

[2] See Chapter 8, "Ready to Read Labels?"

Remember that the Pyramid is only a general guideline to help you choose nourishing meals and snacks. It wasn't designed to be a rigid dietary system—there's always room for detours.

Drink Up

You've probably heard the advice about drinking 8–12 glasses (8 oz. each) of water a day. This recommendation comes from the American Dietetic Association, and it's great advice because water does more than just quench your thirst. Drinking lots of water every day is a great way to:

- hydrate your body (and skin)
- lubricate your internal organs and your joints
- clean out your system
- prevent bloating caused by fluid retention

Don't wait until you're thirsty before picking up a glass of water. Drinking the liquid throughout the day keeps you hydrated and healthy. It's even more important to drink lots of water while you're exercising.[3]

Going Vegetarian

Many teens (and adults, too) are choosing a vegetarian lifestyle because a vegetarian diet tends to be low in fat and cholesterol, making it a healthy eating alternative. Others are saying no to meat due to environmental concerns. Less of the earth's resources are used to grow vegetables and grains than to raise cattle for meat. In addition, you can feed more people with plants like veggies, fruits, and grains than you can with animals. Many people choose not to eat meat for ethical or moral reasons—they feel that animals raised for food consumption are treated inhumanely and/or that eating animals is a form of animal cruelty. Whatever the reason for choosing a vegetarian lifestyle, there are different categories of vegetarians. You may already be a "semi-vegetarian" without knowing it.

---

[3] Read more about water and working out on pp. 165–166.

- *Semi-vegetarians* mostly follow a vegetarian diet but will sometimes eat meat, poultry, or fish.

- *Ovo-lacto vegetarians* say no to all meat, including chicken, turkey, and fish, but will eat eggs and dairy products.

- *Ovo vegetarians* exclude meat and dairy products from their diet but will eat eggs.

- *Lacto vegetarians* won't eat eggs or meat, including fish and poultry, but they will eat dairy products.

- *Vegans* are the strictest group of vegetarians; they don't eat any animal products at all. Some vegans don't use any animal products (such as leather), either.

If you already follow a vegetarian diet, or would like to, it's important for you to eat a wide variety of plant foods so you can get all the nutrients you need for good health. You'll still need to watch your intake of saturated fats, sugars, sodium, and salt. Because meat is a major source of protein, and protein is the building block of your entire body, it's essential to include other kinds of protein-rich foods in your vegetarian diet. Grains, nuts and seeds, dry beans or peas, and soy products like tofu and soymilk pack a protein punch.

It's also important to get enough iron and calcium. Good vegetarian sources of these nutrients include:

Calcium

- almonds
- broccoli
- calcium-fortified breakfast cereals
- calcium-fortified orange juice
- cheese
- collards
- kale
- milk
- spinach
- tofu

Iron

- apricots
- black beans
- canned salmon
- dried fruit
- kidney beans
- lentils
- navy beans
- peanut butter
- pinto beans
- spinach

Teen girls need to pay special attention to getting enough calcium each day for strong, healthy bones that won't become brittle later in life. According to the National Institutes of Health, *1 out of every 4* women over age 60 has osteoporosis, which can be prevented in part by a diet rich in calcium. To consume adequate levels of calcium, make sure to select plenty of dairy products and dark green leafy vegetables every day.

Iron, which carries oxygen to your cells, is another important nutrient that you shouldn't overlook (especially when you have your period—iron is lost in menstrual bloodflow). If you feel tired or fatigued a lot, it may be because you're not getting enough iron each day. To keep your body's iron stores at an adequate level, eat iron-rich foods like iron-enriched pasta, rice, cereals, and leafy green veggies.

Take a look at the Vegetarian Food Guide Pyramid below for further information on meeting your daily nutritional needs.

The Vegetarian Food Guide Pyramid

Fats, oils, and sweets group
Eat sparingly

What does a "serving" mean? See p. 81.

Milk, yogurt, and cheese group
2–3 servings per day

Tofu, beans, eggs, and meat substitutes group
2–3 servings per day

Vegetable group
3–5 servings per day

Fruit group
2–4 servings per day

Bread, cereal, rice, and pasta group
6–11 servings per day

SOURCE: Many versions of the Vegetarian Food Guide Pyramid exist, and all of them are basically similar. We've adapted our version from what we believe to be a good source of information on the vegetarian diet: *Journal of the American Dietetic Association*, volume 93, number 11.

One serving equals:

Bread, cereal, rice, and pasta

- 1 slice of bread
- ½ cup cooked pasta
- ½ cup cooked cereal
- ½ cup cooked rice

Vegetables

- ½ cup cooked vegetables
- 1 cup raw vegetables

Fruits

- 1 piece of fruit
- 1 cup of 100% fruit juice
- 1 cup canned or cooked fruit

Milk, yogurt, and cheese

- 1 cup milk
- 1 cup yogurt
- 1½ oz. of cheese

Tofu, beans, eggs, and meat substitutes

- 4 oz. tofu
- ½ cup cooked dry beans
- 1 egg/2 egg whites
- 1 cup soy milk

Resources for Vegetarians

There are tons of resources available on vegetarianism, including cookbooks, magazines, organizations, and Web sites. So if you're serious about a plant-based diet, be smart. Talk with a registered dietitian or your family doctor, read up on all of the latest information, and stay informed.

Books/Cookbooks

A Teen's Guide to Going Vegetarian by Judy Krizmanic (NY: Puffin, 1994). This helpful guide covers the basics of going vegetarian. Learn all you want to know about nutritional requirements, health benefits, and how to deal with anxious parents.

Beyond the Moon Cookbook by Ginny Callan (NY: Harper Collins, 1996). This cookbook features an extensive selection of breakfast and pancake ideas, soups, pizza, desserts, and more. Beginner-friendly recipes are highlighted.

101 Meatless Family Dishes by John Ettinger (Rocklin, CA: Prima Publishing, 1995). Your family will love this collection, even if they're not vegetarian. It includes a guide to selecting and cooking popular fruits and veggies, plus delicious and satisfying recipes for soups, stews, chili, pizza, pasta, and more.

One Thousand & One Low-Fat Vegetarian Recipes: Easy Great-Tasting Recipes for Everyone by Sue Spitler with Linda Yoakam (Chicago: Surrey Books, 1997). You guessed it: 1,001 recipes for vegetarians—from appetizers and soups to entrees and desserts.

Magazine

Vegetarian Times Magazine
P.O. Box 420235 • Palm Coast, FL 32143-0235
1-800-829-3340 • *www.vegetariantimes.com*
This publication includes recipes, shopping tips, and lots of news and features about the vegetarian lifestyle. Find out about "veggie-friendly" restaurants, clip the recipes, and read about the latest eco-friendly products.

Organizations

The Vegetarian Resource Group

P.O. Box 1463 • Baltimore, MD 21203
(410) 366-VEGE • *www.vrg.org*
A nonprofit organization dedicated to promoting the vegetarian way of life, the Vegetarian Resource Group offers free pamphlets and brochures about vegetarianism, and has vegetarian cookbooks and resources for sale. VRG also publishes *The Vegetarian Journal*.

Vegetarian Awareness Network

P.O. Box 321 • Knoxville, TN 37901
1-800-872-8343
Dedicated to promoting eco-friendly attitudes through informed eating, this nonprofit network answers questions, promotes events, sells books and other materials, organizes a speakers' bureau, and refers callers to other vegetarian resources and services.

Vegetarian Youth Network

P.O. Box 1141 • New Paltz, NY 12561
www.geocities.com/RodeoDrive/1154/
This grassroots organization is run by and for teens who support vegetarianism. If you contact the Network by mail, enclose a self-addressed, stamped business-size envelope.

Web sites

The North American Vegetarian Society Home Page

www.cyberveg.org/navs/
The North American Vegetarian Society (NAVS) is a nonprofit educational organization dedicated to promoting vegetarianism and the health benefits of a meatless diet. NAVS founded and promotes World Vegetarian Day (October 1) and Vegetarian Awareness Month (October).

The Vegetarian Pages

www.veg.org/veg
Packed with information, this huge Web site (based in Great Britain) is a guide to everything "veggie" on the Internet. Includes links to vegetarian organizations in the U.S. and around the world, vegetarian news, profiles of well-known vegetarians, plus access to books, articles, recipes, other organizations, and a network of vegetarians you can reach online.

8
Ready to Read Labels?

"People have the power to make a difference in their lives."

Oprah Winfrey, talk-show host

The clock is ticking. Your friends are on their way to pick you up, and you want to eat before you go. You look for a quick and healthy snack. Then you spot it: Emblazoned on a bag of corn tortilla chips are the words "low fat." The label on a jar of salsa claims the spicy stuff is low in sodium and totally fat free. Sounds great, but can you believe what the label says? The good news is you can.

The Food and Drug Administration (FDA) and the Food Safety and Inspection Service (FSIS)[1] of the U.S. Department of Agriculture have made it mandatory for manufacturers and grocers to put *factual* labels on their food products. Labels are required to meet strict federal guidelines, and the information they contain must be stated in clear, understandable language so that consumers (like you) know what they're getting. This gives you the knowledge you need to make healthier food choices. Now you can have your chips . . . and salsa, too! In this chapter you'll find out what to look for the next time you cruise through a supermarket or convenience store.

---

[1] Contact information for the FDA and FSIS can be found on p. 92.

The Front of the Food Package

The front of a package may have a few words (usually in a bright color) about the food's nutrient content. You're probably already familiar with many of these claims, such as "low fat," "cholesterol free," "extra lean," or "a good source of vitamin C." Here's a rundown of how the FDA defines the following terms:

- **Fat free:** less than ½ gram (g) fat per serving
- **Low fat:** 3 g fat or less per serving
- **Reduced fat:** at least 25% less fat than the regular or reference food
- **Low calorie:** 40 calories or less per serving
- **Cholesterol free:** less than 2 mg cholesterol and 2 g saturated fat per serving
- **Low cholesterol:** 20 mg or less cholesterol and 2 g or less of saturated fat per serving
- **Sodium free:** 5 mg or less of sodium per serving
- **Low sodium:** 140 mg or less of sodium per serving
- **Reduced sodium:** at least 25% less sodium than the regular or reference food
- **Lean:** less than 10 g fat, 4.5 g or less of saturated fat, and less than 95 mg cholesterol per serving and per 100 g (about 3 oz.)
- **Extra lean:** less than 5 g fat, less than 2 g saturated fat, and less than 95 mg cholesterol per serving and per 100 g
- **Good source:** each serving contains 10% to 19% of the daily value[2] for a particular nutrient
- **High in:** each serving contains 20% or more of the daily value for a particular nutrient

The Side or Back of the Food Package

On the side or back of the package, you'll find a nutrition panel with the heading "Nutrition Facts," which provides details about the food. You'll also

[2] Read more about daily values on p. 88.

find the ingredient list, which tells you exactly what's in the food you're about to eat—*whatever appears at the top of the list is the ingredient of the highest weight.* Scanning food labels not only helps you choose healthier foods but can also save you from eating extra fat and calories.

Here's a detailed breakdown of what a typical food label includes:

1. up-to-date, easy-to-understand nutrition information

2. information about how the food fits into your overall diet

3. the amount of saturated fat, cholesterol, dietary fiber, sugar, and other nutrients each serving contains

4. uniform definitions describing a product's nutrient content so the terms mean the same thing on every product

5. standardized serving sizes to make nutritional comparisons between similar products a whole lot easier

6. claims linking a particular food or nutrient to a disease or health-related condition, as long as they're supported by scientific evidence. Some examples include:

- "Too much fat can increase the risk of cancer and heart disease."

- "High-fiber products like whole grains, fruits, and vegetables can reduce the risk of some cancers and heart disease."

- "A high-sodium diet can lead to a greater risk of high blood pressure."

- "Adequate calcium can lower the risk of osteoporosis."

Label-Reading Know-How

Don't let the prospect of reading food labels overwhelm you. Start slowly, comparing one type of product at a time. For instance, you might start with something you frequently buy, such as beverages. Say you zip into the store in search of the ideal thirst quencher. Try reading the labels on 100% fruit juice, a fruit-flavored drink, a soda, and a carbonated, flavored water. Once you check the facts, it's pretty easy to tell which choices are healthiest.

Check out the sample label that appears on p. 86 (serving size, calories, daily value percentages, and calories per gram are explained on pp. 87–90).

Nutrition Facts

Serving Size 1 cup (228 g)
Servings Per Container 2

Amount Per Serving
Calories 250   Calories from Fat 110

	% Daily Value*
Total Fat 12 g	18%
Saturated Fat 3 g	15%
Cholesterol 30 mg	10%
Sodium 470 mg	20%
Total Carbohydrate 31 g	10%
Dietary Fiber 0 g	0%
Sugars 5 g	
Protein 5 g	

Vitamin A 4%	•	Vitamin C 2%
Calcium 20%	•	Iron 4%

*Percent Daily Values are based on a 2,000 calorie diet. Your daily values may be higher or lower depending on your calorie needs:

		Calories:	2,000	2,500
Total Fat	Less than:		65 g	80 g
Sat Fat	Less than:		20 g	25 g
Cholesterol	Less than:		300 mg	300 mg
Sodium	Less than:		2,400 mg	2,400 mg
Total Carbohydrate			300 g	375 g
Dietary Fiber			25 g	30 g

Calories per gram:
Fat 9   •   Carbohydrate 4   •   Protein 4

Sample Label for Macaroni & Cheese

SOURCE: Adapted from a sample created by the U.S. Food and Drug Administration and the U.S. Department of Agriculture.

Serving size

The *serving size* tells you how big a portion actually is. You'll find it expressed in common household measurements (cup, teaspoon), as well as metric measures like grams (g), milligrams (mg), etc. Standard serving sizes have been designed to reflect what the average person typically eats in one sitting.

Read the label to see what's considered one serving. Serving sizes should be consistent for all brands of the same product. For example, one serving of Pop Secret microwave popcorn will be the same size as a serving of Jiffy Pop or Orville Redenbacher's. This makes it easier to tell which brand gives you the least or most fat, calories, and sodium per serving.

Calories

The amount of calories per serving is listed under *calories*. If you eat two or three servings of a food, you'll need to double or triple the calories listed to figure out how many calories you've actually eaten.

Calories from fat lets you know how many of the calories contained in each serving come from fat. Because the USDA and the USDHHS recommend getting no more than 30% of your calories from fat, pay attention to this part of the food label. If the label on a bag of light potato chips says the chips have only 85 calories per serving, but 50 of them come from fat, they're pretty fattening.

When you start scanning labels, you'll see that some foods get most of their calories from fat (margarine and creamy salad dressings are examples). The *calories from fat* section of the label will show a high number of calories compared to the total calories per serving, which makes sense because these food items are part of the fats, oils, and sweets group of the Food Guide Pyramid.[3] It's perfectly okay to eat these kinds of foods, so don't become "fat phobic" or panic if you eat a high-fat product. Enjoying foods that have lots of fat shouldn't give you pangs of guilt. Moderation is the key. It's your *total* diet that counts, not what you eat during one meal on any given day. If you keep your overall diet lean and healthy, you're doing great.

---

[3] See Chapter 7, "Your Road Map to Healthy Eating."

Daily value percentages

This part of the label starts with *% Daily Value* and ends after the asterisked (*) explanation of *Percent Daily Values* toward the lower end of the label. What's included in this list will give you an idea of how healthy or unhealthy the food is by showing how much of each essential nutrient it contains per serving. The nutrients in this list are the ones that many people are concerned about these days:

• total fat (and saturated fat)

• cholesterol

• sodium

• total carbohydrate (including dietary fiber and sugars)

• protein

The *% Daily Value* column shows you how the food fits into your overall diet. When it comes to fat, saturated fat, cholesterol, and sodium, you want to make sure that you don't exceed 100% of your daily value. For nutrients like fiber or vitamin A, your goal should be to eat a variety of foods that add up to at least 100% per day.

Lower down on the label where it says *Percent Daily Values, you can see that the values are based on a 2,000-calorie-a-day diet (some labels may also list values for a 2,500-calorie-a-day diet). Since the USDA recommends that teenage girls consume an average 2,200 calories a day, your daily values are as follows:

• Total fat: 73 g

• Saturated fat: 24 g

• Total carbohydrates: 330 g

• Dietary fiber: 25–30 g

For fats, the grams listed above are your *maximum* amounts for a healthy diet. The amounts listed for total carbohydrates and fiber are the *target* amounts to shoot for. (TIP: Remember that these are dietary suggestions *only*. Some days you may consume more than the recommended amount of fat or less fiber, and that's okay. Just try to eat a balanced diet as often as possible.)

By looking at a food label, you can figure out whether the food you're eating offers a lot or a little of a given nutrient. In general, it's healthier to eat foods that are high in carbohydrates, fiber, and vitamins and minerals, while consuming less fat, saturated fat, cholesterol, and sodium. Look at the sample food label on p. 86 for macaroni and cheese: If you want to decrease your fat and sodium intake and increase your fiber intake, for example, this sample product may not be your best choice. By comparing labels, you would probably be able to find another brand that meets your needs (lower in fat and sodium), or you might decide to eat something else.

What About Vitamins and Minerals?

Your *Reference Daily Intake* (abbreviated as RDI or DRI) is a set of dietary references for essential vitamins and minerals, based on the Recommended Dietary Allowances for Americans (RDA) established by the National Academy of Sciences. Look below to see the amount of vitamins and minerals you need each day. To meet these daily requirements, eat a balanced diet of a variety of foods.

Nutrient	General RDI	RDA for Girls 11–18
Vitamin A	5,000 IU*	5,000 IU
Vitamin C	60 mg*	50–60 mg
Thiamin	1.5 mg	1.1 mg
Riboflavin	1.7 mg	1.3 mg
Niacin	20 mg	15 mg
Calcium	1,000 mg	1,300 mg
Iron	18 mg	15 mg
Vitamin D	400 IU	400 IU
Vitamin E	30 IU	30 IU
Vitamin B-6	2.0 mg	1.4–1.5 mg
Folic Acid	150 mcg*	180 mcg
Vitamin B-12	6 mcg	2 mcg
Phosphorus	1,000 mg	1,200 mg
Iodine	150 mcg	150 mcg
Magnesium	400 mg	280–300 mg
Zinc	15 mg	12 mg

IU = International Units (the unit of measurement for certain vitamins), **mg** = milligrams, **mcg** = micrograms

Calories per gram

The sample food label on p. 86 contains a *calories per gram* portion, but not all food labels do. The calories per gram reference usually only appears on larger food packages and explains that there are:

- 9 calories in 1 gram of fat

- 4 calories per carbohydrate gram

- 4 calories in a protein gram

Regardless of the food you choose, these numbers remain the same.

Label-Reading Quiz

Just for fun, here's a label-reading quiz. See if you can guess the products the following labels are describing. The answers are on p. 92.

LABEL #1

Nutrition Facts

Serving Size: 1 container (64 g)

Amount Per Serving

Calories 300 Calories from Fat 130

	% Daily Value*
Total Fat 14 g	22%
Saturated Fat 6 g	30%
Cholesterol 0 mg	0%
Sodium 1,120 mg	47%
Total Carbohydrate 37 g	12%
Dietary Fiber 2 g	8%
Sugars 2 g	
Protein 7 g	

Vitamin A 20%	•	Vitamin C 0%
Calcium 2%	•	Iron 10%

*Percent Daily Values are based on a 2,000 calorie diet. Your daily values maybe higher or lower depending on your calorie needs:

	Calories:	2,000	2,500
Total Fat	Less than	65 g	80 g
Sat. Fat	Less than	20 g	25 g
Cholesterol	Less than	300 mg	300 mg
Sodium	Less than	2,400 mg	2,400 mg
Total Carbohydrate		300 g	375 g
Dietary Fiber		25 g	30 g

INGREDIENTS: ENRICHED FLOUR (WHEAT FLOUR, NIACIN, REDUCED IRON, THIAMINE MONONITRATE, RIBOFLAVIN, FOLIC ACID), PARTIALLY HYDROGENATED VEGETABLE OIL (CONTAINS ONE OR MORE OF THE FOLLOWING: CANOLA OIL, COTTONSEED OIL, PALM OIL), DEHYDRATED VEGETABLES (CORN, CARROT, GREEN PEA, ONION, GARLIC, TOMATO, PARSLEY, CELERY), SALT, HYDROLYZED WHEAT AND CORN GLUTEN, LACTOSE, MONOSODIUM GLUTAMATE, SUGAR, MALTODEXTRIN, AUTOLYZED YEAST EXTRACT, NATURAL FLAVORS, CHICKEN POWDER, HYDROLYZED SOY PROTEIN, CHICKEN FAT, SPICES, SODIUM TRIPOLYPHOSPHATE, POTASSIUM CARBONATE, SODIUM ALGINATE, SODIUM CARBONATE, BUTTER POWDER, CITRIC ACID, NONFAT MILK, DISODIUM GUANYLATE, DISODIUMINOSINATE, TURMERIC COLOR, TOCOPHEROLS, ARTIFICIAL FLAVOR.

LABEL #2

NUTRITION FACTS: Serving Size: 1 pack

Calories 250, Fat Calories 120, Total Fat 13 g (20% DV), Saturated Fat 5 g (25% DV), **Cholesterol** 5 mg (1% DV), **Sodium** 25 mg (1% DV), **Total Carbohydrate** 30 g (10% DV), Fiber 2 g (7% DV), Sugars 25 g, **Protein** 5 g, Vitamin A (0% DV), Vitamin C (0% DV), Calcium (4% DV), Iron (2% DV), Thiamine (2% DV), Riboflavin (4% DV), Niacin (8% DV). Percent Daily Values (DV) are based on a 2,000 calorie diet.

INGREDIENTS: MILK CHOCOLATE (SUGAR, CHOCOLATE, MILK, COCOA BUTTER, LACTOSE, PEANUTS, SOY LECITHIN, SALT, ARTIFICIAL FLAVORS), SUGAR, PEANUTS, CORNSTARCH, LESS THAN 1%– CORN SYRUP, GUM ACACIA, COLORING (INCLUDES RED 40 LAKE, BLUE 2 LAKE, BLUE 1 LAKE, YELLOW 5, YELLOW 6, RED 40, BLUE 1), DEXTRIN.

LABEL #3

Nutrition Facts
Serving Size: 1 container (128g)

Amount Per Serving

Calories 350 Calories from Fat 180

	% Daily Value*
Total Fat 20 g	31%
Saturated Fat 11 g	55%
Cholesterol 70 mg	23%
Sodium 1,760 mg	73%
Total Carbohydrate 22 g	7%
Dietary Fiber 1 g	4%
Sugars 5 g	
Protein 20 g	

Vitamin A 10%	•	Vitamin C 0%
Calcium 25%	•	Iron 10%

*Percent Daily Values are based on a 2,000 calorie diet.

INGREDIENTS: ROAST TURKEY BREAST & WHITE TURKEY–CURED–SMOKE FLAVOR ADDED–TURKEY BREAST, WATER, WHITE TURKEY, SODIUM LACTATE, MODIFIED CORN STARCH, CONTAINS LESS THAN 2% OF SALT, DEXTROSE, CARRAGEENAN, SODIUM PHOSPHATE, SMOKE FLAVOR, SODIUM ERYTHOR-BATE (MADE FROM SUGAR), SODIUM NITRITE. CHEDDAR PASTEURIZED PROCESS CHEESE FOOD–CHEDDAR CHEESE (MILK, CHEESE CULTURE, SALT, ENZYMES), MILKFAT, WHEY PROTEIN CONCEN-TRATE, WATER, SODIUM CITRATE, SALT, SORBIC ACID AS A PRESERVATIVE, ANNATTO (COLOR), OLEORESIN PAPRIKA. WHEAT CRACKERS– ENRICHED FLOUR (WHEAT FLOUR, NIACIN, REDUCED IRON, THIAMINE MONONITRATE [VITAMIN B1], RIBOFLAVIN [VITAMIN B2]), VEGETABLE SHORTENING (PARTIALLY HYDRO-GENATED SOYBEAN AND/OR COTTONSEED OILS), WHOLE WHEAT FLOUR, SUGAR, SALT, CONTAINS 2% OR LESS OF MALT, LEAVENING (SODIUM BICARBONATE, SODIUM ACID PYROPHOSPHATE, MONOCALCIUM PHOSPHATE), ONION, CORN SYRUP, WHEY, CARAMEL COLOR.

Now that you have an idea of the meaning behind different parts of a food label, why not put your label-reading expertise to work? Get into the habit of comparing a few similar items before making your final choice. Don't stress out about all of the nutrients at once, though. After all, the Mall of America wasn't built in a day, and neither is a well-rounded nutritional plan. Work on one thing at a time. Soon reading labels will become totally natural, and so will reaching for the healthiest choice.

For more information about the new food labels, contact:

The Food and Drug Administration

5600 Fishers Lane (HFE-88) • Rockville, MD 20857
1-800-FDA-4010

Labels—Public Awareness

Food Safety and Inspection Service, USDA • 14th & Independence, SW
Room 1180 South • Washington, DC 20250

Answers for Label-Reading Quiz:

Label #1: "Cup Noodles" Ramen Noodle Soup
(chicken vegetable flavor)

Label #2: M&M's peanut chocolate candies

Label #3: Oscar Mayer Lunchables: lean turkey breast,
cheddar cheese, wheat crackers

9

The Skinny on Fat-Free Junk Foods

"I make the best oatmeal-raisin cookies in the world. Well, I don't make them a lot because I don't think it's fair to the other cookies."

Phoebe, from TV's _Friends_

Mmmm . . . it's tempting to think that you can devour a fat-free muffin, munch on a bag of low-fat potato chips, and gulp down a handful of reduced-fat chocolate-chip cookies and still be "eating right." The truth is, many so-called fat-free or low-fat products can be a sweet invitation to overindulgence. You might mistakenly believe that you can eat a whole bunch of fat-free foods and still be giving your body what it needs for good health. But eating fat-free junk food isn't nutritious and doesn't mean that you no longer have to think about the fat, oil, and sweets group of the Food Guide Pyramid.[1] Here's why: Most snack foods—fat free or not—don't contain the nutrients that your body needs for good health (fiber, vitamins, minerals, etc.). And whether they're from carbohydrates, fat, or protein, _calories are still calories._ When you consume more calories than your body needs, the extra calories are stored as fat, which might mean that you'll gain weight.

When you're reaching for a fat-free or reduced-fat snack, take a look at the label on the package.[2] If possible, compare the lower-fat version with the

---

[1] See Chapter 7, "Your Road Map to Healthy Eating."
[2] See Chapter 8, "Ready to Read Labels?"

regular brand. You may discover that there's not as much of a calorie difference between them as you would think. The chart below shows how several lower-fat brands compare to the originals. Notice that the serving sizes for the fat-free and reduced-fat portions are sometimes *smaller* than the regular portions. Many low-fat and fat-free versions have more sugar, too.

Product	Low-fat version Calories per serving	Regular version Calories per serving
Hostess Twinkies	130 (1 cake)	150 (1 cake)
Wheat Thins	120 (18 crackers)	140 (16 crackers)
Ruffles Potato Chips	140 (1 oz.)	160 (1 oz.)
Oreo Cookies	130 (3 cookies)	160 (3 cookies)
Milky Way Bar	170 (1.57 oz.)	270 (2.05 oz.)
Chips Ahoy! Real Chocolate Chip Cookies	150 (3 cookies)	160 (3 cookies)
Kellogg's Blueberry Pop Tarts	190 (1 pop tart)	200 (1 pop tart)
Ritz Crackers	70 (5 crackers)	80 (5 crackers)
Jolly Time Butter Flavored Microwave Popcorn	120 (5 cups)	140 (4 cups)

NOTE: The calories listed for this chart reflect the 1998 versions of these products and may be subject to change.

Everywhere you look, you're going to find reduced-fat and lower-fat versions of snack foods. Most of these foods are processed, which means that the food is manufactured and packaged (vs. natural). Processed foods are usually high in calories, sugar, sodium, or fat, and they almost always contain chemicals and additives to make the food look and taste better and last longer on the shelf. You have to be careful not to equate reduced-fat junk foods and sweets with foods that nourish your body.

Many of these tantalizing snacks—reduced fat or not—are high in sugar and low in fiber and vitamins. If you tend to fill up on reduced-fat chips, ice cream, cookies, and diet sodas, your body isn't going to get the vitamins and minerals it needs to function. Substituting junk foods for healthier ones deprives your body of important nutrients. To stay fit and healthy, choose foods that are naturally low in fat and loaded with nutritional value.

If you think healthy snacks are boring, think again. It's easy to get creative with nature's huge assortment of naturally low-fat and flavorful fruits and veggies. Smart snacking not only satisfies a case of the munchies but also keeps you energized so you can push it to the limit on the field, on the court, or in the classroom. The next time a snack attack occurs, reach for a healthy treat that will satisfy your taste buds and your "5-a-day" (a total of at least five fruits and vegetables).

Simply Delicious Smoothies

When it comes to satisfying your hunger or sweet tooth, smoothies (fruit, juices, and other ingredients blended together) are a great choice. With smoothies, there really aren't any rules or magic combinations. Be bold and creative. Toss a handful of fruits in the blender, throw in a few other ingredients, hit the puree button, and whip up a fruity, frosty concoction. Here are some recipes to get you started:

Peach Smoothie
- 1 cup peach or apricot nectar
- 1 cup frozen peaches
- 3 or 4 ice cubes

Tofu Smoothie
- 4 oz. soft tofu
- 1 cup berries (any kind)
- ½ cup 100% fruit juice
- 3 or 4 ice cubes

Berry Smoothie
- 1 cup apple juice
- ½ cup low-fat plain or vanilla yogurt
- 1 cup berries (blueberries, raspberries, strawberries, or mixed)

Strawberry Banana Smoothie
- 1 banana
- 1 cup strawberries
- 1 cup 100% fruit juice
- 3 or 4 ice cubes

Tropical Smoothie
- 1 banana
- 1 cup orange juice or 100% tropical fruit juice
- 1 tablespoon shredded coconut (optional)
- 1 scoop pineapple or orange sherbet
- 3 or 4 ice cubes

By now you're probably wondering if it's ever okay to indulge in the reduced-fat snacks and sweets lining the grocer's shelves. These treats do have a place in your overall diet—they're fine for an occasional tasty snack, as long as they don't become a dietary staple. If junk food is a habit for you, ask yourself why:

• are you hungry from skipping meals?

• are you using food for comfort when you're stressed out?

• are you growing quickly and staying really active?

Consider the reasons behind your eating habits, then figure out how to change them gradually.

The good news is, snacking is perfectly fine. In fact, YOU SHOULD EAT BETWEEN MEALS. When you have a snack before lunch, after school, or late in the evening, you're not doing anything wrong. You're probably hungry, and your body needs the calories for energy. Just make sure that you indulge in healthy treats like a smoothie, fruit, a bagel, or some raw veggies as often as possible.

If you feel like giving in to a junk-food craving, going for the "real thing" may actually be a better choice than the reduced-fat or fat-free version. That's because when the fat is missing from foods, some people find that they need to eat more to feel satisfied (which may mean consuming more sugar and sodium). Many people simply don't like the taste and texture of lower-fat products. If you enjoy the reduced-fat versions just as much as the real thing, no problem. Go ahead and have a snack (guilt-free), then eat a few extra vegetables at dinner.

The bottom line is: If you're going to snack, try to keep it healthy. And when the urge to indulge in something sweet or salty strikes, indulge without going overboard.

10

Food Makeovers That Fit Your Social Life

"I finally said, 'I'm a happy person. I'm not going
to let my life revolve around losing weight.
I have other things to do.'"

Rosie O'Donnell, talk-show host

Food is often the center of get-togethers, dates, and family gatherings, but these situations shouldn't make you anxious that you'll blow your commitment to eating right. As long as your *overall* eating habits are healthy, occasional indulgences are perfectly fine.

When you're in any social situation, *you* have the power to make healthy food choices. Once you know which foods are nutritious and which ones aren't, eating right in social settings is easy. Choose foods that will nourish your body, and remember the basics of the USDA's Dietary Guidelines and the Food Guide Pyramid.[1] Following is a little refresher:

- Eat a variety of wholesome foods to give your body all the nutrients it needs.

- Balance the foods you eat with physical activities.

- Eat a minimum of five servings of fruits and veggies daily; they're low in fat and chock-full of fiber and vitamins. Load up on complex carbohydrates (bread, cereal, pasta) to keep yourself energized.

- Keep your diet low in cholesterol and fat for a healthy body.

- Don't consume too much sugar.

- Keep your intake of salt and sodium low. (Processed, frozen, and fast foods are loaded with sodium.)

- Use alcohol in moderation. (*This particular guideline is meant for adults. If you're underage, you shouldn't be drinking alcohol.*)

---

[1] See Chapter 6, "How to Eat Right," and Chapter 7, "Your Road Map to Healthy Eating."

❀ ☀ ❀ ☀ ❀ ☀ ❀ ☀ ❀ ☀ ❀ ☀ ❀ ☀ ❀ ☀ ❀ ☀ ❀ ☀ ❀ ☀ ❀ ☀

Old Attitude	**New Outlook**
❀ It's impossible to eat healthy and still have a social life.	☀ The choice is mine to eat smart no matter where I am.

❀ ☀ ❀ ☀ ❀ ☀ ❀ ☀ ❀ ☀ ❀ ☀ ❀ ☀ ❀ ☀ ❀ ☀ ❀ ☀ ❀ ☀ ❀ ☀

Read on for tips for healthy meals and snacks that won't take a bite out of your social life. Bon appétit!

Dining Out

Eating right is great for your body and mind, so why not set an example for your family and friends and dare to be a healthy-food trendsetter? It doesn't matter if you're luxury dining at a four-star restaurant or chowing down a burger—eating should be enjoyable, not something to agonize over. Here are some tips for healthy eating while dining out:

1. If you're on a date at a nice restaurant, don't assume that you have to pick at a plate of lettuce leaves all evening. Anyone who ever told you that guys don't like to see a girl with a big appetite was simply WRONG! Order your best meal choice and eat with pleasure.

2. Ordering high-fat dishes (like a plate of fettuccine Alfredo or a slice of cheesecake) shouldn't leave you feeling guilty for the rest of the night. Just be sure that your overall diet is lean and healthy.

3. Split an entree with someone, and you'll be splitting the extra calories and fat. Order a dinner salad or a plain baked potato with your meal.

4. Green salads with an oil and vinegar dressing, shrimp cocktail, and fresh pasta with a tomato-based sauce are lighter appetizers.

5. Skip over menu items with the words "au gratin," "creamed," "sautéed," or "fried" in their descriptions—they're usually very high in fat. So are quiches, gravy, and oil-based dressings. If you want to eat lean, pass on those items and on cream-based sauces and soups (such as cream of broccoli). Choose grilled, poached, steamed, or baked meats, poultry, and fish instead of fried.

6. Salad bars are a healthy choice if you load up on lettuce, raw veggies, kidney beans, and other low-fat items. Skip the pre-made macaroni salads, and go easy on croutons, bacon bits, cheese, seeds, and nuts. Top your salad off with a mix of vinegar and olive oil or a reduced-fat salad dressing. If you order a salad, ask for the dressing on the side.

7. Bread has lots of carbohydrates, so it's a good choice. But go easy on the butter if you want to decrease the fat in your diet.

8. Order water or milk instead of a sugary soda.

9. If nothing on the menu appears healthy and you really want to eat light, ask the waiter for a plate of steamed vegetables and a plain baked potato, or find out if the chef can make you a low-fat dish.

Hanging Out

When it comes to snacking at home, you've got lots of healthy options.[1] Try these tasty snacks to satisfy a case of the munchies, whether you're studying solo or hanging out with friends:

*   air-popped popcorn or low-fat microwave popcorn, sprinkled with a dash of garlic powder and Parmesan cheese

*   raw veggies with a dip made from low-fat plain yogurt, low-fat cottage cheese, or a low-fat salad dressing

*   pretzels (low-salt varieties are available)

*   frozen fruit-juice bars or fruit smoothies[2]

*   mini pizzas made with English muffins, pita bread, or bagels; tomato sauce; and part-skim mozzarella cheese

*   quesadillas made with low-fat cheese and salsa

*   nonfat or low-fat frozen yogurt topped with bananas or berries

*   graham crackers or fruit-juice-sweetened granola bars

*   rice cakes or bagels with low-fat cream cheese, peanut butter, or 100% fruit spread

---

[1] See Chapter 10, "Overhaul Your Kitchen for Healthy Eating at Home."

[2] For recipes, see p. 95.

PMS and Junk Food

PMS, or premenstrual syndrome, is a set of symptoms that many girls and women get before their period starts. If you're about to get your period and notice that you're irritable, a little depressed, crampy, bloated, tired, and/or craving junk food, PMS may be the culprit. You can cut down on these symptoms by avoiding certain foods.

PMS often triggers cravings for foods that are sweet or salty. If you devour a plate of French fries, quench your thirst with a cola, and have a chocolate bar for dessert, you're likely to make your PMS symptoms much worse. Salty foods can lead to bloating (and you probably don't want any more of *that* before your period), and the sugar in colas or chocolate can make you feel jittery and then really tired. Caffeine (found in chocolate and colas) is a stimulant that often makes you irritable, and like sugar, can lead to fatigue once the effects have worn off.

Instead of reaching for junk foods, choose fresh fruits and veggies, whole grain products, and low-salt/low-sugar snacks. Drink lots of water, too. Fresh, wholesome foods will keep your energy up and help stabilize mood swings. You'll feel a lot better.

Fast Food

Surprise! You *can* make healthy choices at fast-food restaurants. Most fast-food places offer grilled sandwiches, salads, baked potatoes, and lighter versions of their regular menu items; many even provide nutrition information for their menu selections, making it easier to choose wisely. We don't recommend that you make fast-food cuisine a staple of your diet, but when you do give in to the temptation, follow these guidelines:

1. Choose grilled or broiled chicken over burgers.
2. Lean, grilled, or broiled meats are better selections than fried.
3. Skip the fattening extras like cheese, bacon, mayonnaise, guacamole, sour cream, and/or tartar sauce.
4. Choose soft taco shells (they're lower in fat than fried hard ones).

5. Avoid anything called "super," "double," "extra," or "deluxe." These catchy terms often mean "extra fat and sodium."

6. Beware of hidden fat and high levels of sodium in salad dressings.

7. Avoid fried foods like French fries and fish sandwiches.

8. Skip the meat toppings and extra cheese on pizza. Plain cheese, pineapple, or fresh veggies are healthier choices.

9. Don't load a healthy baked potato with mounds of sour cream, butter, cheese, salt, and/or bacon bits. Pile on steamed vegetables instead.

Get the Facts

If you want to be a smart shopper when it comes to fast-food dining, get the "Fast Food Facts." This free brochure will tell you about the calorie, fat, sodium, and cholesterol counts of popular menu items at national fast-food chains. Write or call:

Fast Food Facts
The Attorney General's Consumer Division
1400 NCL Tower • 445 Minnesota Street • St. Paul, MN 55101
1-800-657-3787

Or visit the interactive "Food Finder" Web site based on the book at *www.olen.com/food/* and search for information about specific restaurants and menu items.

At the Movies

Who can resist a snack attack at the movies? When it comes to really salty and fatty foods at the concession stand, you couldn't do much worse than buttered popcorn, nachos, or hot dogs. Here are some better ways to conquer the movie munchies without filling up on fat:

1. Buy fat-free candies like Hot Tamales, Sweet Tarts, Red Vines, Jujyfruits, Gummi Bears, Twizzlers, Good & Plenty, and jelly beans. Or opt for a low-fat chocolate treat like Junior Mints.

2. Choose air-popped popcorn or popcorn prepared in canola oil. Skip the added butter and salt.

3. If you can't make it through a movie without a chocolate bar but are concerned about the fat and sugar, split the candy with a friend.

4. Wash down snacks with mineral water or seltzers flavored with fruit juice, instead of a soda.

Going Out for Ice Cream

If you want an alternative to the Triple Brownie Heavenly Hash, try low-fat frozen yogurt, ices, sorbets, sherbets, and reduced-fat ice cream. With the exception of colossal waffle cones, cones are generally low in fat and calories. If you're having a sundae, skip the fattening nuts and whipped cream; a better idea is to top your sundae off with fruit or reduced-fat hot fudge. But remember, it's fine to indulge yourself sometimes—if a huge banana split is all that will satisfy you, go for it!

At the Mall

If power shopping leaves you hungry, and the food court is your only option, eating healthy is still possible. Snack on a soft hot pretzel or low-fat frozen yogurt. If you need something more filling, a single slice of cheese pizza is a good bet; use a napkin to blot the excess grease from the cheese before you eat it. (TIP: At food court pizza places, the vegetable toppings are often high in fat because they're usually marinated in oil, so you may want to skip the mushrooms and onions.) When your sweet tooth just won't take no for an answer, treat yourself to licorice or other fat-free candy, or try some flavored popcorn. If you indulge in a gourmet cookie or a warm sticky bun, split it with a friend; you'll save yourself half the fat and still satisfy your sweet craving.

Parties

The main purpose of a party is to socialize, not spend all night taste-testing the appetizers. If you're concerned about being surrounded by junk food, offer to bring your own dish to share. Prepare something healthy so everyone will have something nutritious to nibble on. Here are a few ideas:

- fat-free tortilla chips with salsa or low-fat bean dip
- raw veggies and low-fat dip
- low-fat whole grain crackers and reduced-fat cheese squares
- fresh fruit kabobs with lemon or raspberry low-fat yogurt for dipping
- low-fat breadsticks with marinara or pizza sauce for dipping
- air-popped popcorn
- angel food cake with fresh strawberries and a low-fat whipped topping

The School Cafeteria

How do you guarantee a healthy lunch at school? Brown bag it. Pack a sack lunch full of healthy foods and you're set. (BONUS: Bringing your lunch can be a lot less expensive than buying it.)

Sandwiches made with whole grain breads or stuffed in a pita pocket are good starts. Fill your sandwich with egg salad made with fat-free mayo, or lean meats like leftover chicken or turkey. Pile on lots of bean sprouts, tomatoes, cucumbers, and lettuce to help meet your daily veggie requirement. Peanut butter and 100% fruit spreads are good options, too. Make it a habit to include fresh fruit in your lunch. Other foods to add to your sack lunch are:

- individually packaged all-natural applesauce
- low-fat cottage cheese or low-fat yogurt
- carrot and celery sticks

- reduced-fat cheese and whole grain crackers
- raisins
- fruit-juice-sweetened granola bars

Steer clear of pre-packaged luncheon meats, which are usually high in sodium. Cookies, candy, chips, and cake are okay as an occasional treat, but don't make them a daily staple. Instead of drinking a sugary soda with your meal, choose skim milk or water. If brown-bagging it isn't your style and the cafeteria calls, remember these tips:

1. Many school cafeterias now offer salad bars, fresh fruit, raw veggies, and healthy sandwiches. Fill up on fresh foods whenever you can.

2. Pass on high-sodium, high-fat foods like fried fish sticks, macaroni and cheese, sloppy joes, burgers, pizza, and canned vegetables (and anything you can't recognize as real food!).

3. When it comes to vending machines, go for the low-fat items (pretzels, licorice, an apple). Don't let this be your entire meal, though.

4. Microwavable burritos and pizzas are usually loaded with sodium and fat, so be careful. Same goes for brownies, candy bars, muffins, doughnuts, and snack cakes.

• •

Your school may be one of many that offer brand-name fast food to students. If you're buying a fast-food lunch but still want to eat healthy, try some of the options mentioned on pp. 100–101. If a greasy cheeseburger is all that will satisfy you, balance it with a salad and a piece of fruit. Skip the soda in favor of skim milk.

• •

Picnics and Barbecues

Who doesn't love a great picnic or summer barbecue? Participate in the fun and work up a hearty appetite playing softball or Frisbee, or flying a kite.

These mouth-watering foods ought to hit the spot:

- corn on the cob (go light on the butter and salt)
- grilled chicken breast, turkey burgers, lean hamburgers, or veggie burgers
- carrot-raisin salad
- watermelon or any other fresh fruit
- grilled veggie kabobs made with mushrooms, squash, zucchini, onions, cherry tomatoes, and red, green, and yellow peppers
- baked potatoes (load them up with veggies, and use only a little butter, margarine, or sour cream)

Picnic and barbecue foods to watch out for:

- mayonnaise-based salads such as macaroni salad and potato salad
- pasta salads made with fattening oils
- fried chicken
- hot dogs
- submarine sandwiches
- chips
- bakery items

Holidays and Family Gatherings

Holidays and other celebrations are extra special days, and a lot of people see them as the perfect excuse to indulge until they can't even get up from the table. You can celebrate and still eat healthy, too. These tips should keep you on the healthy track:

1. Drink lots of water and eat a piece of fruit to curb your appetite before you leave home. This way you'll be less hungry when you arrive and not as likely to eat everything in sight.

2. If your family is hosting, avoid tasting every dish before it goes on the table. Instead, snack on fruit or vegetables.

3. Never starve yourself before the big event just so you can binge once you get there.

4. Focus on the fun, not the food.

5. Stay away from tempting trays of high-fat appetizers, such as sausages or hot dogs wrapped in dough, cheese logs, chips, and mayonnaise-based dips.

6. When it's time to eat, be sure to try the vegetable dishes and other healthy selections. It's fine to eat those holiday staples (mashed potatoes with gravy, ham, turkey), so don't feel guilty. If you want to take it easy on the fats, use less gravy or butter, remove the skin from poultry, and go light on cream-based sauces.

7. Volunteer to bring a raw veggie platter, green salad, healthy vegetable side dish, or low-fat dessert.

Whether you're standing in the buffet line or gathered around the table, these are the foods to take smaller portions of:

- cheesy casseroles and creamy sauces

- high-fat meats and gravy made from fat drippings

- fattening desserts

- fried foods

- vegetable dishes with butter or heavy sauces

- pasta salads made with oil or mayonnaise

Eating right doesn't mean you have to stay in the house for the rest of your life, avoiding restaurants, holiday gatherings, social events, and other people. Food is meant to be savored and enjoyed. It's fine to splurge on a meal that's higher in fat without a guilt trip. Just load up on fruits and veggies so you can still get your "5-a-day" (a total of at least five fruits and vegetables), and make sure that indulging in lots of fats and sweets isn't a habit. Once you learn to include healthy foods in your diet and consume the unhealthy stuff only once in a while, eating right in any situation is easy.

11
Overhaul Your Kitchen for Healthy Eating at Home

"You are what you eat, and you'll definitely be healthier if you give your mind and body the fuel they need."

Barbara A. Lewis, author

Do you find it hard to eat right while at home? Maybe it's time to revamp your kitchen. When you're trying to satisfy a snack attack, it's too easy to reach for unhealthy food choices in a kitchen full of high-fat, sugary, processed foods. Those cookies and potato chips can be really tempting if you're worried about an upcoming test or are glued to a new episode of your favorite prime-time soap. The solution: Transform a kitchen danger zone into a haven for healthy nourishment.

When you're serious about eating more nutritious foods, it's a good idea to let your parents or guardians know and ask for their support. Tell them that their assistance and encouragement mean a lot to you. If they already support healthy eating habits and cook nutritiously, great. But, if mealtime at your house could be a lot healthier, why not lend a hand? Help out with the grocery shopping, then put on your chef's hat and share the responsibility with the person who does the cooking at your house. Have fun surprising your family with meals that are both nutritious and delicious.

Shaping a healthy kitchen means filling the pantry and refrigerator with nutrient-rich foods. Keep lots of fruits, vegetables, breads, and grains on hand, as well as dairy products like skim milk, reduced-fat cheese, and yogurt. Stock up on lean meats, poultry, and fish. Remember to keep the oils, fats, and sweets to a minimum.

Dietary changes don't have to happen overnight, so ease into it gradually, adding more fruits and vegetables each week and eliminating a few junk foods from the usual grocery list. Give the cook in your house the night off once a week or more, and dazzle your family with a healthy dish you've prepared. It's easy to follow a basic recipe, and there are healthy recipes for just about every kind of food you can imagine—from tasty pastas and salads to scrumptious low-fat desserts. Check out cookbooks[1] with healthy dishes and easy-to-follow instructions; they show you how to cook meals that are naturally low in fat and taste great, too. Food magazines,[2] many women's magazines, and the food section of most newspapers also offer recipes for delicious low-fat meals. Clip the recipes out or photocopy them, start your own personal file, and get cooking.

Old Attitude	New Outlook
* I don't even know how to cook, let alone make a healthy dish.	* With some easy recipes and a willingness to try, I can learn to prepare nutritious meals.

Whatever you decide to cook, keep it simple. Recipes requiring lots of time and effort are a major hassle for everyday menu planning. Besides, you don't have to labor over a hot stove for hours to make flavorful meals that are low in fat and healthy, too. Quick and easy dishes are often a better choice. Learn to season foods naturally with fresh herbs, spices, and zesty salsas. Once you have a handle on the basics, let your creative flair loose in the kitchen. The only thing standing between you and an incredibly savory pita pocket sandwich loaded with grilled veggies or skinless barbecued chicken with peach-cilantro salsa is your imagination.

---

[1] See p. 110 for cookbook ideas.
[2] See p. 111 for magazine ideas.

Light and Healthy Foods

Tuna Salad

Liven up a can of water-packed tuna with any of the following:

- 1 cup fresh or frozen, thawed peas
- 2–3 stalks of celery, diced
- ½ cucumber, diced
- 2–3 green onions, thinly sliced
- 1 hard-boiled egg white, chopped

Mix your ingredients with a few tablespoons of low-calorie or low-fat mayonnaise. Season to taste with dill, lemon juice, pepper, and/or a bit of Dijon mustard.

Pasta Salad

Cook a package of fun-shaped noodles, such as shells, rotelle (corkscrew), rigatoni (tubes), fusilli (curls), elbow macaroni, or bowtie pasta. Toss with one or more of the following ingredients:

- 1 tablespoon sesame or olive oil
- 1 tablespoon vinegar (cider, red, or white)
- 1 tablespoon lemon juice

Add lightly cooked veggies (sliced or chopped) of your choice. For broccoli, cauliflower, carrots, or zucchini, boil gently for about 2–3 minutes. For mushrooms, onions, and peppers, sauté lightly in a nonfat cooking spray or in olive oil. Season with a clove of minced garlic, a dash of pepper, or a sprinkle of fresh herbs like basil or dill.

Bagel Toppers

Get creative when it comes to topping your bagel the healthy way:

- marinara sauce and melted low-fat cheese
- 100% fruit spread with all-natural peanut butter
- light cream cheese, a slice of red onion, and a slice of tomato
- tuna salad (see above recipe) with lettuce or alfalfa sprouts
- hummus (a spread made from garbanzo beans)

Fruit Salad

Almost any combination of fruit makes a light and delicious snack. Just peel, slice, or cube any assortment of seasonal favorites, such as melons, berries, grapes, and bananas. A dash of orange juice helps blend it all together into a tasty treat.

Resources for Cooks

Another great way to get into eating light is to check out cookbooks and magazines devoted to tasty, low-fat cuisine. Library and bookstore shelves are packed with selections on everything from how to make the ultimate light pizza to creating no-sugar desserts. If you're overwhelmed by all the choices, ask for a recommendation or at least try narrowing the possibilities by picking a category of cooking that you think you might enjoy. Light-cuisine magazines are loaded with recipes, cooking tips, and fun, informative articles—they usually have special holiday issues, too. Following are some recommendations for cookbooks, and magazines and their Web sites.

Cookbooks

Cookbook for the '90s: Great-Tasting Low-Fat Recipes for Better Health by Helen V. Fisher (Tucson, AZ: Fisher Books, 1990). Talk about simple and easy! The instructions for making each recipe in this book are a snap. Create healthy salads, sandwiches, appetizers, and snacks with over 200 recipes and sample menus that make healthy cooking easy.

LooneySpoons: Low-Fat Food Made Fun by Janet and Greta Podleski (Fairfield, IA: Granet Publishing, Inc., 1997). This bright, colorful cookbook is loaded with tasty dishes, informative tidbits, and anecdotes to entertain the beginning cook. The recipes are simple, and each one gets less than 30% of its calories from fat. Have a blast preparing vegetarian dishes from the "Meatless in Seattle" section or other fun favorites like "Flab-U-Less Fajitas."

Low-Fat Cooking for Dummies by Lynn Fischer (Indianapolis: IDG Books Worldwide, Inc., 1997). The more than 150 recipes in this basic book include estimated prep time and nutritional information. The step-by-step instructions make it easy for anyone to whip up main course dishes, as well as sandwiches, snacks, sauces, and desserts. An extensive resource section lists Web sites and newsletters for the nutrition-conscious cook.

One Thousand & One Low-Fat Recipes: Quick, Easy, Great-Tasting Recipes for the Whole Family by Sue Spitler and Linda Yoakam (Chicago: Surrey Books, 1995). Pizzas, veggies, breads, vegetarian dishes, desserts, meats—the list goes on . . . all the way up to 1,001! The recipes include nutritional information from the Food Guide Pyramid.

Cooking Magazines

Cooking Light: The Magazine of Food and Fitness
P.O. Box 830549 • Birmingham, AL 35282-9810
1-800-336-0125 • *www.cookinglight.com*
Each issue of *Cooking Light* features a different food, fitness and nutrition topics, and tons of low-fat and tasty recipes.

SHAPE Cooks
P.O. Box 37279 • Boone, IA 50037-2279
www.shapecooks.com
This magazine devotes sections to overall nutrition, adventures in eating, seasonal favorites, and of course, recipes.

A.M. Energizers

Girls on the go should never skip breakfast. Breakfast gives you the energy to make it through the day—it's what fuels your body so you can stay alert and concentrate in school; plus studies have shown that students who eat breakfast score higher on tests. If you can't take the time to sit down for breakfast, make a take-along meal like a piece of fruit and a bagel. Try these easy-to-fix, energizing breakfasts:

- a fruit-juice sweetened breakfast bar with a piece of fruit

- an individual-sized carton of 100% fruit juice and an English muffin with peanut butter

- nonfat yogurt topped with sliced fresh fruit

- toast with melted low-fat cheese and a fresh fruit salad

- hot cereal sprinkled with cinnamon and raisins, with a glass of orange juice

- melon wedges with a scoop of low-fat cottage cheese

- whole-wheat or oat-bran pancakes with a fresh-fruit topping

- cold cereal (one low in fat and sugar) with skim milk and berries or raisins

Shopping Smart

A touch of supermarket savvy is all it takes to make sure that you have healthy foods on hand. Give the shopper in your house a few suggestions for snacks and menus, and volunteer to help with the grocery run. By the way, never shop when you're hungry; an empty stomach can lead to impulse buying. If you're ravenous and are confronted with fancy packaging and strategically located goodies as you cruise each aisle, it's way too easy to toss them in the cart. Eat a healthy snack before you head to the store, then make a list of the essentials—and stick to it.

The supermarket is a great place to put your label-reading know-how[3] to work. Simply compare labels and switch to healthier choices whenever possible. For instance, if the ingredients for tacos are on your shopping list, buy ground turkey or chicken instead of beef (or use tofu). When you're at the grocery store, you may find two types of ground turkey in the meat section—lean ground turkey, which is ground dark meat, contains the same amount of fat as hamburger; extra lean ground turkey breast contains only 1.5 g of fat. You can also try reduced-fat cheese and low-fat sour cream. Purchase soft corn tortillas, plus lots of ripe tomatoes, onions, and peppers for some healthy homemade salsa. Experiment with spices to season the taco meat, rather than buying a high-sodium taco seasoning packet. Fill your tacos with extra lettuce, tomatoes, onions, and peppers.

Shop smart by making healthy substitutions like these:

Instead of This:	**Try This:**
whole milk	skim milk
tuna packed in oil	tuna packed in water
canned vegetables	fresh or frozen vegetables
sugar-sweetened cereal	unsweetened or low-sugar cereal
chips	air-popped popcorn or rice cakes
salad dressings	reduced-fat salad dressings or flavored vinegars

---

[3] See Chapter 8, "Ready to Read Labels?"

soda	flavored seltzers or 100% fruit juice
ice cream	sorbet, sherbet, or frozen yogurt
canned fruit	fresh fruit
butter	light margarine
frozen entrees	ingredients to make the "real thing"

As you wander around the market, you can learn a lot about the foods you want to buy. The produce departments of most grocery stores provide nutrition information for the Food and Drug Administration (FDA) list of the 20 most commonly eaten fruits and vegetables:

Top 20 Fruits

1. bananas
2. apples
3. watermelon
4. oranges
5. cantaloupe
6. grapes
7. grapefruit
8. strawberries
9. peaches
10. pears
11. nectarines
12. honeydew melon
13. plums
14. avocados
15. lemons
16. pineapple
17. tangerines
18. sweet cherries
19. kiwifruit
20. limes

TOP BANANA

Top 20 Vegetables

1. potatoes
2. iceberg lettuce
3. tomatoes
4. onions
5. carrots
6. celery
7. sweet corn
8. broccoli
9. green cabbage
10. cucumbers
11. bell peppers
12. cauliflower
13. leaf lettuce
14. sweet potatoes
15. mushrooms
16. green onions
17. green (snap) beans
18. radishes
19. summer squash
20. asparagus

TOP POTATO

The nutrition information for these fruits and vegetables is usually found on large placards next to each produce item or in take-home brochures, charts, pamphlets, posters, or stickers. Sometimes nutrition and cooking information can be found on a label stuck directly on the piece of produce. Using these guides, consumers like you can become more aware of:

- serving size
- calories per serving
- amount of protein, total carbohydrates, total fat, and sodium per serving
- percent of the U.S. Recommended Daily Allowances (RDA) for iron, calcium, and vitamins A and C per serving

Watch for nutrition booklets, recipe cards, and educational shelf-labeling for many other foods at the grocery store, too.

Once you get home, tossing fresh fruits and vegetables in the crisper drawer before you clean them means they're more likely to shrivel up and be forgotten. Get in the habit of washing produce as soon as it's purchased. Slice up raw vegetables like carrots, celery, radishes, broccoli, and cauliflower and refrigerate them using plastic containers or plastic bags (perforated bags are best). Do the same with fruits like berries, grapes, melon, and pineapple so each item is fresh and ready for snacking.

A kitchen stocked with plenty of ready-to-eat fruits and vegetables makes it easy to satisfy your "5-a-day" (a total of at least five fruits and vegetables). Place an assortment of fruits, such as apples, bananas, oranges, and pears, in a bowl on the kitchen counter for easy-to-reach treats. If you know that you won't get around to peeling and chopping veggies before they wilt, buy pre-washed, packaged produce like lettuce, carrots, and celery sticks instead.

No matter how determined you are to eat right, it's difficult to keep on track when hunger hits and you're face-to-face with a cookie jar full of Double-Stuff Oreos. Cover your bases by planning ahead for nutritious meals and snacks. A kitchen full of healthy foods makes the challenge of good nutrition an easy one to tackle.

12

Diet Is a Four-Letter Word

*"Dieting isn't healthy. Health comes from well-being.
And well-being is a thing of the spirit."*

Rene Russo, actress

Having a healthy diet is NOT the same thing as dieting. *Having a healthy diet* means consuming the nutritious foods that your body needs for good health, while eating less-nutrient-rich foods in moderation. *Dieting* means limiting your food intake, obsessively watching your weight, and depriving yourself of things you really want to eat. Throughout this book, you've been learning how to eat in a way that honors your body, mind, and spirit. You've been discovering that eating right and taking care of yourself can lead to a sense of well-being and higher self-esteem. Dieting just doesn't fit into this new outlook.

A trendy crash diet might tease you with the promise of fast and easy weight loss, but don't believe that a quick fix will be a permanent one. Oprah Winfrey is a good example of how diets don't work. In 1988, she lost 67 pounds on a medically supervised liquid diet program; fourteen months later, she had gained it all back and then some. Oprah has once again lost weight, but this time she's toned her body, too, by eating right *and* exercising. The lesson learned: Going on hard-core diets to drop pounds quickly is never a good idea. Besides, does anybody really want to hear about your new bean-sprout-cucumber smoothie diet or that you've dropped seven ounces? Bor-rrring!

Fifteen Reasons to Say No to Diets

If you're still not convinced, consider these reasons for saying no to dieting.

1. Dieting doesn't work.

Remember this: DIETS DON'T WORK. Although going on a diet may allow you to lose some weight, it's not the kind of weight you want to lose. Why? Because depriving your body of the food and calories it needs for good health will most likely lead to a loss of weight from water and muscle—not from fat. (In other words, your muscle tissue is eaten away, and you lose some weight from body fluids. Meanwhile, the fat you thought you'd lose stays right where it was.) When you diet, your body thinks that you're starving it and reacts by slowing down the rate at which you burn calories. The result? Your body copes by hoarding as much fat as it can. The only way to lose weight safely and effectively, and keep it off, is through lifestyle changes that include regular exercise and healthy eating habits.

2. Dieting doesn't make you fit.

Fitness—not thinness—should be your goal. Skinny people aren't always healthy people. Some thin people—not all of them, of course—are actually underweight and may be malnourished. It's also possible to be skinny and still be totally out of shape due to an inactive lifestyle and lack of muscle tone. Instead of worrying about whether you're thin enough, consider whether you're a fit and healthy person. Being fit means committing to healthy eating and regular exercise.

3. Dieting can make you fat.

Research has shown that 90% of all dieters who lose 25 pounds or more on strict diets end up reverting back to their old eating habits and gaining the weight back within two years. Then they diet again and gain even more pounds back, creating a vicious cycle. This frustrating trap is called "yo-yo dieting" or "weight cycling." Victims of weight cycling have difficulty losing weight because their body gets accustomed to being denied food and is forced to store fat as a precaution against future calorie shortages.

It sounds strange, but when you diet, you're teaching your body to get fatter. Your body becomes less efficient at using energy from food—in other words, it trains itself to work on less food, and you burn off less fat. Whenever you eat, your body stores away more fat since it expects to be starving again. Dieting means that you're working against your body. To work *with* your body, you need to nourish it with healthy foods and stay active.

4. Dieting slows down your metabolism.

Metabolism is the process by which food is used to fuel the body. Your body has a genetically programmed weight that it considers ideal, and your metabolism adjusts itself to maintain this set-point. Eat too little, and your body shifts into "survival mode," slowing down your metabolism to conserve energy and store fat.

If you diet because you want to be thinner than what's right for your body, your metabolism may slow down so much that it's nearly impossible to lose an ounce. Exercising helps increase your metabolism. Through exercise, you develop muscle tissue (lean body mass) and lose body fat. As your lean body mass increases, so does your metabolism, which means you can eat more without gaining weight. Your body becomes leaner, stronger, and more efficient at burning fuel.

5. Dieting is a futile fight against your genes.

Your ideal weight is based on your particular body type and size—not on someone else's ideal weight—and your body type is predetermined by your genes.[1] In other words, heredity is what determines whether you'll be thin and angular, round and curvy, or somewhere in between. If you're petite and curvy, dieting won't turn you into a statuesque beanpole.

You and your best friend may be the exact same height, yet she may weigh 10 pounds less than you. Even if you dieted, your body would fight to maintain the weight best suited for your particular shape, not hers. Instead of dieting to look like someone else, focus on yourself. Eat right and exercise to look and feel *your* best.

---

[1] For more information about body types, see pp. 140–141.

6. Dieting is unhealthy.

When people hear the word "dieting," they often assume it means "eating healthy." But when you're on a low-calorie diet, it's nearly impossible to get all of the vitamins and minerals that your body needs. Gulping a handful of vitamins with a frosty mug of diet root beer is no substitute for a healthy meal. And fat-free, chocolate-covered Ding-a-lings and reduced-calorie Quadruple Fudge Ripple ice cream may *seem* like innocent indulgences, but fat-free goodies like these offer little or nothing in terms of fiber, vitamins, and minerals. Same goes for all those diet drinks on the market that encourage you to substitute flavored liquids for an actual meal; they may contain added nutrients, but your body gets more benefits from the natural vitamins and minerals found in wholesome foods.

Think of it this way: A driver wouldn't fill her gas tank with Kool-Aid and expect her car to run properly (if at all!), so don't load up your body with low-fat junk food and/or diet drinks and expect it to run efficiently, either. For peak performance, your body needs balanced nutrition from fruits, vegetables, proteins, grains, and essential fatty acids.

7. Dieting makes you sluggish.

When you deprive your body of essential nutrients, it can't function properly. A drastic reduction in calories puts serious stress and strain on your system, which can make you tired, weak, and less alert. With your energy totally zapped, you'll be reduced to spending evenings glued to the TV watching reruns. Wouldn't you rather be taking a walk in the fresh air or playing fetch with your dog?

8. Dieting can lead to eating disorders.

An obsession with food and weight can contribute to a variety of eating disorders, including Anorexia nervosa, Bulimia nervosa, and compulsive overeating.[2] Food should never rule your life. If you suspect that you might have an eating disorder, *get help now.*

---

[2] See Chapter 13, "Battling Eating Disorders," which includes hotlines you can call for help.

9. Dieting can make you cranky.

Have you ever known anyone to be in a peppy, positive mood while she's dieting?

10. Dieting supports poor food choices.

Pre-packaged diet foods and fat-free junk foods don't teach consumers how to eat healthy, which is the key to long-term weight management. The front of that yummy-looking chicken stir-fry package may boast only 250 calories, but flip it over and read the ingredients. You may find that it's loaded with chemicals and enough sodium to salt a big bag of chips.

11. Dieting doesn't make you more popular or happier.

Picture this: You crash diet and shed 10 pounds. Does your life suddenly change? The answer is no. Being thinner won't magically make you more popular, get you a date, or turn you into a better person. Weight loss isn't the solution for happiness. Don't set yourself up for disappointment by thinking life will be better if the scale registers 10 pounds less.

12. Dieting keeps you from fully enjoying life.

You may think that your life will improve once you lose some weight, but this is unrealistic. In the meantime, you may be putting your life on hold. For example, if you decide to skip your best friend's pool party because you think you have to lose weight to look good in a bathing suit, you're missing out on a great social opportunity. Get out there and enjoy life. Experience every moment, and feel good about having fun, learning, and making the most of who you are . . . as you are.

13. Dieting can lead to amenorrhea.

Losing weight to the point that your percentage of body fat drops drastically can lead to amenorrhea, which is the absence of the menstrual cycle. Menstruation stops because the female sex hormones, estrogen and progesterone, require a certain amount of body fat to be produced. Amenorrhea is frequently seen in hard-core athletes and women who have an eating disorder because they have such a low percentage of fat on their bodies. You may think skipping your period is a good thing, but it can cause all sorts of health problems both now and when you're older.

14. Dieting can lower your self-esteem.

Since dieting isn't the answer to achieving good health and a fit body, as soon as you begin a calorie-restrictive diet, you may be setting yourself up for failure. This lose/lose situation makes it hard to feel good about yourself.

15. Dieting can interfere with growth.

The teenage years are a time of physical growth and development, and your body demands lots of vitamins, minerals, and calories to mature properly. If you don't consume enough of all the nutrients you need, your growth may be affected. This could mean weaker bones, smaller muscles, and amenorrhea. In order to grow up healthy, you have to give your body the nutrition it needs.

"I thought I'd like myself better if I was skinnier,
but now I know that this is who I am. And that's okay,
because it's part of what makes me *me*."

Raina Lowell, "plus-size" model

Say No to Diet Pills

Using over-the-counter diet pills, diuretics, and laxatives to lose weight is dangerous.[3] No ifs, ands, or buts. Just because these products are readily available at drugstores and supermarkets doesn't mean they're safe to use.

Most diet pills contain some sort of stimulant like caffeine; stimulants suppress your appetite, making you less likely to eat. But your appetite is natural—it's your body's way of telling you that it's hungry and needs nourishment. When you suppress your hunger, you're depriving your body of the food it needs for growth and good health.

Weight-loss aids usually have a diuretic component, too, increasing the rate at which your body eliminates fluid. This helps to get rid of bloating and can result in a quick drop in pounds. Sound too good to be true? It is. The fluid loss caused by diuretics can deplete your body of important minerals, since the minerals you need don't get absorbed by your cells before the fluid leaves your body. This may lead to dehydration and prevent your muscles and nerves from working properly. What's more, the quick weight loss is merely water weight, so as soon as you drink liquids, you'll gain the weight back.

In addition, the stimulant action of diet pills can elevate your blood pressure and heart rate to dangerous levels, stressing vital organs in your body. Not only that, stimulants often make people feel cranky, hyper, and restless. Another danger: Diet pills can be addictive. If you're tempted by the quick and easy promises of weight loss advertised on the package of a diet aid, stop and ask yourself if there's a catch. (There always is.) Don't pay the price with your health.

If you think that you're overweight and want to lose a few pounds, be smart about how you go about it. First, see your doctor or school nurse for help in determining if you need to lose weight and how much would be healthy for you to lose. A medically supervised nutrition and exercise plan is the best way to tone your body and maintain good health.

---

[3] For information on the effects of laxatives, see p. 126.

13
Battling Eating Disorders

"Recovery from an eating disorder is possible, although the process may be painful and take longer than most people expect. One meal at a time is sometimes the only way to recover. With each meal, and then each day, it becomes easier and easier to eat without obsession once again."

Shirley Nelson, R.D. (Registered Dietitian)

Eating disorders aren't just a phase of adolescence; they're very real and serious problems—life-threatening illnesses—that require medical attention. Young women with eating disorders often obsess about their weight and their physical appearace. They either starve themselves (Anorexia nervosa), binge and purge (Bulimia nervosa), or eat uncontrollably (compulsive overeating).[1] Some girls exercise excessively to lose weight, which is a related disorder. The statistics on eating disorders are alarming: According to the National Association of Anorexia Nervosa and Associated Disorders (ANAD) and Anorexia Nervosa and Related Eating Disorders, Inc. (ANRED), an estimated 20% of females ages 12–30 are experiencing a major eating disorder.

Although eating disorders can occur at any age, they tend to affect females in their teenage years when the pressure to fit in is so intense. In fact, eating and exercise disorders affect millions of girls and young women around the world (with the highest rates of occurrence in the U.S.). The reasons young women develop eating disorders vary. For some, an eating disorder is a way to cope with change, stress, low self-esteem, depression, family problems, and other anxieties associated with growing up. For others, an eating disorder stems from a fear of being fat and of not measuring up

---

[1] This chapter covers eating disorders such as Anorexia nervosa, Bulimia nervosa, and compulsive overeating; it also discusses compulsive exercising. Another category of eating disorder is known as Eating Disorder Not Otherwise Specified, meaning disorders that don't meet the criteria of any specific eating disorder. For example, a girl may have the signs of anorexia, yet her weight may be in the normal range; or a girl may have the signs of bulimia, except that she binges and purges less than twice a week instead of every day. Eating disorders vary in degree of severity and the type of symptoms. Professional help is recommended for diagnosing an eating disorder.

to the unnatural images of models and celebrities portrayed by the media. Still others feel pressured by parents who make negative comments about their daughter's appearance, or by coaches who want a girl to maintain a particular weight for sports or dance. Most often, eating disorders are the result of a combination of factors that may include depression, the desire to lose weight, perfectionism, and feelings of not measuring up to other people's expectations. As a result, the treatment of eating disorders requires medical attention and counseling.

Eating disorders can cause permanent physical damage, sometimes so severe that the person dies. The emotional effects are also devastating. It's not uncommon for people who have eating disorders to feel lonely, isolated, and terrified that someone will find out about their illness; the nightmare continues with feelings of inadequacy, depression, shame, and guilt.

If you suffer from an eating or exercise disorder, you're not alone. The important thing is to get help before the problem destroys your life. It can be scary telling your mom or dad that you have a problem with food, but reaching out is the first step toward recovery. If there's no way you can talk to your parents, tell someone else you trust—a grandparent, guardian, teacher, school counselor, coach, minister, rabbi, or friend. And if you don't feel comfortable turning to a person you know, call one of the support groups listed on pp. 131–132 for information or a referral. You won't be alone in your recovery; many sensitive and caring professionals can help you get better. It's crucial that you get help right away; your life depends on it.

When you live with an eating disorder, you're not the only one who feels the pain. Your family and friends suffer, too, because they care about you so much. The lies, denial, and fights about eating or not eating can tear a family apart. But, with appropriate treatment, you can overcome your eating disorder and heal your relationships with your parents, siblings, and friends.

Anorexia Nervosa

Victims of Anorexia nervosa, or anorexia, restrict their food intake to the point of starving themselves. Fearful of gaining weight, they eat very little and can become so painfully thin that they look like people who have been in a concentration camp. No matter how skinny and malnourished they become, victims of anorexia believe that their frail bodies are fat. Some girls with anorexia binge and purge, or take laxatives, diuretics, or diet pills. The disorder can start as a reaction to a change of life (such as puberty) or a traumatic event (such as a death in the family), or can be the result of a dieting and exercise program gone awry. Left untreated, anorexia can become a lifelong problem or can even be fatal.

If you suspect that you or a friend may be suffering from anorexia, watch for the warning signs below.

Body changes

- significant weight loss (even as much as 25% over several months)
- loss of muscle tissue and body fat
- dull hair or loss of hair on the head; growth of fine, fuzzy body hair
- absence of menstrual periods (amenorrhea)
- dry scaly skin; yellowish skin tone
- sensitivity to cold temperatures
- difficulty sleeping; fatigue
- abdominal bloating; constipation
- dental problems due to damage of teeth and gums
- low blood pressure and slower pulse
- muscle cramps and/or tremors

Prolonged self-starvation does tremendous harm to the body. Some of the long-term results include:

- a weakened heart
- a decreased rate of metabolism
- liver and kidney damage
- brittle bones
- dehydration
- death (up to 20% of people with anorexia die from the disorder)

Behavior changes

* strict dieting or fasting, or a refusal to eat except for small amounts of very low-calorie, low-fat foods
* a distorted body image (believing you're fat even when you're bone-thin)
* low self-esteem
* an abnormal fear of gaining weight
* an unnatural preoccupation with calories, fat, and how much food weighs
* ritualistic eating habits, such as eating very slowly, cutting food into minuscule bites, or chewing each bite a certain number of times before swallowing; secretiveness about food
* denial of hunger pains; lying that you've eaten when you haven't
* withdrawal from family, friends, and social activities
* cooking and baking for others but not eating the food
* exercising too much
* perfectionism (striving to be the perfect student, daughter, athlete, etc.)

"Girls with anorexia have tried too hard to be slender, feminine, and perfect. They have become thin, shiny packages, outwardly carefully wrapped and inwardly a total muddle."

Mary Pipher, Ph.D., author

Bulimia Nervosa

People who battle Bulimia nervosa, or bulimia, generally eat large quantities of food in a short period of time (binge), then purge to get it out of their system. Purging can take the form of vomiting; abusing laxatives, diet pills, or diuretics; or exercising intensely. A girl with bulimia may also binge and then go on a fast or start an extreme diet.

• •

Laxatives, diuretics, and/or diet pills should never be used for weight loss.[2] Overuse of laxatives can cause bloating, constipation, and loss of vital nutrients (because your body doesn't have enough time to absorb them). The fact is, laxatives don't make you lose fat; all you lose is water and other nutrients. Diuretics, which increase urination, dehydrate your body. This can cause a loss of vital nutrients, an irregular heartbeat, and increased stress on your kidneys. Like laxatives, they don't help you lose fat.

• •

Bulimia often starts as a reaction to emotional stress or as a desire to lose some weight. Bingeing leads to feelings of guilt and fear, and purging seems like the only way to get rid of the feelings and the food. The nasty cycle of bingeing and purging gets so out of control that most young women can't stop on their own. Ashamed and guilt-ridden about their behavior, they withdraw to hide their bingeing and purging from their family and friends. The resulting feelings of isolation, fear, shame, and loneliness lead to more bingeing.

> " . . . bulimics feel totally out of control with eating, in contrast to their high-achieving, well-regulated life."
>
> **Kaz Cooke, author**

Just as with anorexia, the effects of bulimia can be extremely damaging to the body. Watch for the following signs:

Body changes

- weight fluctuations due to episodes of bingeing and purging
- a puffy face due to swollen salivary glands; bulging eyes
- broken blood vessels in the face and eyes
- vomiting of blood
- blurred vision

---

[2] For more on the dangers of diet pills, see p. 121.

- severe tooth decay, loss of tooth enamel, gum disease, and mouth ulcers from regurgitated stomach acid
- sore throat; pain/bleeding of the esophagus (tube that carries food to the stomach)
- dependency on laxatives and/or diuretics
- irregular or no periods (amenorrhea)
- heartburn, indigestion, stomach cramps, bloating, gas, or constipation

Bingeing and purging can have extreme consequences, such as:

- electrolyte (sodium and potassium) imbalance, which can cause de-hydration and may lead to death
- internal bleeding
- liver and kidney damage
- death

Behavior changes

- bingeing on large amounts of food in a short period of time, especially high-fat, sugary foods
- throwing up after meals
- vomiting or abusing laxatives, diuretics, or diet pills after bingeing
- sneaking or hiding food to binge on when alone
- feeling guilty about eating large amounts of food
- low self-esteem
- abnormal concern about body weight and shape
- fear of not being able to stop bingeing and purging
- obsession with food; secretiveness about food
- fasting or dieting between binges
- exercising compulsively to burn the calories from bingeing
- depression, mood swings, isolation, or suicide attempts

Check It Out

Lots of great books have been published on the topic of eating disorders, providing information, help, and hope.

Food Fight: A Guide to Eating Disorders for Preteens and Their Parents by Janet Bode (NY: Simon & Schuster Books for Young Readers, 1997). Filled with first-person testimonials, this book covers the symptoms, causes, diagnoses, and treatments of eating disorders.

Surviving an Eating Disorder: Strategies for Family and Friends by Michele Siegal, Ph.D., Judith Brisman, Ph.D., and Margot Weinshel, M.S.W. (NY: Harper Perennial, 1997). If you know or care about someone who has an eating disorder, this book can help you—it offers information, insights, and strategies for coping with the situation.

Your Dieting Daughter: Is She Dying for Attention? by Carolyn Costin (NY: Brunner/Mazel, Inc., 1997). Sections help readers tell the difference between a diet and a disorder, answer questions like "What Do I Do When . . ." and share personal letters and journal entries from dieting daughters to parents. If you suffer from an eating disorder, this book can help you and your parents to communicate.

See also p. 68 for information on *Taking Charge of My Mind and Body: A Girls' Guide to Alcohol, Drug, Smoking, and Eating Problems.*

Compulsive Overeating Disorder

Girls who have compulsive overeating disorder, or binge eating disorder, consume large quantities of food but don't purge to control their weight. The result is that they're overweight or obese and tend to use food as a substitute for intimate relationships with family and friends.

A compulsive overeater gets caught up in a cycle where she:

1. overeats

2. gains weight

3. diets to lose weight

4. feels miserable while dieting

5. breaks the diet, then feels guilty

6. finds temporary comfort in eating

7. gains back the weight and then some

8. diets again

All her attention is focused on eating, and she pulls away from family and friends to concentrate on food. The cycle of gaining and losing weight is extremely hard on the body.

The signs and symptoms of compulsive overeating may include the following:

Body changes

- excessive weight gain or obesity
- an increased risk of high blood pressure, clogged arteries, heart attack, stroke, and some forms of cancer
- slow metabolism leading to sluggishness
- bone and joint problems
- circulatory problems

Behavior changes

- eating a normal amount of food while with others, but bingeing in private
- snacking constantly
- eating even when full
- obsessing over calories and weight loss
- dieting repeatedly
- eating to relieve stress or cope with painful feelings
- using food as a reward or to provide comfort

Compulsive Exercising

Exercise helps you stay healthy and fit, and boosts your self-esteem. But when working out becomes your primary focus and interferes with school, family, and your social life, you've crossed the line into excessive exercising. For compulsive exercisers, working out can become an addiction.

If you're wondering if you or a friend may be a compulsive exerciser, watch for the following warning signs.

Body changes

- stress fractures
- bone injuries, including wear and tear that could lead to arthritis
- shin splints, pulled or torn muscles, tendons, ligaments, and damaged cartilage
- exhaustion

Excessive exercise can lead to even more dangerous physical problems:

- heart and lung damage
- dehydration
- death from overexertion

Behavior changes

- feeling overly anxious about a missed workout; feeling stressed out or upset if unable to exercise
- exercising more than once a day; exercising even when sick
- calculating how much exercise is needed based on the amount of food eaten or the amount of weight to be lost
- making workouts a #1 priority
- fear of gaining weight if a workout is skipped
- a total fixation on the next workout to the point that nothing else matters

Talk It Out

If you think that you or someone you care about may have an eating disorder or problem with excessive exercise, you don't have to deal with the situation on your own. Devoted health-care professionals have helped countless others recover from eating disorders; they can help you, too. It's crucial to get help now—don't wait another minute. Talk to your parents or another trusted adult about the problem.

Confronting someone who has an eating disorder is very difficult. If your friend doesn't want to admit she has a problem, she may just blow you off or get angry with you for suggesting that she needs help. If you suspect a friend has an eating disorder, let her know that you're concerned, that you care about her, and that you really want to help. Tell her how important she is to you and that you'll be there for her. Suggest she tell an adult about her eating disorder. If she refuses to get help, you need to confide in a trusted adult—a parent, teacher, coach, school counselor, or relative. Reaching out could save your friend's life.

Call for Help

Help is just a phone call away. Your local phone book has listings for crisis hotlines and mental health counselors (look under Community Services). You can also find Overeaters Anonymous, a 12-step group that welcomes people of all ages. You can contact one of the following national eating disorder organizations to receive professional referrals, newsletters, self-help groups, fact sheets, educational materials, and recommendations for books about eating disorders. Early treatment of eating disorders has saved thousands of lives and could save yours, too.

Organizations

(847) 831-3438 connects you to the National Association of Anorexia Nervosa and Associated Disorders (ANAD). They are available Monday through Friday 9 A.M. to 5 P.M. CST. This organization provides help to sufferers of eating disorders and their families. ANAD's free services include access to a network of support groups and referral sources, a newsletter, and educational programs. If you're online, go to: *members.aol.com/ANAD20/index.html*

(212) 575-6200 is the number for the American Anorexia/Bulimia Association (AABA) in New York. Call Monday through Friday 9 A.M. to 5 P.M. EST. This association sends task forces to high schools and colleges to help students with eating disorders and also provides information on treatment, recovery, and support groups. If you're online, go to: *members.aol.com/AmAnBu*

(541) 344-1144 puts you in touch with Anorexia Nervosa and Related Eating Disorders, Inc. (ANRED), a research and information organization. A prerecorded message will refer you to the National Eating Disorders Organization (see below) for further information and materials on eating disorders. If you're online, go to: *www.anred.com*

(918) 481-4044 is the number for the National Eating Disorders Organization (NEDO), an educational, treatment, and referral resource for victims of eating disorders, their families, and health-care professionals. Call Monday through Friday 8:30 A.M. to 4 P.M. CST. If you're online, go to: *www.laureate.com*

(505) 891-2664 contacts the World Service office of Overeaters Anonymous. You can call their offices Monday through Friday 8 A.M. to 5 P.M. MST for information on this 12-step group. The program helps overeaters, as well as those with anorexia or bulimia. If you're online, go to: *www.overeatersanonymous.org*

Part Three

Bodies in Motion

"I don't think being an athlete is unfeminine.
I think of it as a kind of grace."

Jackie Joyner-Kersee, two-time Olympic gold medalist, heptathlon

Quiz
Test Your Fitness IQ

Calling all fitness buffs! How much do you really know about exercise? This quiz puts your knowledge to the test as you sift through common myths and misconceptions about fitness. Write your answers on a separate sheet, have fun, and don't forget to check your score once you cross the finish line.

1. Wearing heavy sweats while working out will:

   a) make you perspire more so you can lose a lot of weight.
   b) heat up your body and burn more fat.
   c) cause a loss of water weight and, potentially, dehydration.
   d) make your muscles work harder.

2. True or false:

   To achieve total fitness, aerobic exercise is all you really need.

3. Drinking water before and during exercise:

   a) makes you bloated.
   b) helps cleanse your pores.
   c) gives you sideaches.
   d) helps your body work more efficiently.

4. Exercising regularly can:

   a) improve your looks.
   b) burn body fat.
   c) speed up your metabolism.
   d) all of the above.

5. "No pain, no gain" is:

   a) the ultimate workout motto.
   b) a philosophy reserved for the serious workout enthusiast.
   c) completely false.
   d) what your P.E. teacher says if she's any good.

6. Endorphins are:

   a) chemicals released in the brain that make you feel good when you exercise.

   b) the main ingredient in McDonalds' secret sauce.

   c) aliens from the planet Endorph.

   d) hormones that cause zits.

7. Warming up and stretching:

   a) are one and the same.

   b) are two different things.

   c) can be accomplished with a hot shower and a few toe touches.

   d) only need to be done when it's cold out.

8. True or false:

   If you look in the mirror after just a few weeks of working out, you'll see noticeable changes.

9. You can prevent injuries, relieve boredom, and achieve a more balanced body by:

   a) cruising the Internet.

   b) cross-training.

   c) getting more sleep every night.

   d) training yourself to walk, read, and chew gum at the same time.

10. If you stop exercising, the muscles you've sculpted:

    a) turn to fat.

    b) stay the same.

    c) shrink in size.

    d) will never be as strong again.

11. Which of the following requires the least amount of aerobic endurance?

    a) cross-country skiing

    b) soccer

    c) jogging

    d) tennis

12. True or false:

    Exercise zaps your energy, leaving you too tired to do anything afterward.

13. Cooling down after you exercise:

    a) allows your heart rate to return to a normal level and helps reduce your risk of injury.

    b) is a good time to contemplate the extra cookies you can devour as a reward for working out.

    c) is only necessary if you've done a particularly grueling training session.

    d) means your body will stop sweating.

14. If you can't sing along with your favorite tunes without huffing and puffing while exercising aerobically:

    a) don't sweat it—you should really stay focused on your workout, not the tunes.

    b) you're exercising too hard.

    c) it's probably safe to say a singing career isn't in your future.

    d) the tempo of your music doesn't suit the activity you're doing.

15. True or false:

    Exercising during your period can make you feel better.

Answers

1. **C.** Wearing sweats can leave you dripping wet, but all you lose is water, not fat. If you hop on the scale after a grueling workout in heavy sweats, you might notice a slight drop in your weight; but as soon as you replenish your body with water or any other liquid, the weight is quickly regained. The fact is, you can't sweat off fat; it must be burned by doing aerobic exercise, which uses fat as fuel.

2. **False.** Aerobic exercise is great for burning body fat and working your heart and lungs, but you should still strengthen and stretch your muscles, too.

3. D. Drinking water before and during exercise allows your body to work more efficiently. Proper hydration helps regulate body temperature, replaces lost water, and keeps the chemical balance in your muscles on track so you're less likely to cramp.

4. D. Can you believe it? Exercising regularly can improve your appearance, burn body fat, *and* speed up your metabolism.

5. C. "No pain, no gain" means no brain! Fitness fanatics used to believe that for exercise to count, it had to hurt. Nowadays, experts know this isn't true. A little soreness is normal as you push yourself during a workout. However, if you experience pain that doesn't subside within 48–72 hours, you need to see a doctor.[1]

6. A. Endorphins (chemicals released in the brain when you exercise) produce a euphoric, relaxed sensation. Exercises that involve rhythmic, repetitive movements help release endorphins, making exercise a safe and healthy high.

7. B. Warming up and stretching are two different things.[2] Warming up is a way to heat up your body. The most effective way to warm up is by doing a slower, gentler version of your workout (for instance, if you're going to jog, warm up with a brisk walk first). Stretching loosens the muscles, making them more elastic. This prepares them for the extreme motions to come during exercise. Muscles that are more elastic are less likely to get pulled or strained.

8. False. The reality is, you may have to work out for a few months before you see visible changes in your body. However, there are immediate results you can count on, such as increased energy, improved concentration, and a good night's sleep. Don't be disappointed waiting for the "big payoff." Stay motivated by focusing on the positive benefits that can't be measured but are worth being proud of: a sense of accomplishment for tackling a tough workout, the camaraderie you feel when you're part of an athletic team, or the pride of learning to stick to an exercise program that's good for your body. The physical changes will come in time, and they'll definitely be worth the wait.

---

[1] See Chapter 21, "The Agony and the Bliss," for information on sports injuries.
[2] See Chapter 19, "Vroom Vroom: Warming Up," for information on warming up, and Chapter 20, "Head-to-Toe Flexibility," for more on stretching.

9. **B.** Cross-training[3] is a great way to spice up your workouts. By doing a lot of different activities, you can relieve boredom, rest some of your muscles while you work on others, prevent injuries, and give yourself a more balanced fitness program. These benefits will make you more likely to stick with exercising, which is crucial if you want to reap the rewards of a fit body.

10. **C.** If you quit working out, the muscles you've developed will shrink, but it's impossible for muscle to turn to fat. If you don't adjust your caloric intake for your decreased activity level, you'll lose muscle *and* gain fat. The fat sits on top of the shrinking, once-fit muscles, and this makes them appear soft and mushy.

11. **D.** Tennis requires the least amount of endurance since it's an *anaerobic* activity. This means the activity demands short bursts of energy instead of continuous, rhythmic movements. Activities that last 15 minutes or more are defined as *aerobic* since they kick in your body's demand for oxygen-rich blood to be delivered to your working muscles. Examples of aerobic activities include cross-country skiing, brisk walking, jogging, in-line skating, aerobic dance classes, and soccer.

12. **False.** A moderate workout won't zap your energy. Exercise gets your heart pumping and your blood moving, and this increased bloodflow can relieve stress and make you feel ready to tackle just about anything.

13. **A.** Cooling down[4] after a workout gives your body a chance to return to a resting level by slowing down your pulse and breathing rates. When stiff, tight muscles suddenly stop moving, painful cramps may result. A good cool-down also reduces the chance of injury.

14. **B.** If you can't sing along to music during an aerobic workout without gasping for air, you're exercising way too hard. A "talk test" is a simple way to determine whether your workout pace is appropriate. Exercise of moderate intensity—which would enable you to gab with a workout partner or sing (whether you're on key or not is another story)—is more effective for cardiovascular conditioning and fat burning than pushing yourself until you can hardly breathe.

---

[3] See Chapter 16, "Cross-Training Fun."
[4] For more on cooling down, see pp. 198–199.

15. True. Contrary to popular belief, having your period isn't a legitimate excuse to blow off a workout. Exercise can relieve symptoms associated with menstruation, such as bloating, irritability, and body aches. Working out helps reduce stress and gets you sweating—both of which may ease the pain of your period. However, if you're bleeding heavily or feel weak (like on the first or second day of your cycle), exercise may be too taxing. Wait until you feel better before resuming your aerobic workout. In the meantime, continue with stretching exercises, which are gentle and relaxing.

Your Score

Give yourself one point for each correct answer.

1–7 points

You definitely need to catch up on the latest fitness facts. The good news is, you're moving in the right direction by reading this book and making a promise to yourself to get fit. If exercising is new to you, it's totally understandable for you to be a little confused about the do's and don'ts of working out. To get on the fitness fast track, keep reading and start exercising. You'll gain expertise in no time.

8–12 points

You're off to a great start! With a solid foundation of knowledge, you're less likely to fall for outdated exercise myths. Listen to your body and be open to new things. Fitness is a rapidly growing field, and it's fun to learn something new every day while you get in shape.

13–15 points

What a pro! You've got the inside scoop on fitness facts. Apply all your knowledge to your workouts for a safe, well-rounded exercise program.

14
What Does Fitness Really Mean?

*"I respect my body and make changes in it
to help me achieve my goals."*

Rebecca Lobo, 1996 Olympic gold medalist, women's basketball

One of the glorious things about the human body is that it comes in so many shapes, sizes, and colors. Take a look at your own body. Instead of thinking that you're too fat or too thin, not athletic enough, or hopelessly out of shape, tell yourself how graceful, feminine, and powerful you are. Your body is a unique treasure, and taking care of it is essential.

Beneath your skin lies the skeleton, or framework, for your body. Your frame or "body type" is uniquely yours, and as you grow and develop, your body takes on its predestined shape. Your parents' genes are the seeds that determine what your genetically programmed shape will be, and this basic structure can't be altered. Girls with large frames will never have small ones, petite girls will never be tall, and broad-shouldered girls will never have narrow shoulders. It's all in your genes.

Your body type fits somewhere into three main categories known as ectomorph (thin), endomorph (curvy), and mesomorph (athletic). Maybe you match one of the categories perfectly; maybe you have a combination of features. One category isn't superior to another, and you can't change from one to another. Learn to love what you've got.

Your Unique Body Type

Take a look at the following descriptions to see what body type you have. The illustrations can help you, too.

If you're an ectomorph, you have a thin body type characterized by:

- a naturally slender shape
- narrow shoulders and hips
- long arms and legs
- small or medium-sized breasts
- a flat stomach
- difficulty building muscle
- a tendency not to gain weight

If you're an endomorph, you have:

- a soft, round figure
- a pear-shaped body
- a short neck
- full breasts
- a tendency to gain weight easily, especially around the buttocks, hips, and thighs
- a well-defined waist

If you're a mesomorph, you have:

- a more athletic body
- well-defined muscles
- a narrow waist
- broad shoulders and hips
- potential for great strength

No matter which type of body Mother Nature has blessed you with, it's up to you to make the most of what you've got. Eating right and exercising regularly helps ensure that your bones and muscles are as strong and healthy as they can be. Even if you have a tendency toward small muscles, it's important to build them up so they're more lean and firm. As you strengthen your body, you'll find that you feel more fit and powerful.

As you think about what type of exercise program is right for you, you may wonder if your body type is suited only for certain sports and activities. Classifying yourself as one particular type shouldn't prevent you from enjoying—and even excelling—in any athletic activity, however. Having a thin body doesn't mean you can't triumph in softball, and a curvy physique doesn't prohibit you from becoming a graceful dancer. If your body isn't very muscular, don't convince yourself that there's no way you can ever be a jock. Regardless of your size and shape, you can reach your optimum fitness level and have a lot of fun in the process.

• •

If you want to build muscle to look lean and strong, or to help yourself excel in a sport, do it *naturally*. In other words, stay away from steroids. Anabolic steroids, used by some people to increase muscle mass, contain the male hormone testosterone. Use of steroids increases the concentration of muscle-building hormones (like testosterone) in the blood, which means the body develops larger muscles than it would normally. Women who use steroids may get a deepened voice, acne, and increased masculine characteristics. Research has linked long-term steroid use with physical and psychological problems like liver cancer, heart disease, infertility, and psychotic episodes.

• •

Think about different famous female athletes—Michelle Kwan, Gabrielle Reece, Dominique Moceanu—and how they've made the most of their different body types. Michelle, a World Champion figure skater, is willowy with long, lean muscles. Technically superb at executing difficult jumps, she demonstrates amazing flexibility while gliding across the ice, her legs creating fluid, graceful lines. At six-foot-three, Gabrielle is a pro beach volleyball player who's tall, quick, and physically strong. She's known for her explosive spikes and digs, and she gives everything she's got to send the ball zooming over the net. Dominique, a member of the '96 Olympic gold medal-winning gymnastics team, is small and compact, all muscle and might. Her amazing strength and balance help her to flip, tumble, and vault high in the air. Each of these athletes has learned to use her unique shape to her advantage, and one thing they all share in common is a positive attitude about their bodies. You can see it in the way they move and carry themselves—like winners. Their bodies don't define who they are but instead help propel them toward their goals.

* *

Old Attitude	New Outlook
I hate my body and how I look.	My body is right for me, and I'm going to take good care of it.

* *

Whether you're an athlete or an artist, petite, angular, muscular, or anywhere in between, what really counts when it comes to your physique is fitness and confidence. This means accepting and making the most of the way nature intended you to be.

Being fit means:

1. You can tackle the day's challenges and have plenty of energy left for play.

2. Your heart, lungs, bones, and muscles are strong, and your body is firm and flexible.

3. Your percentage of body fat is low, and your weight is within a normal range.

4. You feel good about yourself and have a positive outlook on life.

Think of fitness as a recipe with four equal parts all mixed together. Here's the list of essential ingredients.

Recipe for Fitness
Endurance
Strength
Flexibility
Body composition

Endurance

Whether you're an elite athlete training for a triathlon or a recreational exerciser playing a game of pick-up basketball, you need stamina, or endurance, so you don't tire out. Having endurance gives your body the ability to work more efficiently for extended periods of time so you can swim, bike, and run longer or shoot more hoops without getting tired.

When muscles are worked continuously for 15 minutes or more, they need more oxygen to function properly. Your level of endurance, also called cardiovascular fitness, refers to how well your heart and lungs pump oxygen-rich blood to your exercising muscles. The miles of vessels running through your body are the delivery route for oxygen-carrying blood, which is deposited directly where it's needed—in your muscles. This process provides the necessary fuel to keep your body working longer and harder, with less effort.

Aerobic exercise improves your endurance. The word aerobic means "with oxygen." Aerobic (also called cardiovascular) activities use the body's largest muscle groups—namely the legs and torso—in continuous, rhythmic action, and you need more oxygen when you move your body this way. Running, power walking, cycling, in-line skating, aerobics classes, dance, and soccer are good examples of aerobic activities.

Anaerobic, by contrast, means "without oxygen." Activities that involve lots of starting, stopping, and short bursts of energy (like tennis, volleyball, and softball) don't tap into the body's need for oxygen and are considered anaerobic. While sports like these won't necessarily improve your cardiovascular endurance, they're very effective for building strength, power, and coordination as part of a total fitness plan.

Being aerobically fit is important for several reasons. First and foremost, aerobic activities strengthen your heart and lungs. A strong cardiovascular system boosts your body's supply of energy, making it easier to do all sorts of things, from lugging books home from school, to babysitting, to whizzing around an amusement park without panting. Aerobic exercise also burns more fat and calories than any other type of physical activity. A regular aerobic exercise program uses stored body fat for fuel, resulting in a leaner body. Finally, a strong cardiovascular system can reduce the risk of illnesses like heart disease, high blood pressure, and diabetes.

Strength

Strength is defined as the ability to move a muscle against a resistance. Say you want to rearrange your bedroom furniture. You'll need strength to push the bed, drag your desk across the floor, and lift heavy boxes of prized mementos. The more strength you have, the easier it will be to get the job done.

When a muscle tries to move and meets resistance, a contraction results. Muscle contractions can be either static or dynamic. A static contraction occurs when the resistance is so great that the object can't be moved, like if you tried to push a parked car. Static or isometric contractions improve strength, but only in the muscle that's contracting. For instance, squeezing your fist as hard as possible can make your grip stronger since you're using your forearm muscles. However, your shoulder muscles aren't being used, so you won't develop a more powerful tennis serve.

A dynamic contraction occurs when you use your muscles to actually move against something. Lifting weights, doing squats, pushing the vacuum, and taking out the trash are all movements that cause dynamic contractions. The more intense the contraction, the bigger the improvement in strength. For example, a professional weight lifter will gain more strength by lifting a 100-pound box once than by lifting a one-pound box 100 times.

To move with resistance *quickly* requires a different type of strength—power. Power is what gives your soccer kick its snap and your softball throw its distance. Activities such as bench-stepping, in-line skating, and boxing not only increase your endurance but also improve your power.

To become stronger, your muscles need some form of resistance to conquer. You can use the resistance of your own body by doing push-ups, chin-ups, lunges, or squats. Weight machines and dumbbells can also be used for resistance training, but they can be dangerous if you don't know what you're doing. Make sure a qualified instructor sets you up with a safe program.

Flexibility

Having a flexible body means that your joints and muscles are able to move through their full range of motion. Every joint in your body has a particular range of motion that's determined by the shape of the joint and the structures surrounding it—ligaments, tendons, and muscles. When your body is flexible, your joints have some give, which allows you to reach, bend, and stretch with ease.

The best way to become more limber is by stretching.[1] For stretching to be effective, it should be static and sustained. This means slowly extending your body to the point where you feel tension in the muscle and holding it for at least 20 seconds. Try not to bounce when you stretch. If a muscle is jerked while it's being stretched, the nerves within the muscle fibers think they're being damaged and respond by tightening up, which may result in pain or injury. To improve your flexibility, you've got to hold a stretch long enough for the muscle fibers to stretch gradually, relax and let go.

Being flexible can help prevent injuries such as pulled muscles.[2] If your muscles are tight and you attempt to move your body in a way it's not accustomed to (like doing a high kick in cheerleading tryouts), you could be asking for trouble. When your thigh muscles are taut instead of elastic, you run a greater risk of tearing something if they're stretched further than you've trained them to go. A muscle that's strong and flexible is more resistant to sudden stress than one that's strong and tight.

Body Composition

Put simply, body composition is what makes up your body. A fit, healthy person has a lower amount of body fat (expressed in pounds or percentages)[3] compared to her lean body mass—muscles, bones, and organs (also expressed in pounds or percentages). A ratio of these two factors determines your body composition. For example, a ratio of 10:1 means for every 10 pounds of lean tissue, you have 1 pound of fat. The higher the ratio, the better shape you're in. However, it's crucial to realize that having too little body fat is dangerous and can be a sign of an eating disorder.[4]

Body composition is a better gauge of how fit you are than weighing yourself on a scale. The scale can't take into consideration the fact that muscle weighs more than fat, or that each of us is blessed with our own

---

[1] See Chapter 20, "Head-to-Toe Flexibility," for more on stretching.
[2] See Chapter 21, "The Agony and the Bliss," for more about exercise injuries.
[3] For more information on body fat percentages, see p. 57.
[4] See Chapter 13, "Battling Eating Disorders."

unique body type. If you play soccer, for example, you may weigh a little more than your friend who's the same size but doesn't work out. While the scale may register a higher number while you're on it, you may actually be more fit than your friend. That's because people who exercise regularly tend to have more lean tissue and a lower percentage of body fat.

As your fitness level improves, you may notice changes in your body— your clothes may become looser and you may see more muscle tone when you look in the mirror. These changes could be indications that you're losing body fat as a result of your exercise program. No matter what your shape, exercise is the tool you can use to create a trim and toned body. Strive for a lean physique that suits your frame, and you'll be well on your way to achieving fitness.

If you're interested in a specific calculation of your lean-to-fat ratio, talk to your P.E. teacher, a trainer at a gym or athletic club, or someone in the physical education department of a local college. Any of these experts should be able to test you using one of several scientific methods, such as the following:

- *skin-fold calipers:* similar to a "pinch-an-inch test," where the calipers measure the thickness of folds of skin and fat at different points on your body.

- *hydrostatic weighing:* a dunk test where you sit in a "scale" and get submerged in water while a computer calculates your body fat.

- *bioelectrical impedance:* this method uses electrodes and a current that you can't feel to measure your lean-to-fat ratio.

- *BOD POD:* a high-tech, egg-shaped device that you sit in while a computer figures out your body-fat percentage based on the amount of air you displace in the pod.

If You Have a Disability

Maybe you have physical limitations because of a disability. This may make it tougher, but not impossible, for you to stay in shape. Like many other people with disabilities, you can find the courage to see beyond your disability and realize your full potential.

Many people who have disabilities participate in a variety of sports and fitness activities. In fact, the Paralympic Games for athletes with disabilities have provided outstanding athletic opportunities since 1960; the number of nations participating in the Paralympics grows each year. The Special Olympics, a sports program and competition for people with mental disabilities, has programs across the United States and offer challenges for more than one million athletes. If competition isn't your thing, you can still participate in a variety of sports and physical activities and have fun meeting other people who enjoy the challenges exercise can provide. Just check with your doctor before starting a fitness program to be sure that your activities are safe and right for you.

Don't be afraid to join a team or find solo activities that suit your particular style. The physical and emotional benefits that you'll gain from exercise are worth it. Aimee Mullins, who had both legs amputated below the knees because she was born without fibula bones in her legs, is a great example of a young woman who refuses to give in to her limitations. Aimee runs track for Georgetown University and is a World Champion Paralympic sprinter. She also plays softball and soccer, and skis. She does all of this with two prosthetic legs. During races against single-leg amputees (who have an advantage over her), Aimee's powerful arm motions and stamina help her compete with confidence and win.

Getting involved in athletics can improve *your* stamina and confidence, too. According to the Centers for Disease Control and Prevention, people with disabilities can use regular physical activity as a way to gain strength and endurance, feel better mentally and emotionally, and improve their quality of life by increasing their ability to perform daily activities.

Exercise will make you feel more energized and stronger, and you may gain a better sense of self-esteem from having a fit body, competing athletically, or being involved in team sports. With improved self-confidence, you may find that you're better able to manage other challenges in your life, too.

Organizations

If you have a disability and want to get started on a fitness program, contact one of the following organizations or check the Yellow Pages for services in your area. There are organizations that can teach you skiing, sailing, horseback riding, whitewater rafting, biking, in-line skating, and lots of other skills.

Disabled Sports USA
451 Hungerford Drive • Suite 100 • Rockville, MD 20850
(301) 217-0960 • *www.dsusa.org*
Disabled Sports USA is dedicated to providing people who have disabilities with access to all types of sports and fitness activities. More than 80 community-based chapters nationwide offer year-round recreational and competitive sports programs. Choose from activities like swimming, volleyball (sitting or standing), power lifting, cycling, table tennis, bowling, archery, and skiing (standing and sitting).

National Ability Center
P.O. Box 682799 • Park City, UT 84068
(801) 649-3991 • *www.utahrec.com*
This organization is a recognized chapter of Disabled Sports USA and an accredited operating center for the North American Riding for the Handicapped Association (see below). The National Ability Center provides low-cost sports and recreational activities for people with disabilities and their families.

National Sports Center for the Disabled
P.O. Box 1290 • Winter Park, CO 80482
(303) 780-6540 • *www.nscd.org/nscd/*
"No mountain too high" is this organization's motto. The Center offers recreational and competitive challenges year-round, including skiing, snowboarding, biking, hiking, in-line skating, sailing, and whitewater rafting.

North American Riding for the Handicapped Association
P.O. Box 33150 • Denver, CO 80233
(303) 452-1212 • *www.narha.org*
NARHA gives children and adults with disabilities (physical or emotional) the opportunity to experience the feeling of freedom and autonomy that comes from riding a horse.

Special Olympics International
1325 G Street NW • Suite 5008 • Washington, D.C. 20005
(202) 628-3630 • *www.specialolympics.org*
This organization offers sports training and competition for young people and adults who have mental disabilities. Currently, about 25,000 communities across the United States have Special Olympics activities.

United States Cerebral Palsy Athletic Association
200 Harrison Road • Newport, RI 02840
(401) 848-5280 • *www.uscpaa.org*

Swimming and track and field are some of the fitness choices for young people with cerebral palsy. This association arranges competition at national events.

U.S. Association for Blind Athletes

33 North Institute Street • Brown Hall, Suite #015 • Colorado Springs, CO 80903
www.usaba.org
USABA offers sports programs at the state, regional, national, and international levels and is dedicated to changing public perception of the capabilities of the blind and visually impaired. Programs include skiing, track and field, power lifting, cycling, wrestling, and judo.

U.S. Olympic Committee/Disabled Sports Services

One Olympic Plaza • Colorado Springs, CO 80909
(719) 578-4818
This office serves as a clearinghouse of information on sports programs for people who have disabilities. It also sanctions organizations that govern teams of physically disabled athletes chosen to represent the U.S. in competitions like the Paralympics.

Wheelchair Sports USA

3595 East Fountain Boulevard, #L-1 • Colorado Springs, CO 80910
(719) 574-1150 • *www.wsusa.org*
Recreational and competitive programs for all age groups are available through Wheelchair Sports USA. Regional organizations offer activities like swimming, track, archery, table tennis, and basketball.

Exercise shouldn't be about sculpting your body into the "perfect" shape. Instead, think of exercise as an important part of taking great care of yourself. When you work out, experience the pure enjoyment of physical movement and the fun of challenging your body. No matter what your capabilities, exercise can help you feel good about who you are and all that you can accomplish in life. Make fitness a part of your routine—it's a recipe for success.

> "There is no person who cannot reach a healthy
> fitness level—and you don't have to train like an Olympian.
> All you need is a goal and a little discipline."
>
> **Florence Griffith-Joyner, five-time Olympic medalist, track and field**

15

A Fitness Plan That Fits You

"Whenever I want to skip a workout, I think about how I'll feel when it's over. One, I'll be in a great mood. Two, I'll have a lot of energy. And three, because I'll have energy, I'll be able to stay up later with my friends—I won't wimp out."

Jennifer Love Hewitt, actress

Committing to fitness means that you look forward to exercising, enjoy the challenges of physical movement, and remain active for your whole life. When designing a fitness plan, the single most important factor to consider is whether you like the activities included in your workout. If they're fun, you probably won't be tempted to quit. Whether you choose cycling, team sports, or dance classes, all that matters is that you get your body moving. It's okay to experiment—how else will you know if something excites you unless you give it a try? If you get bored or burned out with one activity, choose another. Or alternate your activities by trying cross-training.[1] No excuses! And don't give up.

Old Attitude	**New Outlook**
Exercise is one big bore.	If I find physical activities that I enjoy, working out can be lots of fun.

With so many possibilities for your workout program, where do you begin? To help take the confusion out of selecting physical activities that you'll stick with, think about the following ten questions for each activity you're seriously considering.

---

[1] See Chapter 16, "Cross-Training Fun."

Ten Questions

The more often you answer yes to these questions, the greater the odds that you'll remain faithful to your workout routine.

1. Is it fun?

You'll want a workout that's going to excite you so much that you can't wait to get moving. After all, as long as you're going to exercise, why not opt for something fun? How about mountain biking, power walking with a friend, or hip-hop aerobics for a change of pace?

2. Does it make you feel good?

The activities you choose should make you feel good and boost your self-esteem. If the thought of swinging a racquet bores you, tennis or racquetball may not be your thing. A dance class that makes you feel like a total klutz is one you'll dread going to, so why bother? Give new workouts a fair shot, and if they don't thrill you, try something else.

3. Is it practical?

Scuba diving and windsurfing are wet and wild adventure sports, but if you don't live near the ocean or a lake, how will you keep your commitment to exercising? Choose practical activities that require little fuss—like walking, jogging, or dancing. The fewer the obstacles, the better. You'll be less likely to skip your workouts.

4. Is it safe?

Any sport can be dangerous if you don't follow the rules and safety requirements, which may include wearing protective gear and training with a qualified coach or instructor. Thrill sports[2] such as rock climbing and white-water rafting are naturally more risky than, for example, playing basketball, so check with your parents before you sign up for lessons.

If physical activity hasn't been a part of your life until now, it may be a good idea to see a doctor before getting involved in an exercise routine. A doctor or other health professional can help you start a fitness program that matches your ability level and needs. You don't want to take on too much too soon because you're more likely to get hurt.[3]

You should *always* exercise in a safe place. Never work out alone in an isolated area. If you prefer the school field for getting in shape, exercise at times when other people are around, such as team members, coaches, or teachers. If you like to take solitary bike rides, choose paths or trails that are familiar and always let someone know where you'll be and when you plan to return. If you wear headphones while working out, keep the volume low or listen through one earphone only, so you know what's going on around you. Use common sense—safety comes first, no matter what activity you try.

5. Is it available to you?

Make it a priority to work with what you've got, and do your best to pick an activity that you can do almost any time. If you're the outdoorsy type, you may love downhill skiing, and that's great if you live near a ski slope and can afford the cost of lift tickets for the entire snow season. But if you live in the desert, maybe you'd better think about hiking nature trails with a qualified guide instead. Cycling, jogging, and dancing are great activities you can do almost anywhere, anytime, for minimal cost and hassle.

6. Is it affordable for you?

If you're on a budget (and who isn't?), make selections that fit your price range. There are lots of physical activities to choose from, with costs to match most budgets. Many require nothing more than a pair of supportive athletic shoes.

---

[2] See Chapter 22, "Pros and Cons of Your Workout Options," for more information about thrill sports.
[3] See Chapter 21, "The Agony and the Bliss," for more information about sports injuries.

7. Is it YOU?

A workout has to feel right, as if it were tailor-made for you. And with *you* in charge of creating your own fitness plan, there's no reason it should feel any other way. If team sports turn you on, great. If they turn you off, don't worry. Maybe you prefer solitary activities like swimming or running. The only thing that matters is that you're happy with your decision, so choose a workout that matches your personality and interests.

8. Is there a big time commitment involved?

If an activity is a hassle before you even get started, you'll be more likely to kiss it good-bye. Maybe you've decided to try ice-skating but the rink is far away, requiring you to rely on the bus or a ride from your parents. Once you arrive at the rink, you have to drag your gear into the locker room, change your clothes, and lace up your skates—probably more than once to get them just right. If this tires you out just thinking about it, stick with activities that don't require a lot of "getting ready" time.

9. Is it versatile?

Doing the same exercise the same old way gets tiresome quickly. Your best bet is to develop a workout that you can vary according to your mood. For instance, some days you may be bursting with so much energy that you could take a brisk walk, then turn on music videos and jam for an hour nonstop, and other days you may opt for a de-stressing yoga session instead. Having a variety of physical activities to choose from ensures that you can work out rain or shine, at home, or with a friend—no matter what your mood.

10. Does it inspire you?

Exercise should spark your imagination, not put a damper on it. If you find yourself falling into an exercise rut, try a different physical activity before your motivation is zapped. Switching gears may be just what you need.

Another way to stay motivated is to bring along a friend or two (the more the merrier) to double or triple the fun. Workout partners can be an unbeatable source of encouragement, and they provide healthy competition so you push yourself to reach your highest potential.

If you answered yes to most of the ten questions, the activities you've chosen are probably the right match for you. Fun fitness options that suit your lifestyle are the kinds that will inspire you now and in the future. As you develop a fitness plan that suits you, you may want to keep a Fitness Journal for recording your thoughts, goals, successes, feelings, and hopes for the future. A journal can help you stay on track and record the changes that are happening in your body and in your way of thinking. Below are some suggestions for what to keep in your Fitness Journal; use these ideas to get started. Make your journal a unique and personal tool. You can fill it with motivating quotes, tips for staying healthy, affirmations, and anything else that will inspire you to get fit and feel good.

 My goals for staying fit and active:

Goal #1 . . .

Goal #2 . . .

Goal #3 . . .

Other goals . . .

Sports/activities I'd like to try . . .

Steps I need to take to get involved . . .

Ideas for staying motivated . . .

Ways to de-stress . . .

Supportive people I can talk to . . .

Other resources . . .

How I feel after exercising . . .

Healthy foods I like to eat . . .

Ways to reward myself for taking good care of my body . . .

16
Cross-Training Fun

"Finish what you start. . . . Meeting goals builds your self-esteem; you just feel like you're on top of the world."

Cynthia Cooper, Women's National Basketball Association's first "Most Valuable Player"

If your exercise program has become too routine, mix it up. Cross-training, or a fitness program combining two or more activities, is a sure way to say good-bye to boredom. You can use any combination of activities to get in shape. Alternate jogging with in-line skating; try stair-climbing one day and cycling the next; or trade off between intervals of aerobic dance and weight lifting. You've got the power to build a cross-training program that's custom-designed to suit your taste.

How Cross-Training Got Its Start

The steadfast pursuit of one sport was once the norm for serious athletes, as well as those interested in fitness. Competitors trained by practicing their sport exclusively, and exercise enthusiasts followed suit. If you were a runner, you ran, and if you were a cyclist, you cycled. Then, in the '70s, someone came up with the idea of combining three activities into a single event—the Ironman Triathlon. This mega-endurance contest involves swimming 2.4 miles in the ocean, cycling 112 miles, and running a marathon (26.2 miles). Amateurs were awestruck by the incredible stamina, strength, and determination of these athletes. Fans of the Ironman began applying the same "alternating" concepts to their own workouts, and cross-training was born. Today, cross-training isn't just for elite athletes; it's for anyone who wants to break out of a dull routine and have a great time getting in shape.

Why Cross-Train?

The benefits of starting a cross-training program are as diverse as the activities that you can choose to include, and only as limited as your imagination. Variety is the spice of life (corny, but true), and that applies to fitness as well. The choices for designing your cross-training program are limitless. You can ride your bike Monday, go to a water aerobics class Wednesday, and take a power hike over the weekend, or try any other combination that gets your heart pumping and spirit soaring. There aren't any rules, so make the most of your playfulness and creativity.

The best benefit of all? A more thoroughly trained body. Cross-training gives you the opportunity to use more muscles and work them in many different ways. If you were to limit your fitness program to jogging only, your body would become proficient at jogging. This concept, known as specificity of training, means that muscles adapt specifically to the demands placed on them. Cross-training gives you the freedom to become adept at more than just one activity. It also helps you develop a body that's athletic, toned, flexible, strong, and aerobically fit.

Cross-Training Means Fewer Injuries

Cross-training not only perks up a stale routine, conditions your muscles, and strengthens your heart—all at the same time—but also reduces your risk of injuring yourself.[1] Performing the same type of exercise over and over can put lots of stress on your body, increasing your risk of an "overuse" injury (when a muscle or group of muscles is overused, a strain or sprain, for example, may result). Adopting a cross-training program reduces the risk of getting an overuse injury because alternating your activities allows some muscles to rest while others work. The possibility of overusing muscles decreases when you allow them to recover from one workout before tackling the next.

Cross-training also enables you to maintain an exercise program when you have a minor injury; it's possible to work part of your body while resting the afflicted area. You can stay in shape, let the injury heal, and try out a few new activities—all while you're recovering.

Getting Started

Cross-training opens up a world of fitness possibilities, providing an opportunity to exercise your muscles as well as your options. Be daring and

---

[1] See Chapter 21, "The Agony and the Bliss," for more information about sports injuries.

experiment! Try activities that you may never have considered (ballet, martial arts, track and field) and get motivated at the same time. Your confidence will grow as you become more fit. Follow these five tips for cross-training success:

1. Pick enjoyable activities.

If you like quiet, solitary activities, don't force yourself to join a team or a bustling health and fitness club. Instead, opt for individual sports like in-line skating, cycling, or walking. Steer clear of anything that leaves you feeling discouraged. If you're itching to try something really different, like synchronized swimming, but can barely dog-paddle, you may be setting yourself up for failure. A better choice would be to sign up for swimming lessons first and move up to synchronized swimming when you feel more confident in the water. Fitness activities should empower and encourage you, not stress you out.

2. Start new activities slowly.

If you jump full force into a multisport cross-training program, the only thing you'll achieve is sore muscles.[2] Any time you try a new sport or activity, your body needs time to adapt. If you switch gears too often or try several new sports all at once, you'll end up a sore, achy mess (which isn't very motivating). To avoid injured muscles, limit your cross-training program to just two activities for the first few weeks. As your body gets used to exercising regularly, feel free to add other activities, one at a time. Don't zap all of your energy right away—take it slow and have fun molding your program to suit your style.

3. Warm up thoroughly.

Because cross-training puts so many muscles to work, a thorough warm-up[3] is important before beginning your program. Design a warm-up routine that matches the demands of your workout. With the right pre-exercise warm-up, you'll be ready to give your cross-training program everything you've got.

---

[2] If your muscles do get sore, read pp. 188–190 for muscle-soothing tips.
[3] See Chapter 19, "Vroom Vroom: Warming Up."

4. Create your own program.

Put together a custom-made cross-training routine. Start by listing the activities that you already love, then add ones you've always wanted to try. To help choose which cross-training choices will work best for you, make a list of the resources you'll need for the activities you plan to do—a fitness club, special equipment, training, a field, certain weather conditions, etc.

If you'll need some special gear or equipment, figure out how you can rent or buy what you need. Perhaps finding the necessary equipment or facilities isn't an option for you—instead of giving up, try a compromise. For example, maybe you want to get involved in yoga but there isn't a class available to you—try renting an instructional yoga video instead. Just remember that your program needs to be convenient, realistic, and fun, too.

5. Get fit in the great outdoors.

Ahhh . . . the free feeling of running with the wind (and no gym fees, either). Take your cross-training routine outside and add some fresh air to your workout. With a little imagination, you can turn your local park or school football field into a cross-training playground. Either locale can be turned into an obstacle course, chock-full of possibilities to improve your endurance, strength, power, and coordination. Take advantage of all there is to offer and have a blast constructing a program to suit your individual exercise needs.

Three Steps to Cross-Training Fun

Follow these three simple steps to develop a cross-training program that combines fitness with fun.

Step 1: Scope out your surroundings.

Take a look around a local park or field and identify props and activities that can be incorporated into your workout. On pp. 160–163 are some examples of how you can use a variety of locations for different exercises, plus how-to's for the suggested exercises.

Track: Use it for power walking, jogging, or jog/walk combinations.

Hills: Use them for power work.

Trees, bushes, or goalposts: Use them for agility drills.

Fences, walls, and trees: Use them for arm strengthening (push-ups, pull-ups).

Monkey bars: Use them for arm strengthening (pull-ups).

Benches: Use them for leg strengthening (step-ups).

Bleachers: Use them for leg toning (squat steps).

Exercise How-To's

Power walking: To power walk, pump your arms and walk really fast, as if you're in a hurry. Keep your shoulders relaxed and your back straight. Your elbows should be bent at an angle that feels natural, with your hands loose and relaxed. Use the muscles in your hips, thighs, and lower legs to move yourself forward.

Jogging: The proper technique for jogging requires striking the ground first with your heel, then rolling onto the ball of your foot and toes as you push off. Your arm swing should be relaxed, and your hands should be held loosely with your arms at a natural angle (about 90 degrees). Pick a comfortable stride—if you can't chat with your workout partner or sing along with the tunes on the radio, you're going too fast. Let your body find its natural stride, stay light and springy, and don't forget to breathe.

Jog/walk combos: An easy way to perform jog/walk combos is to run the straight part of the track and walk the curves. Or alternate walking a lap with jogging a lap. At the park, try walking for a minute, then jogging for a minute; or run a lap around the park, then walk a lap.

Power work: While walking quickly up hills, use long, powerful strides and pump your arms. You can also sprint uphill. But never, ever run downhill (it's dangerous); always walk downhill using controlled strides.

Agility drills: Run zig-zag patterns between a pair of trees or bushes, or around goalposts. Start by slowly jogging the pattern two times. Increase by one set each week until you can do it five or six times. Making your turns tighter as you round each obstacle, or going faster, makes the drill more difficult.

Push-ups (off a vertical surface): Stand with your feet together, and your hands placed at shoulder height on a sturdy fence, wall, or tree. The further away your feet are from the wall, the harder the exercise will be. Your hands should be shoulder width apart. Keeping your back

straight, slowly bend your elbows and bring your chest toward the wall. Exhale and push away gently while straightening your elbows. Start with a set of 10 repetitions; increase by 5 reps per week up to three sets of 10–15 reps.

Pull-ups: This exercise is best with a workout partner. Hold onto a monkey bar, using either an underhand or overhand grip (overhand is more difficult). Bend your knees and have your workout partner hold your feet. Pull yourself up as high as you can without swinging your body back and forth, and have your friend push you up as you pull. Slowly lower your body without letting your elbows lock. Do as many pull-ups as

you can with a maximum of 5 repetitions; increase by 2 repetitions per week if you're up to it.

Step-ups:* Stand upright, facing a step or low bench (no more than 12–15 inches high). Place your left foot completely on the step. Your left knee should be directly over your heel. Step up, straightening your left knee and placing your right foot next to your left. (As your left leg straightens, tighten your left thigh and your rear.) Then step down, leading with your left foot and lowering your body slowly using your right leg. Keep the landing soft.

Finally, bring your right foot down to meet your left. Now repeat the same moves, only stepping up with the right foot first. Begin with a couple sets of 10 steps each way. Increase by 5 steps per week until you can perform 30 steps in each direction.

Squat steps:* Stand sideways on the upper bleacher, so you're not looking down. Start with your feet together and your legs straight. Your left side should be facing the field below. Step to your left, placing your entire foot on the next bleacher down. Bend both knees, keeping your back straight, squatting as low as you are comfortable. Keep the heels of both feet flat. Look at your knees; you should be able to see your feet. If you can't, slowly shift your weight back until you can.

Next, stand up, bring your right foot to meet your left, and straighten both knees. Go back to the starting bleacher, turn and face the other way, and perform another set. Begin with 5 squat steps in each direction. Increase by 5 repetitions per week until you can squat step the entire set of bleachers.

---

*Whenever you perform step-ups or squat steps, climb stairs, or exercise on bleachers, be sure to place your *entire* foot on the step. Also, check that your knee is directly over your heel—you want the knee bent at a right angle.

Step 2: Practice the moves.

Before going full speed ahead, practice the exercises that you want to include in your outdoor cross-training program. Familiarize yourself with the different stations so you know exactly what you're doing. This allows you to move continuously, eliminates down time, and results in a better workout. For example, test the height of the benches or bleachers so you're comfortable with the step size. Walk through your zigzag agility drill to judge the distance between shrubs or trees and the angle of each turn. Look for running/walking paths that aren't hidden so you'll always be visible (for safety). Preparing in advance also gives you a chance to rate the difficulties of each exercise—you'll know if you need to add or subtract time or repetitions at each station to fit your needs.

Step 3: Customize your program.

Decide how long you want your workout to last, then break it down into sections. If you're a beginner, start with 10–15 minutes of aerobic work and two stations per session for the first week. Add 5–10 minutes of cardiovascular work and one station per week from there. Aim for a workout of about 30–45 minutes total. The idea is to vary your routine, using short intervals of different exercises; there's no need to do more than 30–45 minutes of continuous aerobic activity in a cross-training program. You can always break the routine up like this: Do 10–15 minutes of cardiovascular exercise (power walking), then two stations (stride up and down a hill five times and do 20 step-ups), then another 10–15 minutes of cardiovascular work (walk/jog), and two more stations (zigzags and push-ups).

Every session of a well-designed cross-training program should include:

- a thorough warm-up
- a cardiovascular segment
- strengthening exercises
- power work or agility drills (include one or both, depending on your fitness level)
- a cool-down and static stretching[4]

---

[4] For more on cooling down, see pp. 198–199; for stretching tips, see Chapter 20, "Head-to-Toe Flexibility."

17

Why Sweating Is Cool

"Sweat is your body leaking fuel."

Nike

"Women don't sweat, they glow," the old saying goes. Yeah, right. Whoever dreamed up that notion must not have envisioned the power, strength, and grace of women athletes in motion. Check out the athletic beauty of Kristi Yamaguchi on the ice, Sheryl Swoopes on the basketball court, Martina Hingis on the tennis court, or Shannon Miller on the uneven bars. None of these elite athletes could have achieved glory without huge doses of dedication, determination, and sweat. The truth is, whether they're recreational athletes or prima ballerinas, women *do* sweat.

Sweating is a sign of fitness. Perspiration is totally natural and necessary to keep your body functioning properly. The next time you complete a workout drenched in glistening sweat, don't be grossed out—be thankful that your body's thermostat is working. Just like an air conditioner, your body has a thermostat to help regulate its temperature. When things heat up internally, your cooling system is triggered into action. If you've danced nonstop to five or six of your favorite songs, you've probably noticed flushed cheeks, a faster heartbeat, and little beads of sweat rolling off your body. The reason? Your body's air-conditioner has clicked on.

As your body temperature rises during a workout, the tiny blood

164

vessels close to the surface of your skin, called capillaries, open up. This allows the blood, which carries heat away from vital organs and working muscles, to get closer to the skin. As the hot blood flows near the skin's surface, water escapes through your sweat glands and onto your skin, which makes you perspire. And finally, when the air brushes over your sweaty skin and dries up the moisture, your body cools down.

While sweating is cool, body odor generally isn't. To combat stinky underarms, bathe or shower daily with an antibacterial soap and use a deodorant or antiperspirant for added protection. Deodorants mask odors, and antiperspirants help fight wetness. They come in so many different scents, you can arm your "pits" with the fragrance of anything from an ocean breeze to baby powder to a bouquet of fresh flowers.

To avoid smelly feet, use a medicated foot powder, antifungal spray, or odor-absorbing shoe inserts. Be sure to air out damp athletic shoes after every workout, too. Foot lotions scented with peppermint or other pleasant-smelling aromas make nice indulgences for tired feet.

Tips for a Sweat-Healthy Workout

1. Drink lots of water.

Drinking water before, during, and after you exercise is one way to keep your body's air-conditioning system in tip-top shape.[1] Failing to keep your muscles well hydrated can leave you feeling weak and sluggish. Dehydrated muscles can also lead to:

- decreased stamina (you'll tire sooner)
- slower muscle response (you'll be less coordinated)
- diminished sports performance (you might not achieve your personal best)

You shouldn't sabotage your workout or game by forgetting to drink enough water. But how much is enough?

---

[1] See p. 77 for more information on the benefits of water.

Follow these guidelines, and you won't have any trouble keeping your thirst quenched:

- The more you sweat, the more water you need.

- Always keep a water bottle or thermos nearby whenever and wherever you exercise, and drink 4–8 oz. every 15–20 minutes.

- When it comes to the amount of water you need, the American Dietetic Association recommends this rule of thumb: Start with 8 glasses of water a day and drink an additional 1–3 cups per hour as you increase the intensity and length of your physical activity.

- Avoid drinking coffee, tea, and colas to replace lost water; they usually contain caffeine, which is a diuretic. Diuretics cause you to eliminate water by making you urinate more often, so they defeat the purpose of drinking liquids to keep your body hydrated.

• •

Consuming lots of caffeine isn't a great idea, whether you're exercising or not. Caffeine is a stimulant, which causes an increase in your heart rate, blood pressure, and the acid secretions in your stomach. Over prolonged periods, use of caffeine can lead to ulcers, insomnia, high blood pressure, and heart irregularities. The short-term effects of too much caffeine include nervousness, irritability, nausea, or a jittery feeling.

• •

- Skip the sugary drinks during and immediately following your workout because your digestion stops during exercise (the blood and energy required for digestion is diverted to your exercising muscles). If you drink soda or fruit juices while working out, the concentrated calories and sugar sit in your stomach longer. That sugar draws water from your muscles into your stomach, which can result in cramping and diarrhea.

- Choose liquids that are cool instead of ice-cold or warm—they'll get into your bloodstream quicker.

- Thirst is your brain's way of letting your body know that it hasn't been getting enough water. But here's the problem—once you realize you're thirsty, your body is already dehydrated. Think of thirst as a smoke alarm. The alarm doesn't go off until *after* it senses the danger of fire. Thirst isn't much different, so it's important to drink water throughout your workouts, even when you don't feel thirsty.

- The harder you exercise, the more you'll sweat. So drink up. It doesn't matter if you gulp designer water from a fancy bottle or plain old tap water. The important thing is that you stay hydrated.

2. Try a sports drink during strenuous workouts.

For workouts under 90 minutes, water is all you need to keep your body properly hydrated. If you're training for an endurance event like a marathon or planning a strenuous workout lasting more than 90 minutes (which you shouldn't do unless you're in excellent shape), you'll lose more water than usual and may need the extra boost of a sports drink to go the distance.

Sports drinks (like Gatorade or Hydra Force) help your body stay hydrated more effectively than water alone. These popular beverages are often promoted for their added electrolytes—the fancy term for the minerals sodium, potassium, and chloride. The job of these minerals is to keep your body's fluid levels balanced. The main reason electrolytes are added to sports drinks is to keep you thirsty so you'll be more likely to keep guzzling and less likely to get dehydrated.

Recreational athletes don't really need the added electrolytes found in sports drinks, since the amount of sodium and potassium lost during a regular workout is pretty minimal. Sodium is easily replaced by the salt contained naturally in foods, and eating a banana will take care of lost potassium. A final thought—if you decide to try a sports drink, make sure to read the label because some of them contain lots of sugar.

3. Wear well-ventilated clothing.

Wearing clothing that allows your body to breathe is another way to keep cool while exercising. Natural fibers like cotton absorb perspiration, and as you get more and more sweaty during a workout, they can become saggier and heavier. If damp, droopy drawers aren't appealing, shop for high-tech synthetic fibers such as Coolmax, Supplex Lycra, Dri-F.I.T., and Tactel. They're designed to draw sweat away from your skin (called "wicking") to the outside of the fabric so you stay dry.

If you think wearing heavy sweats during a rigorous workout burns lots of fat and extra calories, guess again. What you lose is strictly water weight. What you gain is an increased risk of throwing your body's cooling system out of balance. When you exercise in heavy clothing, air can't get to the skin to evaporate sweat, so your system is forced to work overtime to reduce the extra heat. If you feel cold when you begin a workout or can't imagine exercising in anything but oversized comfy sweats, layer your fitness apparel so you can peel off the outer layers as your body warms up.

4. Check your heart rate.

Checking your Target Heart Rate (THR) is a good way to tell if you're getting the most out of your physical activity. It's also a way to find out if you're exercising too hard. Here's how to calculate what your THR should be:

$$(220 - \text{your age}) \times 70\% = \text{Your THR}$$

Your THR is the heart rate to aim for as you work out, and you should check it after about 20–30 minutes of continuous exercise (walking, biking, swimming, jogging, etc.). All you do is feel for your pulse—at your wrist or on your neck at the carotid artery. Count the number of beats that you feel in 15 seconds, then multiply this number by four for your heart rate. (NOTE: Do this while you're still active. If you wait until you start to cool down, your heart rate is already returning to normal.) If your pulse is way above your THR, you're working out too hard. Take it easy on yourself. If your pulse is far below your THR, find ways to make your workout more difficult. Move faster, for example, or add more resistance (with hills, steps, swim fins, etc.). You can also use a multiplier of 60% or 85% in the formula (instead of 70%) because your THR is really a range to aim for. Your goal when exercising is to keep your heart rate somewhere *above* the lower number (60%) and *below* the higher number (85%).

5. Don't let yourself get overheated.

Exercising in high temperatures calls for water, water, and more water. When the temperature outside soars, your body heats up more than it does during a cool-weather workout. Your internal thermostat works overtime to keep up with the amount of heat generated inside your body. Remember these tips for working out when the weather heats up:

- Drink lots of water, and if you're exercising outdoors, splash cool water on your body.

- On hot days, cut back on the length and intensity of your workouts. Gradually increase the time you spend exercising by 5 minutes every couple of days until you're better acclimated to the heat. It can take 9–14 days for your body to adjust to warmer temperatures.

- Try to exercise during cooler times of the day, like early morning or evening (not when it's too dark out, though).

- How about a change of scenery? Work out indoors or go to a park that has lots of shade. Take a refreshing dip in a pool and try brisk walking or jogging in the shallow end.

- Wear light colors, since they reflect sunlight, and loose-weave fabrics so more air can get to your skin.

- Be sure to cool down after exercising. Gradually lowering the intensity of your activity will help keep you from feeling dizzy or light-headed.

- Use waterproof sunscreen and protect your head and eyes with a hat and sunglasses.

- Avoid exercising on concrete or near buildings —they can intensify the heat. Opt for heat-absorbing dirt or grass instead.

Hot Flash! Avoid Heat-Related Illnesses

Even if you're careful when working out during a heat wave, you might still overheat. It doesn't have to be really hot and sunny for you to get overheated, either; the humidity and your fitness level are important factors. If your body's air-conditioning system can't work fast enough, or you're dehydrated from excessive sweating, you run the risk of getting sick. Watch for the three stages of heat-related illnesses:

Stage #1—Heat Cramps: These usually occur in the stomach or legs. Nausea, tingling in the arms and legs, and clammy skin may accompany the cramps. If you experience any of these symptoms, find a cool spot to rest and drink water. This helps your internal air-conditioner to get back on track.

Stage #2—Heat Exhaustion: This can happen in as few as 30 minutes. Signs of heat exhaustion include profuse sweating; cool, clammy, pale skin; and a weak, rapid pulse. Your body is working so hard to keep your temperature balanced that everything is thrown out of whack. Get out of the heat, lie down, and slowly drink cool liquids.

Stage #3—Heat Stroke: This is the most serious stage and requires medical attention. Your sweating mechanism shuts off, causing your internal thermostat to overheat. Your body temperature can rise to dangerous levels. Signs of heat stroke include red, hot, dry skin; dizziness; and confusion.

(TIP: If you notice someone suffering from heat-stroke symptoms, immediately get to a phone and dial 911. The victim's clothes should then be removed down to the underwear; sponge the skin with cool water.)

18

Gearing Up to Get Moving

"When more women play, everybody wins."

Women's Sports Foundation

Here are a few pointers on exercise clothing, athletic shoes, hair solutions, skin-care, music, and magazines to help you kick your routine into high gear.

Choosing a Workout Outfit

Selecting workout wear can make you break out in a sweat if you feel pressured to look picture perfect. What should you wear when working out? Whatever suits your style. There's no reason to be a fashion fiend when you exercise because working out is about doing something good for your body, not impressing everyone at the gym. Keep the focus on your workout, not on what you're wearing. Comfort is the key, so wear whatever feels good.[1] As long as the outfit you choose lets you move easily and helps you stay cool, anything goes. Great options include bra tops, tank tops, bike pants, baseball jerseys, leggings, unitards, shorts, leotards, baggy T-shirts, and tights. Mix and match your favorite pieces to reflect your personality.

A supportive athletic bra is essential to any workout ensemble. Frilly, lacy lingerie may be pretty, but it won't do for exercising. Running, jumping, leaping, and twisting may cause your breasts to bounce uncomfortably (and uncontrollably), so adequate support is needed to protect tender breast tissue. Some manufacturers (such as Lily of France, Champion, and Speedo) have even created sports bras versatile enough to wear when you're not exercising but just need some extra control and support.

---

[1] See Chapter 22, "Pros and Cons of Your Workout Options," for information on specific apparel needs for various sports.

Look for an exercise bra with plenty of coverage in the front and wide straps across the back (thin straps can dig into your shoulders when you move your arms). Working out in a regular underwire bra may chafe your skin as well as irritate the glands beneath your breasts. Choosing bras with minimal hardware against the skin can eliminate such problems. Because they allow total freedom of movement, materials like lycra, mesh, net, supplex, stretch cotton, and spandex are good choices for bras. They'll also keep you cool and help pull sweat away from your body, which is a plus if your chest or back tend to get pimples.

Be sure that your workout wardrobe reflects the climate you live in. When exercising indoors or outdoors in warm weather, wear clothes that keep your body cool by allowing air to get to your skin. Fabrics that draw or "wick" moisture from your skin, while resisting the moisture from the air around you, include Capilene by Patagonia and Dri-F.I.T. by Nike. If you're cold when you begin working out, wear sweats or a lightweight shell over your outfit; these items can easily be peeled off as your body warms up.

For outdoor winter or altitude sports such as skiing, snowboarding, and climbing, layers are your best bet. Again, "wickable" fabrics such as Polypropylene, Thermolite, and DryLete are best to have closest to your skin, then add layers. Options include a thermal shirt, sweater, turtleneck, or fleece sweatshirt. Top it off with a shell or parka made of water-resistant fabrics like nylon or Gore-Tex. The outer layers can be removed once you heat up and put back on once you cool down.

Don't forget safety equipment.[2] Helmets, elbow and knee pads, wrist guards, and gloves are a must for injury prevention when it comes to sports like in-line skating, cycling, and snow boarding. All athletes and recreational sports enthusiasts need to put their personal safety first and wear protective gear whenever it's recommended.

Selecting Athletic Shoes

With so many different athletic shoes on the market, choosing a pair can bewilder even the savviest shopper. Manufacturers use cool-sounding terms to describe the impact cushioning and functional support of the shoe. Words like

---

[2] See Chapter 22, "Pros and Cons of Your Workout Options," for information on safety equipment for various sports.

"nitrogen," "phylon," "hexalite®," "hytrel foam," and "GraphLite®" scream for your attention. If you've visited an athletic shoe store lately, you know that many shoes also boast flashy gizmos, from lights to pumps. There are lots of shoes to pick from, but the most important concern is *how they feel on your feet.*

We don't recommend spending your life savings on a pair of titanium-filled, glow-in-the-dark street stompers. Athletic shoes don't have to cost a fortune to do the job. Although some shoes are quite expensive, finding a reasonably priced pair to suit your workout needs is possible. Check out end-of-season sales for discontinued styles. You may discover that last year's model is almost the same as this year's, only a different color . . . and at a clearance price. Warehouse stores, discount sporting goods stores, and outlets are also good hunting grounds for bargains.

Aside from fit and cost, another factor to consider when shopping for fitness shoes is what you're going to do in them. If your workout mainly revolves around one specific sport or activity, the shoes you wear should provide support for that particular type of movement. For example, if you jog more than two miles three times a week, you're better off with a running shoe. Then again, if you power walk, take a dance class, and shoot hoops at the park all in the same week, you'll need an athletic shoe that's more versatile—look for a "cross-trainer."

Depending on the sport, you may put from two to seven times your body weight into every step, so choose a shoe with adequate cushioning. You'll need more cushioning for high-impact activities. If the activity involves a lot of side-to-side (lateral) motion—such as dancing, tennis, or basketball—good traction and extra ankle support are also helpful. When you're ready to purchase a new pair of workout shoes, consider the five footwear facts on page 174.

1.   **Running shoes are designed to cushion impact from heel to toe.** This usually results in an elevated heel, assisting with the rolling motion of the foot, which propels you forward. They provide good forefoot stability (that's your arch and instep), but lack lateral support since running is strictly a straight-ahead movement. They're also suitable for weight training, walking, low-intensity hiking, and stair-climbing.

2.   **Court shoes (high-tops or low-tops) score big on lateral support and traction for quick stops and starts.** You won't find much cushioning for impact, though. Court shoes can be used for all racquet sports, as well as weight training, boxing, basketball, walking, and low-impact dancing such as hip-hop. (NOTE: Sometimes court activities like tennis, basketball, racquetball, and squash require players to wear shoes with certain types of soles to protect the playing surface. Check first.)

3.   **Aerobics shoes tend to be lightweight and padded mostly under the ball of the foot and heel.** They have good lateral support, a smooth outsole, and are usually cut higher around the ankle for stability when you twist and turn. They're ideal for dancing, boxing, tennis, and stair-climbing.

4.   **Cross-trainers are generally suitable for a wide variety of sports.** You can use them for aerobics, stair-climbing, walking, jogging (less than two miles three times a week), tennis, dancing, boxing, hiking, and weight training. You get cushioning, lateral support, and traction all in one durable, lightweight package. Be sure to try on a few brands so you can find the one that fits the specific shape of your foot.

5.   **Hiking boots should have rounded toes with room for your foot to slide forward as you descend a hill.** If you're a serious climber and intend to scale rugged terrain that includes streams and rocks, look for good traction and weatherproof material. Rugged "walkers," a cross between a walking and hiking shoe, work well for flat hikes and all-terrain power walking.

How long a pair of athletic shoes should last depends on how hard and how often you exercise in them. Working out in shoes that are no longer supportive can lead to injury.[3] To figure out if it's time to give your tried-and-true tennies the old heave-ho, try this test: Place your shoes on a flat surface and take a good look at them from behind. Does the upper part of

---

[3] See Chapter 21, "The Agony and the Bliss," for more information on sports injuries.

the shoe sag to one side? Are the heels worn down, causing the shoe to sit at an angle? If the answer is yes to either or both of these questions, it's time to retire your shoes. Peek at the inside, too. Holes and frayed lining can add blisters to your woes. Finally, if your feet, knees, or back have begun to ache, or if you can feel every bump in the ground through the sole, it's time to buy a new pair. Try these suggestions for finding athletic shoes that suit your needs:

- Visit a store with a large selection of shoes so you'll have plenty of options.

- Tell the sales associate which activities you're involved in and ask for suggestions for what shoes to buy so you're sure to purchase the right ones.

- Try on shoes wearing the socks you'll be working out in; otherwise you may find that the shoes are too tight once you get them home.

- Put the shoes to the test by simulating the motions of your sport: jump, jog in place, and pivot from side to side. Do they give you free range of movement? Are they comfortable? Do they offer enough support?

- Resist thinking "Oh, they'll be fine once I break them in." If the shoes don't feel right at the store, they won't feel right later either. Don't buy them just because they seem like a good deal or are a popular shoe among your friends.

- The pair you ultimately decide on should feel supportive and comfy so you're ready for action. Be picky . . . your body will thank you.

Here are tips to make your workout shoes last:

- Use them only for exercising. Wear an old pair for beach trips, pulling weeds, and other activities that don't require a supportive athletic shoe.

- Air them out after each workout. If foot odor is a problem, sprinkle deodorizing powder inside each shoe; wash the insoles if they're removable.

- Replace worn insoles with new ones—sometimes the inside of the shoe gets worn out before the outside does. You can find replacements (such as Dr. Scholl's) at the drugstore or supermarket.

- If your budget allows, buy two different pairs of shoes and alternate them. This may help prevent injuries and increase the life of your shoes.

Hair Strategies

No matter what kind of hairstyle you've got, keep it out of the way when you work out. Wet, stringy hair flopping in your eyes can really dampen your exercise enthusiasm (and your ability to concentrate on what you're doing). Develop a hair-management strategy based on the style and length of your locks, and how vigorous your training routine is. Butterfly clips, scrunchies, and button tiebacks are perfect for keeping medium-to-long hair in line. Pull it back into a ponytail, braid, or twist, add some barrettes or bobby pins for stray strands, and you're ready for action.

Another tidy way to tame those tresses is with a baseball cap. Caps are great for hair of any length and may help deter the wild frizzies once you get heated up. A fabric headband or folded bandanna tied behind your head or neck and under your hair can help keep sweat off your face.

If you're seriously into athletic endeavors, consider choosing a hairstyle that's simple to maintain and easy to keep neat when exercising. Between racing to practices, games, competitions, or daily workouts, who has time and energy to waste fussing with hair? Keep it simple.

To counteract the effects of sports-induced hair damage due to sweat, sun, dirt, or pool chemicals, wash and condition your hair as soon as possible after working out. As for styling, select a lightweight gel or spray that won't get totally sticky and run into your eyes once you start perspiring.

Skin Care

Put your best face forward with a good skin-care regimen. Clean skin is always important, but it's an absolute necessity when you work out.

Sweat combined with makeup can add up to clogged pores and irritated eyes. Make a clean start by removing any trace of makeup before you exercise. After your workout, wash your face with a cleansing gel or soap and water. Don't worry about having perfect hair and makeup while working out; it's more important to be comfortable and to feel good while you're exercising.

If your training takes you outdoors, be sure to protect your skin with waterproof or sweatproof sunscreen. You need to apply sunscreen whether it's sunny or not, since 80% of ultraviolet (UV) rays can penetrate clouds. Make sure to reapply sunscreen after you sweat or get out of the water.

Although some people mistakenly consider deep tans and sunburns "healthy," overexposure to the sun can lead to premature wrinkling, dark spots, and skin cancer. To minimize these risks, use a sunscreen with a sun protection factor (SPF) of at least 15. A minimum SPF of 30 is recommended if you're fair-skinned, work out at high elevations (mountain biking, hiking, or snow sports), or if prolonged sun exposure is unavoidable. Rub the sun protection generously over all exposed skin, especially your face, lips, nose, ears, shoulders, arms, and legs. Hats will also help you avoid a sunburned face and head.

Tunes That Move You

Music is guaranteed to jump-start your workout if the tunes move you. Because musical preference is a very personal thing, choose songs that charge your spirit and pick a sound that sets the mood for your particular workout. For activities like jogging and walking, you may want a tempo that creates a meditative mood. For aerobic dance and in-line skating, a fast beat can help you pick up the pace. If you need a motivation boost, make a tape of your favorite songs to play while you exercise. Feel the rhythm as you pump up your body and soul.

Magazines That Go the Distance

If you want more information on workout gear, getting fit, and feeling good about yourself, check out some of the following magazines. They can help get you excited to take great care of your body while improving your mind.

Fitness—Mind, Body, Spirit for Women
P.O. Box 5309 • Harlan, IA 51593-2809
1-800-888-1181
This publication covers fitness for the mind, body, and spirit. It includes personal stories, diet and nutrition tips, travel features, exercise how-to's, and health information.

JUMP: for Girls Who Dare to Be Real
P.O. Box 55954 • Boulder, CO 80323-5954
1-888-369-JUMP
This teen magazine is all about fitness and feeling good, and it's made just for you. Articles give you the jump on sports, style, health, nutrition, exercise, and much more.

19
Vroom Vroom: Warming Up

"I hope I just show women that it's okay to inhabit
your own body . . . it's important to me that
people see you can be an athlete and
be strong—and also be a girl."

Gabrielle Reece, pro beach volleyball player, model

Warming up is exactly what it sounds like—a way to heat up the body. It helps ensure a safe exercise session by preparing your muscles, tendons, joints, heart, and lungs for the effort to come. Consider this: A beginning jogger wouldn't begin a running program by sprinting a marathon (unless, of course, she's looking for a sore, potentially injured body). It's crucial to warm yourself up gradually for whatever sport or recreational activity you're doing to get the best performance possible out of your body.

Physical Preparation

The ideal warm-up involves performing movements similar to those your activity demands, only slower and gentler, for about 10–15 minutes. You'll notice some definite changes in the way your body feels if this pre-exercise routine has been effective.

First, you may break a slight sweat, or at least feel warm. Your heart will beat faster, causing an increase in bloodflow, improving the delivery of oxygen and nutrients to working muscles. Your metabolism also speeds up, boosting energy production so you'll have enough energy to finish working out. Your muscles should feel looser, and your entire body should be easier to move. Because warming up prompts your nervous system into action, your coordination will be a lot better, too. Motions that once seemed sluggish will become more fluid as you limber up. While a warm-up doesn't have to be exhausting, you should feel like you've exerted some effort.

Mental Preparation

The time you spend warming up is ideal for getting yourself mentally prepared to exercise. Clear your mind of any unwanted thoughts as you focus on what you're doing right now. Think about how your body feels. Can you feel your heart beating faster, your breathing rate increasing? Good! This means your cardiovascular system is getting geared up and ready to work. Do you sense any tightness in your muscles? If so, they may be telling you that they're not quite ready to exercise full force. Continue warming up, then spend a little extra time stretching these areas.

As you move through your warm-up, become aware of the strength you've developed and anticipate the feeling of accomplishment you'll have after completing the workout. If your program involves competition, the warm-up period is a great time to go over plays and strategies. Being mentally prepared for a game or fitness routine can enhance your performance, as well as the whole exercise experience.

Injury Prevention

Prevention is the best medicine when it comes to sports injuries, and a thorough warm-up is a great way to ward off an injury.[1] The increased circulation created by warming up makes your muscles, tendons, and ligaments more pliable. This means they'll be ready for the stretching phase that follows the warm-up, as well as for the demands of your sport.[2]

Warm-Up Basics

How do you wake up your muscles so they're ready for action? By doing a slower version of the activity you're about to perform. The goal is to promote warmth and flexibility in your body, so relax and get loose.

Try the following sport-specific warm-up suggestions. You'll want to warm up for about 10–15 minutes for each one.

---

[1] See Chapter 21, "The Agony and the Bliss," for more information on sports injuries.
[2] See Chapter 20, "Head-to-Toe Flexibility," for more information on stretching.

Aerobics: Most aerobics classes (and home videos) start with a warm-up that uses rhythmic, full-body motions, low-impact steps, and a variety of movements to make you more limber while gradually increasing your heart rate. If you get to class late and miss the warm-up segment, do some marching or stepping on your own, or take it easy during the first few minutes of the routine.

Basketball: Do a little bit of each movement you'll be doing on the court. Include some jogging and sprinting, jumping, side-to-side cutting, dribbling, quick stops and starts, and shooting.

Boxing: Jump rope, jog in place, or do jumping jacks to get your blood flowing. Follow up with some shadow boxing before beginning round one.

Cycling: Start with several minutes of leisurely pedaling. Use lower gears (which have less tension) and stay away from hills. Shrug your shoulders up and down, and perform wrist circles to loosen your upper body.

Dancing: Break down some of the more complex steps and combinations in your routine and perform each of them for several minutes. Begin with slower music, then speed it up once you're ready to start jamming.

In-line skating: Use long, flowing strokes as you begin. Add some shoulder shrugs to warm up your arms and torso, and you're ready to roll.

Jogging/running: Start by walking, then increase your speed to a slow jog. Avoid hills or inclines. Save any sprints for after your warm-up.

Tennis: Jog or walk for a few minutes, then start simulating the lateral (side-to-side) movements you'll be using during your match. Hit the ball lightly for a while to loosen up your arms and get in the groove of the game.

Weight training: Either ride a bike, walk, use a stair-stepper, or jog slowly for at least 10 minutes. Then go through each exercise in your circuit at least once using lower weight and higher repetitions before pumping serious iron. If you use light, hand-held weights in your routine, go through a set of each exercise once without them.

Swimming: Do several easy laps, tread water, or walk back and forth briskly in the shallow end. Include low-intensity versions of each of the strokes that you'll be doing, as well as arm circles to loosen your upper body.

It's easy to get into the habit of skipping your warm-up and jumping right into your activities, but resist the temptation. The warm-up is the most important part of any workout. Why? The warm-up is what prepares your body to work efficiently and safely when you exercise at full speed. Once you've properly warmed your body up, you're ready to stretch.

20
Head-to-Toe Flexibility

"To keep a lamp burning, we have to keep putting oil in it."
Mother Teresa

When a body is flexible, its muscles and tendons are pliable, not rigid, which allows every joint to move through a full range of motion. A little more flexibility may be just what it takes to lunge for that tennis shot, put the perfect snap in a karate kick, or scale the most challenging boulders on the way up a mountain. Your best bet is to limber up through a comprehensive stretching program.

While stretching alone won't boost your endurance, make you stronger, or tone your muscles, it's still a vital part of a balanced fitness program. It's the next step in your workout after a thorough warm-up, helping you feel looser, avoid injuries, and perform better. Flexibility exercises, done independently of a full workout, can also be totally relaxing. Stretches are a nice finish to any exercise routine, too. Do yourself a favor and take some time to loosen up.

Types of Stretching

Ever try yanking a comb through wet, tangled hair? Ouch! You probably discovered that slow, gentle strokes result in considerably less pain and fewer split ends. Performing stretches is like pulling a comb through wet hair—fast, jerky motions are not only ineffective but can cause pain and damage, while slow, gentle movements give the best results. The two main approaches to stretching are known as ballistic and static. A ballistic stretch occurs when you bring a muscle to the point where a stretch is felt, then you bounce up and down. When you do this, a protective response called the stretch reflex occurs. Nerves within the muscle fibers detect the intense stretch being applied and, to protect the muscle from injury, reflexively cause it to contract. The result: Instead of relaxing, the muscle tightens up.

You not only lose out on becoming more limber, but you may even injure yourself. Static stretching, on the other hand, is a better method. With this technique, you ease into a stretch and hold it when you feel a gentle pulling in the muscle. This creates a slow buildup of tension in the muscle, causing it to relax. Stretches can then be taken further, resulting in increased flexibility. To get the best possible result from your flexibility program, follow these stretching tips:

DON'T force it! Stretching to the point of pain will only backfire, increasing your risk of injury.
DO ease into each movement gently, until you feel a stretch.

DON'T clench your fists, grit your teeth, or hold your breath.
DO exhale slowly as you stretch. Let your body and mind go. Relax.

DON'T bounce and jerk.
DO hold stretches at the point of tension, then gently ease beyond it once the tension subsides.

DON'T rush. Stretching is a noncompetitive sport.
DO hold stretches 15–20 seconds (take your time) and repeat each one 3–5 times.

DON'T skip stretching if you're pressed for time.
DO make stretching a regular part of your workouts.

DON'T stretch when your muscles are cold.
DO warm up before you stretch. Warm muscles are supple and will stretch more easily.

DON'T settle for being tight.
DO stretch all the muscles you'll be using when you work out.

Limber Up

While it's true that some people are naturally more flexible than others, each person has the potential to become more limber by stretching. The most important thing is to stretch regularly so you can make the most of how loose your body can be and prepare yourself for upcoming workouts. Sample the stretches that follow by incorporating some or all of them into your workout. Remember—go slow and be gentle. Repeat each of the stretches 3–5 times, holding each 15–20 seconds.

NECK STRETCH
(TRAPEZIUS MUSCLE)

Sit or stand with your back straight, shoulders down and relaxed. Look forward and slowly tilt your head to the right side until you feel a gentle stretch in the neck and/or shoulder. Hold 15–20 seconds, then return to the starting position. Repeat, only this time tilt your head to the left.

CHEST STRETCH
(PECTORALIS MAJOR/MINOR)

Stand in a doorway, one foot in front of the other. Place your forearms on the doorjambs so your elbows are level with your shoulders and bent at right angles, with your hands above your elbows.

    Look straight ahead and slowly lean your body forward until you feel a comfortable stretch in your chest and/or shoulders. Keep your back straight. Hold 15–20 seconds, then relax. Raising or lowering your arms helps you to feel the stretch in a different part of your chest or shoulders.

SHOULDER STRETCH
(POSTERIOR DELTOID AND RHOMBOID)

Sit or stand with your back straight, shoulders down and relaxed. Without twisting your torso, bring your left arm across your body, elbow level with your chest. Keeping your left shoulder down, grasp your left elbow from underneath with your right hand and pull it gently toward your chest. Hold 15–20 seconds, then release. Repeat, alternating your arms.

ARM STRETCH
(TRICEPS)

Stand upright and bring both arms overhead. Bend your right elbow so your hand is resting behind your neck. Grasp your right elbow with your left hand and gently pull downward until you feel a stretch in your arm. Keep your shoulders relaxed. Hold 15–20 seconds, then release. Repeat, reversing your arms.

THIGH STRETCH
(QUADRICEPS)

Stand next to a chair or wall and hold on with your left hand. Bend your right knee and grasp your shin using your right hand, bringing your heel toward your rear. If you can't grab your shin, hold onto your ankle. Stand up straight (don't arch your back) and relax your knee. Keep your knees together and pull gently until you feel a stretch in the front of your thigh; hold 15–20 seconds, then release. Turn around, hold on with your right hand, and repeat, stretching your left leg.

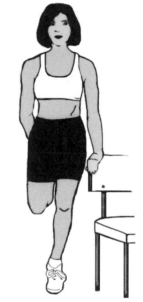

BACK STRETCH

This is a three-step stretch. Start on your hands and knees, with your back straight. Repeat the sequence three times.

Step 1: Begin by slowly arching your back, letting your belly button sag down, and tilting your hips forward. Look straight ahead, and don't drop your shoulders. Hold 5 seconds.

Step 2: Now round your back, pulling your stomach in and tucking your hips under. Keep your neck relaxed. Hold 5 seconds.

Step 3: Sit back on your feet. Drop your head and shoulders, keep your hands down, and reach both arms forward. Hold 5 seconds, then return to the starting position.

CALF STRETCH (GASTROCNEMIUS)

Stand upright, hands against a wall or table. Place your left foot back, right foot forward. Keeping both heels down and your back leg straight, slowly lean toward the wall, bending your front knee, until you feel a stretch in your left leg. Keep your back straight. Hold 15–20 seconds, then release. Switch legs and repeat.

CALF STRETCH (SOLEUS)

Stand in the same position described above. This time, slowly bend your back leg until you feel a stretch in your lower leg, just above your left ankle. The stretch comes on fast, so do this gently. Hold 15–20 seconds. Straighten your left knee to release. Switch legs and repeat.

THIGH STRETCH
(HAMSTRING)

Sit on the floor with your right leg straight, left leg bent. The sole of your left foot should gently touch the inside of your right knee. Rest each of your hands on the floor on either side of your body.

Keeping your back straight and leading with your chest, press your body forward until you feel a stretch in the back of your thigh. (If you have a hard time keeping your back straight when you do this, put a towel around your foot and use it to gently pull your body forward.) Don't lock your right knee. Hold 15–20 seconds, then relax. Switch legs and repeat.

THIGH STRETCH
(HAMSTRING)

Lie on your back with both knees bent, feet flat. Bring your left knee toward your chest and place both hands behind your thigh.

Slowly straighten your leg so your foot goes upward, until you feel a stretch in the back of your thigh. If you place your right leg flat, you'll intensify the stretch. Hold 15–20 seconds, then bend your knee to release. Switch legs and repeat.

21

The Agony and the Bliss

*"No matter what adversity you face,
if you strive to improve every day and set high
goals, you will always bounce back."*

Sheryl Swoopes, 1996 Olympic gold medalist, women's basketball

Exercise is an amazing thing. It energizes you, improves your health, and makes you feel stronger. Exercise also has the power to liberate you and drive you toward your personal best. The rewards are limitless, but as incredible as exercise can be, the pursuit of fitness sometimes results in pain.

Learning to recognize sports injuries, and knowing what to do if they occur, may help prevent a minor injury from becoming a full-blown trauma. As you get to know your body, it becomes easier to tell if something doesn't feel right. Recognizing an injury is extremely beneficial, yet no amount of knowledge can take the place of medical attention. If you have any doubt about the severity of an injury, see a doctor immediately. This will help you get back to your fitness program as quickly as possible and ease your mind, too.

Muscle Soreness

You've moved and grooved through your first workout with no problem. But if channel-surfing was your old workout of choice, brace yourself. There's a good chance that you're soon going to feel the effects of your new fitness routine. How? Most likely with an amazing sense of accomplishment . . . and a body that's stiff and sore.

Muscle soreness that hits a day or two after exercising is called delayed onset muscle soreness, or DOMS. It's normal, especially if you dive into something new. Suppose you shift gears and give up leisurely walks to school in exchange for an all-night dance-a-thon to your favorite music. A few days later you might notice that you can barely bend over to tie your

188

shoes, let alone climb the stairs to your room. Turns out the added effort of all that hip-hopping was a major wake-up call for your muscles.

What do you do when muscle soreness sets in? Don't give up. Make a deal with yourself to give exercising another try. Imagine—you've literally discovered muscles you never knew you had. Even though soreness can be a "pain," you've found new ways to work your body and you've pushed beyond old limitations in the process.

Don't worry—it *is* possible to have a great workout without being sore. Sure, if you push yourself extra hard on some days, you may feel it later, but your body eventually adapts to whatever physical challenges you give it. When that happens, soreness will no longer be a major problem.

If what you're experiencing is normal post-exercise discomfort, it will go away. After about 72 hours, you should notice less and less soreness each time you work out. Best of all, once your muscles stop hurting, you can feel good about the stronger, more resilient body that you're building.

If soreness does strike, try these five tips to ease your aching body:

1. Rest a day between workouts.

Rest gives your body a chance to heal and get revved up for the next workout. The recovery period between training sessions is the time when your body reaps the physiological benefits of exercise—namely tissue healing, which results in increased strength and a boost in your metabolism.

2. Stretching can work wonders on stiff muscles.

When muscles contract over and over during exercise, lactic acid builds up. The acid sits in your muscles, giving them a stiff, almost "congested" feeling. Lactic acid buildup tells you that your muscles have been doing their thing; it's a sign of a job well done. By gently stretching and drinking lots of water, you release this "junk," and your body feels more limber.

3. Work out again!

Getting your body moving is one of the best things you can do. When you're really sore, take it easy while working out. Spend an extra 5 or 10 minutes on your warm-up, and don't add anything new to your fitness program. Chances are, you'll feel more energized when you're done.

4. For relief, use ice during the first 24–48 hours.

Ice reduces swelling and eases pain by numbing the injured area. A bag of frozen peas makes a great ice pack because the pieces are small, and you can use it over and over. About 10–15 minutes a few times a day should do the trick. If you don't feel relief after a few days of using ice, try soaking in a warm bath. (WARNING: If three or four days go by and there's no change in your pain or it gets worse, you may have a full-blown sports injury. See a doctor.)

5. Try the R.I.C.E. approach.

R.I.C.E. is a common first-aid method referring to Rest, Ice, Compression, and Elevation. In other words: Sit down, chill out, wrap it, and prop it up! It's important to stop what you're doing so no more damage occurs. Place ice on the sore spot for 10–15 minutes several times a day. Be sure to place a towel between your skin and the ice so you don't add frostbite to your woes. Apply mild pressure by wrapping the area with an Ace bandage, towel, or T-shirt. This will also help control swelling and lend support to the injury. Prop it up above the level of your heart to keep the area from getting too puffy. This way, gravity can help keep fluid from collecting at the site of the injury. This treatment should ease the pain within a couple of days.

Sports Injuries

Sports injuries can range from slight pangs of soreness to absolute agony. Minor, nagging pains usually don't have to disrupt your workout or your life, but you know they're there because of the discomfort they cause. Examples include a tweaked ankle, a stiff neck, and tired feet. Mild injuries like these can easily be treated using the R.I.C.E. approach. However, if the pain is strong and continues for more than 48 hours, the injury could be serious and you'll need medical attention.

To determine whether you might have a sports injury, consider the following questions:

1. Does your knee look like a grapefruit?
2. Does your back ache before, during, and after a workout, as well as while you sit around the house?
3. Do you get a sharp pain in your shoulder every time you reach over your head?
4. Does your leg hurt when you start a run, get worse with each mile, and absolutely throb by the time you're finished?
5. Is the purple hue of your ankle beginning to clash with your favorite outfit?

If you answered yes to any of the above questions, you probably have a sports injury. Read on for the lowdown on some of the more common ones.

Sprains

Picture this: You're goofing around in the park, playing Frisbee with a friend. While your hands grope the air for the soaring neon disc, your foot finds a hole and before you know it, you're flat on your back with a throbbing ankle. What happened?

When a joint is forced to move further than it should, as it did when your foot had an unexpected rendezvous with the hole, something has to give—in this case, the fibers in the ligaments that hold your ankle together began to tear. The result? A sprain. The more fibers torn, the more severe the sprain.

Symptoms of a sprain include:

- tenderness to the touch
- pain with movement
- swelling
- discoloration

191

Ligaments can be sprained from mild, repetitive overstretching such as dragging your foot whenever you dive for a volleyball shot. Sudden, extreme stresses like when you step on a teammate's foot (which results in your ankle "rolling"), often cause more severe sprains and are usually accompanied by a loud "pop." If your finger is bent at a strange angle or your ankle swells so much that your shoes don't fit, there's a good chance that you've got a serious sprain—see a doctor right away. You may need to wear a brace, wrap the afflicted area, or wear high-tops to give the injury some extra support once you're ready to start training again.

Parts of the body most susceptible to sprains include:

- *the ankle:* if you fall off a curb, trip, or slip on water or loose gravel

- *the knee:* if you get hit on the side of your knee or twist your body while your foot remains stationary

- *the fingers and wrist:* if a finger gets jammed catching a ball or trying to break a fall; or if your wrist gets bent back at an angle

Accidents happen (there's not a whole lot you can do to prep your foot for a blind date with a hole), but you *can* reduce their likelihood. For example, choose your workout location carefully. Stay away from areas where there could be hidden holes, cracked pavement, or other obstacles. Also, wear shoes with good traction to keep yourself from slipping on loose gravel or damp surfaces.

If your sense of balance (a.k.a. proprioception) is good, you'll easily bounce back from a momentary loss of footing. To improve your proprioception, try activities that involve coordination and quick changes of direction. Running, walking, and biking are excellent exercises, but they're strictly straight-ahead activities; you can make your body more sprain-resistant by adding in-line skating or dancing to your fitness routine.

Strains

Strains occur when a muscle or tendon (which connects a muscle to a bone) is pushed beyond its normal limit. If you attempted 100 lunges with 50 pounds in each hand as a quick fanny-firmer, you'd very likely strain a muscle. Like a sprain, the more fibers torn, the greater the severity of the injury. Symptoms of a muscle pull or strain include:

- weakness
- stiffness
- pain when you move the area
- swelling
- tenderness to the touch

In the case of a severe strain, you may feel or see a deformity in the muscle, such as a bump or gap, and be unable to move the area. If this is the case, get medical attention immediately. A completely torn muscle usually needs surgical repair.

Some of the more common strains and their causes include:

- *low back pain:* often a result of lifting incorrectly, weak abdominals, or poor posture
- *hamstring and quadricep (thigh muscle) strains:* usually caused by sudden, forceful movements, or inadequate strength
- *shoulder strain:* sometimes the result of repetitive overhead motions or a strength imbalance in the shoulder muscles

Warming up your muscles before your workout can help ward off strains.[1] Not only do warm muscles feel more flexible, they're less likely to get pulled. And just as important as warming up is knowing when to stop exercising. Your fitness program will be more productive and there will be less chance of injury if you call it quits when you're tired. If you push yourself too hard when your body is fatigued, you're practically begging for a muscle strain. Do plenty of stretching and make sure your training regimen is well rounded. This way, every muscle will have a chance to become strong, fit, and flexible.

Tendinitis

Put your fingers in the crook of your elbow. Now bend your arm. Did you feel something pop up? These are tendons, which are the ropy ends of your muscles. Their purpose is to connect muscle to bone. When you get a strain near the end of a muscle, the tiny tears affecting the tendon result in tendinitis.

---

[1] See Chapter 19, "Vroom Vroom: Warming Up."

Symptoms of tendinitis include:

- sensitivity over a specific spot (also called localized tenderness)
- a burning sensation
- loss of motion
- sharp, stabbing pain with movement
- warmth to the touch
- swelling

The more severe the tendinitis, the more intense the symptoms. If an area remains inflamed for too long, the tendon can become weakened and seriously damaged. If this happens, you're susceptible to even more types of injuries. Applying an ice pack may chill out the early symptoms of tendinitis, but if ice doesn't help, see a doctor.

The more common types of tendinitis you may experience include:

- *Tennis/golfer's elbow:* caused by sports that involve a lot of gripping, pulling, or twisting, such as weight lifting, hockey, and racquetball. The sides of the elbow, where the forearm muscles attach, become inflamed and sore.
- *Achilles tendinitis:* affects the heel or back of the ankle. Achilles tendinitis can flare up from the repetitive stress of bench-stepping or running hills.
- *Rotator cuff tendinitis:* affects the group of muscles in your shoulder that allows activities such as throwing, swimming, and swinging a racquet. These muscles are small and can be easily overworked with repetitive movements.

A balanced program of stretching, strengthening, and conditioning will help prevent tendinitis. Be sure to include stretching in both your warm-up and cool-down. Flexible tendons don't pull as hard on their attachments, so they're less likely to become inflamed. Be consistent with your training, too. Strong, well-conditioned muscles won't tire as quickly when you exercise and are less likely to become overworked from the effort.

Shin splints

"Shin splints" refers to pain that occurs along the shin and can actually be the result of anything from tendinitis of the lower leg muscles to a fracture of the tibia, the bone between the knee and ankle.

Symptoms of shin splints include:

- dull, achy pain along the outside, inside, or front of the shin

- major tenderness to the touch (usually to an area about 3 inches in size)

- tightness in the lower leg

In some cases, the pain of shin splints will feel sharp; other times it may feel like your lower legs or feet are falling asleep while you exercise. If either of these situations apply to you, see a doctor immediately. You may be suffering from one of the more severe types of shin splints—either a stress fracture or compartment syndrome, both of which must be diagnosed by a physician and demand medical attention.

The best medicine for minor shin splints is to figure out what may be causing them. Read through the following list of common culprits to see if you can pinpoint the origin of the problem, then make some changes to alleviate your pain:

- *speed*: a too-sudden increase in how hard and how often you work out

- *shoes*: athletic shoes that don't support and cushion your entire foot[2]

- *surface*: training on a surface that's too hard or one that's different from what you're accustomed to

- *structure*: having flat feet or super high arches

- *strength*: not having enough strength in your lower leg muscles

- *stiffness*: not doing enough stretching to limber up your shins and calf muscles

Shin splints are painful and preventing them is the best "medicine." Begin by stretching your lower leg muscles frequently. Loosen up your shins and calves before and after your workout, as well as whenever they start feeling tight or sore. Picking up small items, such as marbles or tubes

---

[2] For more information on choosing athletic shoes, see pp. 172–175.

of lip balm, with your toes will help strengthen your arch. Wear supportive athletic shoes, exercise on soft surfaces, and try cross-training[3] to lessen the pounding on your legs. And, at the first sign of pain, use ice. Massage your lower legs with an ice cube or homemade water popsicle (water frozen in a paper cup) for 8–10 minutes several times a day. As with any other sports injury, if it doesn't feel better in two or three days, see a doctor.

Runner's knee

If sitting through a movie, climbing a flight of stairs, or squatting to pick something up bothers your knees, you could be suffering from "runner's knee." Known in medical lingo as *chondromalacia patella* or *patellofemoral stress syndrome*, runner's knee refers to pain underneath or around the kneecap. Runner's knee occurs when the cartilage on the undersurface of the kneecap, or patella, becomes irritated and inflamed. Pain is experienced when the quadriceps or thigh muscles contract, compressing the patella on the femur or thigh bone. You don't have to be a runner to get runner's knee. A single incident—such as lunging too deep when you go for a forehand shot on the tennis court, or repetitive stress from overdoing activities like bench-stepping, aerobics, basketball, or skiing—can result in runner's knee, too. Symptoms of runner's knee include:

• pain during squatting, stair-climbing, or prolonged sitting

• swelling around the kneecap

• stiffness in your joint

• weakness

• grinding (also called crepitus) when you bend and straighten your knee

The more inflamed the undersurface of the patella gets, the more painful your knee becomes. If it hurts to use your knee, you end up favoring it (by limping, for example), which causes your muscles to weaken. Since weak muscles can't support your knee very well, more stress is added to the problem area. This "pain cycle" may get progressively worse until you do something to cool off the inflamed area and restore the strength in your leg.

---

[3] See Chapter 16, "Cross-Training Fun."

Remember, ice is the simplest way to reduce inflammation. Use it 10–15 minutes at a time, as often as every two hours, if you want. Strengthening the quadriceps (thigh muscles) can help correct muscle weakness associated with a condition like runner's knee. Try these two simple strengtheners:

Quad sets: Sit with your legs straight, hands on your thighs. Tighten both thighs as much as you can, like you're trying to lock your legs. If you're in pain, stop. Feel your thighs and make sure the muscles are tightening equally. Hold 10 seconds, then relax. Repeat 20–30 times, working up to doing them 2–3 times per day.

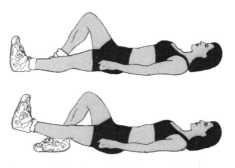

Straight leg raise: Lie on your back, injured leg straight, opposite leg bent so the foot is flat. Tighten your thigh, pulling your toes back and locking your leg; then lift your leg up about 12 inches. Hold 5 seconds, then slowly lower it. Repeat 20–30 times. Ankle weights can be added to this exercise for increased strengthening (start with 1–2 pounds) when 20–30 reps feels easy.

Keeping your legs strong and well-conditioned is a good way to prevent runner's knee. Be sure to include a variety of activities in your fitness program so all your muscles are strengthened and your knees aren't overstressed. Also, work your legs by lifting weights or trying other exercises that use resistance for strengthening, in addition to doing aerobic activities for endurance. If you end up seeing a doctor for runner's knee, physical therapy may be recommended to correct the problem.

Preventing Sports Injuries

When it comes to sports injuries, the best defense is a good offense—avoid getting them in the first place. A chronic injury can nag at you and make working out painful. If the injury is severe enough, you may be tempted to give up on exercise altogether—but don't! The benefits of exercise far outweigh the frustrations. To minimize your risk of injury, develop a strategy that incorporates these five basic suggestions:

1. Wear supportive shoes.

You don't have to spend a fortune. All you need is a comfortable pair of athletic shoes[3] that support your feet. The shoes you pick should feel good not only when you're standing still, but also when you're dancing, climbing, or stepping.

2. Listen to your body.

If your feet, legs, or knees are telling you that they're sore, listen up; something may be wrong. Consider changing your routine so you can rest some muscles, work others, and keep on exercising.

3. Warm up and stretch.

Check out any team at your school, and you'll discover that the players always warm up and stretch out[4] before playing. Basketball players, for instance, are out on the court early, shooting baskets, dribbling the ball, and running through plays to prepare their muscles. Moving until you break a slight sweat, followed by gentle stretching, is your best bet.

4. Cool down.

Exercising until you're in a sweaty frenzy, then plopping on the couch with a diet soda is a no-no. When you're done working out, take at least five minutes to cool your body down.

Keep moving and gradually slow your pace until your breathing returns to normal and your heart rate slows down. This will help you avoid dizziness (caused when the blood circulating through your body drops to your feet) and muscle cramps (which can occur when you suddenly stop moving).

---

[3] For more information on choosing athletic shoes, see pp. 172–175.

[4] See Chapter 19, "Vroom Vroom: Warming Up," for warm-up ideas, and Chapter 20, "Head-to-Toe Flexibility," for more on stretching.

Follow your cool-down with more slow stretching, and you'll have a winning workout. Drink lots of water to quench your thirst and replace lost fluids.

5. Gradually increase the intensity of your workouts.

Escalating from a jog around the block one week to a 5K sprint the next is asking for trouble. Increase the level and intensity of your workout gradually, and only when you no longer feel any post-exercise soreness. Doing *too* much can be as bad for your body as no activity at all; for peak performance, give your body time to adjust.

Listen to what your body is telling you when you exercise. Working out should feel good, challenge and inspire you, and propel you toward your fitness goals. If exercise hurts, stop what you're doing and take action. Don't let an injury get the best of you. Keeping your commitment to making physical activity a part of your life is one of the best things you can do for your health.

22
Pros and Cons
of Your Workout Options

"There is an athlete in all of us."

Reebok

It's true—there really is an athlete in all of us. If you're interested in adding a new activity to your current exercise program, or need a little inspiration to coax yourself off the couch, this chapter is for you. It covers a wide variety of sports and workout options with an emphasis on fun. For each option, you'll read about the pros and cons, body benefits, possible variations of the sport/exercise, and the equipment needed to get started; there's also an "FYI" (For Your Information) section that contains addresses and phone numbers of organizations and publications so you can get more information. Of course, your local phone book is an excellent resource, too.

When you exercise regularly, the rewards are definitely worth the effort. Here's a reminder of what you can look forward to:

• opportunities to meet new friends

• a higher level of confidence, self-esteem, and energy

• a better sense of who you are and what you can become

• a way to feel and look great

• a chance to feel strong, inside and out

• a winning attitude

• better concentration

• stress relief

• improved muscle tone

These rewards can last a lifetime.

Aerobics

Pros

Aerobics classes aren't the same old song and dance anymore. There are many workouts available to fit your mood, style, and individuality. Sweat it out on your own, with friends, at an aerobics class, or in the comfort of your own home with a video or TV fitness program. Aerobics classes generally include a warm-up, toning exercises, and a stretching or cool-down segment, giving you everything you need for a complete workout.

Cons

The continual pounding and jumping of high-impact aerobics may contribute to problems such as low back pain, sore knees, shin splints, and twisted ankles. Selecting proper workout shoes that are designed to support and cushion your body specifically for the activity you're doing will help protect you from this type of stress. To further reduce injury risks, opt for low-impact or step aerobics instead. Since one foot is usually on the ground, these forms of aerobics are less jarring, but you still get a great workout.

Body benefits

Aerobics classes are a great way to strengthen your heart and lungs, since this type of exercise means you're moving continuously for at least 20 minutes. Depending on the type of class you take, you may also tone your inner and outer thighs, buttocks, abdominals, shoulders, and arms. If the instructor does a lot of side-to-side movements and dance combinations, your agility and coordination are bound to get a workout, too.

Variations

High-impact aerobics involve dance-like combinations of hopping, skipping, turning, twisting, and jumping movements—all of which are variations on a basic in-place jog. Low-impact aerobics use the same type of movement combinations, except marching replaces hopping so one foot is always on the ground.

Check out these winning classes for new ways to work it:

African dance aerobics: African dance movements are done to the rhythm of African music or drums, sometimes performed live.

Boxing, martial arts, or kaerobics: These vigorous activities combine aerobics with martial arts techniques such as punches, kicks, jumping rope, and shadow boxing.

Hip-hop/funk aerobics: You perform cutting-edge hip-hop, funk, or street dance moves to the beat of rap music.

Line dancing aerobics: Combines aerobics and line dancing to country-western tunes.

Slide aerobics: You glide back and forth on a slide board (a long sheet of plastic with bumpers on each end) while wearing nylon booties over your shoes.

Spinning classes: Using specially designed stationary bikes, you're led through a grueling ride while you visualize an imaginary touring path and follow the instructor's cues to stand, sprint, and pedal nonstop.

Step aerobics: You step up and down onto a raised platform while you pivot, turn, squat, lunge, and "travel" to music.

Water aerobics/water step aerobics: Movements similar to those in aerobics or bench-stepping classes are done in the pool.

Yoga aerobics: Yoga moves and aerobic dance performed to new-age music add up to a super mind/body workout.

Equipment

All you need to get started is a fun class with a motivating instructor to lead you through the moves. If you don't have access to a gym, studio, or community recreation center, check your local TV listings for a workout program that fits your schedule. Or try an exercise video where you can do the moves at home, at your convenience.

The physical demands of most classes require a supportive pair of workout shoes with good cushioning and side-to-side stability, but there are exceptions. For instance, hip-hoppers can opt for funky street shoes, line dancers may want to wear cowboy boots, and boxers can slip on a pair of high-tops. If your class is meets in a pool, a pair of old tennies or aqua socks will help protect your feet from the roughness of the pool floor. As far as clothing goes, wear whatever feels best—anything from loose-fitting sweatpants and a T-shirt to a sports bra and bike shorts will do.

FYI

Aerobics and Fitness Association of America
15250 Ventura Boulevard • Suite 200 • Sherman Oaks, CA 91403
1-800-445-5950 • *www.afaa.com*
AFAA is a national certifying organization for aerobics instructors and personal trainers.

International Association of Fitness Professionals
6190 Cornerstone Court East • Suite 204 • San Diego, CA 92121
(619) 535-8979 • *www.ideafit.com*
This association offers fitness resources, such as workshops, up-to-date information on workout trends, and educational products for health and fitness professionals.

Ballet

Pros

The romance of ballet easily captures the heart. The orchestra swells, the curtain rises, you enter the stage dressed in a beautiful costume, filled with nervous excitement. The music sweeps you away as you tell a story through dance. Ballet gives you the freedom to express yourself through movement in a way that words alone can't convey. When you dance, your body consciousness is enhanced because you get to know your physical self so intimately. You learn your body's every nuance, and its limitations and strengths, which gives you the confidence to take center stage. Even if your dream isn't to become a prima ballerina, taking ballet lessons can be very rewarding. Learning to move gracefully can help you feel more comfortable with your body, even love it, as you get to know its never-ending potential.

Cons

Ballerinas dedicate their entire heart and soul to dance. For some, the pressure is too intense. Many girls involved in ballet are prone to eating disorders because there's so much emphasis on staying thin. Before the accolades and standing ovations, years of demanding training are required. Pliés and pirouettes aren't perfected overnight; it takes long hours of daily practice to polish the graceful, flowing moves that make ballerinas look so light on their toes. But if you feel the passion to dance, the sore feet and blisters can be worth it.

Body benefits

The movements of ballet promote a lithe body with long lines and taut muscles. Ballet also helps develop a strong back, torso, and legs, as well as grace, flexibility, coordination, and balance. One of the best body benefits of ballet may be improved posture. You'll learn to stand straight and hold your head high, which is admirable because how you carry your body says a lot about how you feel about yourself.

Variations

Ballet classes are a wonderful way to develop grace and poise, and get fit. If you're training to be a ballerina so you can one day dance with a professional company, you may be selected as a soloist, as a member of the corps de ballet, or to dance a pas de deux with a partner.

Equipment

Ballet students wear a leotard, tights, and ballet slippers. Once your leg muscles and technique are strong enough, your teacher may advance you to satin pointe shoes. Performances require costumes and makeup to capture the essence of the story being told.

FYI

American Ballet Theatre
890 Broadway • New York, NY 10003
(212) 477-3030 • *www.abt.org*
The ABT offers dance classes designed to prepare students for a career in ballet. Special outreach programs bring the magic of ballet to inner-city children.

Dance Theatre of Harlem
247 West 30th Street • New York, NY 10001
(212) 690-2800
In addition to an international professional touring company, the Dance Theatre of Harlem offers community education and dance-awareness programs such as "Dancing Through Barriers."

Joffrey Ballet
130 West 56th Street • New York, NY 10019
(212) 265-7300 • *www.joffreyballetschool.com*
This school offers dance programs for aspiring ballerinas of all ages, as well as professional dance performances.

New York City Ballet
New York State Theatre • 20 Lincoln Center Plaza • New York, NY 10023
(212) 870-5656• *www.nycballet.com*
This professional ballet company performs at Lincoln Center in New York City. The School of American Ballet, the official school of the New York City Ballet, trains dancers in this classical art.

Biking

Pros

The road beckons—whether cycling solo or with friends, biking is a lot of fun. Wherever you live, you're bound to find plenty of trails to choose from, so you can enjoy anything from a leisurely to a challenging ride. Blaze a trail on your mountain bike, tackle a long-distance ride, or get in touch with nature while coasting along scenic routes by the beach, park, or lake. Pack a healthy lunch and stop for a picnic along the way.

If you don't have anybody to ride with, joining a cycling club can be a terrific way to get to know other fitness enthusiasts. Many bike shops, health clubs, and sporting goods stores offer free group rides, and the U.S. Cycling Federation licenses thousands of cycling clubs nationwide. You can get more information on clubs, as well as advice on the latest gear, by logging onto your computer (Web sites are listed under "FYI" below). And while you're surfing the net, check out other online sports-related bulletin boards, too.

Cons

You're cruising for trouble if you crank up the miles on a bike that doesn't fit your frame or if you ride with poor technique. You might have problems with aching knees, numb fingers, a sore neck or back, and inner thigh chafing from rubbing against the seat. To prevent "saddle sores" as well as other cycling-related aches and pains, be sure that your bike seat, frame, and handlebars are adjusted to fit your body. Read a cycling book or magazine or ask a bike pro for tips on frame size, appropriate seat height, riding posture, pedaling techniques, proper use of gears, and suggestions for approaching different kinds of terrain.

Biking can be hazardous if you ride out of control, in adverse weather, or in heavy traffic. Minimize your risk by wearing a bicycle helmet, cycling at moderate speeds, riding in light traffic whenever possible, and wearing brightly colored clothing (or reflective gear if you're riding after dark). And of course, it's every rider's responsibility to learn proper hand signals and traffic rules.

Body benefits

Bicycling tones and tightens the legs and can improve your balance and agility, too. Off-road biking will strengthen your arms, shoulders, neck, and lower back, especially when you include hills in your ride. Pedal for at least 20 minutes (about 3 miles) for a cardiovascular workout.

Variations

Whether your goal is to pedal your way through the urban jungle or tear up some rugged terrain, there's a bike for you. There are four basic types, each designed to help you comfortably and efficiently cover whatever path you choose. Hybrids are the perfect set of all-around wheels for recreational riders to zoom about town, go on an occasional distance ride, or cruise basic mountain trails. For longer rides, a touring bike (with around 21 gears) is the rig of choice. Off-roaders or cyclists interested in tackling the hills ought to gear up on a mountain bike with a sturdy frame, good suspension, and fat, knobby tires. Speed demons serious about staying aerodynamic opt for the road racer. For a more mellow ride, rent a tandem (a.k.a. bicycle built for two). It will provide a playful outing for you and a friend.

Equipment

Different bikes offer different types of control, comfort, and components, depending on your riding ability and choice of terrain. Cycling shops, sporting goods stores, or discount or department stores offer choices galore. Some bike shops will even let you test-ride, so you can try before you buy. If you get serious about cycling, be prepared to pay a lot for a high-tech bike; super rugged or ultra-lightweight bikes designed for aggressive or competitive riders are expensive.

No matter what type of bike you choose, you'll need a helmet and reflectors for safety. When choosing a helmet, look for safety certifications such as Snell or ANSI, as well as a ventilated, resilient outer shell for the best protection. You'll add comfort to your ride with accessories like cushioned bike shorts or lycra tights (to reduce chafing), gloves with palm padding, cool shades with maximum UV protection, and sunscreen with an SPF of at least 15. For off-roading, you'll need a frame-mounted pump, spare tube, and patch or repair kit, just in case you get a flat. Don't forget a bike lock to protect your investment, a water bottle to keep you hydrated, and a small pack to strap on your bike frame to hold your student ID and a healthy snack.

FYI

American Bicycle Association
9831 South 51st Street • Suite D135 • Phoenix, AZ 85044
(602) 961-1903 • *www.ababmx.com*
The ABA is the national sanctioning body for Bicycle Motorcross Racing (BMX) competitions.

National Off-Road Bicycle Association
One Olympic Plaza • Colorado Springs, CO 80909
(719) 578-4717 • *www.usacycling.org*
As the governing organization for mountain bike racing, NORBA is dedicated to promoting the growth and safety of competitive and recreational mountain biking.

U.S.A. Cycling Inc.
One Olympic Plaza • Colorado Springs, CO 80909
(719) 578-4581 • *www.usacycling.org*
U.S.A. Cycling, Inc., the national governing body for competitive cycling events, sanctions cycling clubs, teams, and events across the country.

Boxing

Pros

Big math test tomorrow? Did you just have a spat with your best friend? Boxing is a great stress reliever. Lace up your gloves and punch those frustrations away. Whether you're throwing a straight right or a mean left hook, boxing is a super workout. It's easy to do at home and whips you into shape through total body conditioning. Through physical training like boxing, you can increase your self-confidence and gain assertiveness. The aggressive moves and mental concentration contribute to a mind-blowing workout.

Cons

You may get a few bumps and bruises with this sport (that's why it's essential to wear protective gear). Depending on how serious you are about your technique, you may want to work with a qualified instructor. Finding a gym or a recreation center that offers classes is a good idea, but working with a special trainer can get expensive.

Body benefits

Sleek, lean arms and strong leg muscles are some benefits of this sport. Boxing is an excellent aerobic workout for burning body fat and improving your speed, agility, and endurance. The defensive strategies can increase your confidence, too.

Variations

The options include boxing and kick boxing. You can box simply for the exercise, or you can learn different defensive and offensive strategies and combinations. Many gyms offer boxercise classes, which combine traditional aerobics with boxing moves. You'll work up a sweat jumping rope, shadow boxing, and punching a target (speed bags, heavy bags, or pads) to the sound of the latest tunes.

For solo workouts, try shadow boxing. Just practice punching combinations in front of a mirror using your reflection as an imaginary opponent. Hitting a punching bag or a duffel bag filled with old clothes, rags, or pillows is another option.

Equipment

You'll have to pay a membership fee or the cost per session if you take classes at a gym. Working out at home is a cinch, though. Exercise videos can teach you the moves and give you a basic boxing program to follow. Or you can stick with noncontact shadow boxing for a super workout. If you want to actually hit something, you'll need boxing gloves and a punching bag. Don't forget wraps for your wrists to help prevent injury.

FYI

Check the Yellow Pages of your phone book for a boxing gym or a health club or recreation center that offers boxing, kick boxing, or boxercise classes.

Cheerleading

Pros

Does this sound like you? Enough infectious spirit to motivate large spectator crowds, a positive attitude, an outgoing and confident personality, enjoys dance, presents a well-groomed appearance, knows the difference between a fumble and a slam dunk, understands the concept of teamwork, and gets a kick out of performing. If so, cheerleading may be for you.

A cheerleader's primary responsibilities are to engage the crowd, generate enthusiasm for the game, and encourage fan participation with cheers. Cheerleaders also entertain the spectators with dance routines that often incorporate stunts like pyramids, cradle tosses, and shoulder stands, and gymnastic moves like aerial walkovers and cartwheels. In addition to games, cheerleaders often perform at school pep rallies, special events, parades, and charity functions.

Cons

Difficult stunts and gymnastics moves can be very risky if they aren't done properly. To reduce your risk of injury, train with a certified coach who follows national safety guidelines and standards, learn safety spotting techniques, use mats, and never practice advanced moves without proper supervision. Cheerleading camps and clinics are another way to learn how to perform complex moves safely. Don't expect to master stunts overnight— they require lots of hard work, patience, and perseverance.

Unfortunately, there are only a limited number of members per squad. If you don't make the spirit team this year, don't give up. Keep practicing, and give it everything you've got next year. If performing is in your blood and you just can't wait until next year to get involved, consider trying out for the drill team, or taking a dance or gymnastics class instead.

Body benefits

With proper training, cheerleading can burn fat and promote good posture, increase stamina, and improve flexibility, coordination, and rhythm. A good strengthening program will give you the athletic ability and power needed for advanced maneuvers such as jumps, stunts, pyramids, and lifts.

Variations

Cheerleading squads are generally sponsored by schools from junior high through college. Spirit competitions are held at the local, state, and national levels, with scholarships and awards presented to the top finishers. Competitive divisions include dance, individual, and cheerleading, and junior high, varsity, and coed teams. Some women even make careers out of cheerleading, including choreographing, coaching, or cheering for professional sports teams.

Equipment

For practice, all you need is a supportive pair of shoes and neat and clean workout wear. Your attire should reflect that you're a school representative. Unless the school picks up the entire tab, you may have to pay for a uniform and some travel expenses; fundraisers may be held to help defray these costs.

FYI

Eastern Cheerleaders Association
P.O. Box 475 • South Hill, VA 23970
1-800-940-4ECA • *www.ecaeda.com*
The ECA organizes competitions for cheerleading and dance in the eastern U.S. and offers training camps, instructional programs, scholarships, and apparel.

National Cheerleaders Association
P.O. Box 660359 • Dallas, TX 75266
1-800-NCA-2-WIN • *www.nationalspirit.com*
This cheerleading and dance association sponsors team competitions and events, in addition to offering skill development and performance opportunities. Cheer gear is available through NCA, too.

Universal Cheerleaders Association
2525 Horizon Lake Drive • Suite 1 • Memphis, TN 38133
1-800-238-0286 • *www.usa.com/uca/index.html*
UCA organizes camps, competitions, and conferences for cheer and dance. Spirit squads can also get information on fundraising ideas and scholarships.

World Cheerleading Association
10555 Rene • Lenexa, KS 66215
1-800-858-4851 • *www.worldcheerleading.com*
Cheer and dance teams can participate in competitions, camps, and other special events sponsored by the WCA. This organization also provides info on scholarships and event results.

Dancing

Pros

Whether you're hip-hopping to music videos, creating your own moves to favorite tunes on the radio, or taking jazz, ballet, or country-western line dancing classes at a studio, dancing is great exercise. You can dance alone or turn a workout into a party and invite friends to join you. You might consider throwing a learn-to-dance party at your house or going to a dance studio as a group. Imagine the fun you'll have learning how to slow dance like they do in the movies. It's great practice for special dances like the prom and wedding receptions, too. Dancing works your entire body and is great for your cardiovascular system.

Cons

There aren't really any cons—unless you're self-conscious about your dancing ability. But that shouldn't keep you from having a good time. Pick your music and dance alone—there's no pressure to impress anyone.

Body benefits

Keep it moving through five or six songs, and you've got a terrific aerobic workout. Dancing is also super for toning and strengthening the entire body while improving flexibility and coordination.

Variations

Hip-hop, country-western, salsa, jazz, modern, ballet, and tap are just some of the ways you can move. You can dance alone in your bedroom to your favorite CDs or to the radio. Groove to music videos and exercise videos, or take class at a studio.

Equipment

Music that makes you want to move!

FYI

Check the Yellow Pages or contact your local gym, community recreation center, or YWCA for programs in your area.

Exercise Videos

Pros

When it comes to exercise videos, you can work out when you want, at your own pace, and in the privacy of your own home. Variety and low cost are major perks to working out with home exercise videos. You can choose practically any kind of workout imaginable, with props ranging from hand-held weights and exercise balls to step platforms and slide boards. The endless categories include videos that will tone your muscles, make you sweat like a fiend, burn body fat, improve flexibility, or teach you all sorts of new moves. Exercise videos generally range from $15 to $30, which is much cheaper than a gym membership. There are also many instructor personalities to choose from.

Cons

Not using them! Self-motivation is crucial here, and TV talk shows, the telephone, and lounging on the couch are just a few of the distractions that may keep you from using your videos. Try alternating different tapes to avoid getting trapped in a monotonous routine. How about hip-hop aerobics one day, a power-step workout the next, and a yoga session to finish off the week? Some videos on the market may be a bit on the unsafe side, so choose wisely. Many women's and teen magazines rate the safety and effectiveness of current home exercise videos; another resource is "The Complete Guide to Exercise Videos," a catalog devoted strictly to exercise tapes, put out by Collage Video (their 800 number is listed on p. 213).

Body benefits

Treat your body to whatever type of workout it craves. You can target a specific area of your body, work on overall toning and strengthening, improve your cardiovascular fitness or flexibility, or get in shape learning a new sport like boxercise.

Variations

Head to the video store—the choices are endless.

Equipment

A TV, VCR, adequate space to move (an 8-by-8 foot area should do), and a fitness video are all it takes. You may want to rent several different videos before buying one so you don't get stuck with a dud. After all, the goal is to enjoy working out to the video, not to use it as a paper weight. Some tapes require additional equipment, such as weights for specific toning exercises or a bench for a step-training workout. Bench-stepping videos are a great way to combine all the elements of fitness—cardiovascular, strength, and agility training—into a single intense workout. And once your fitness level and stepping proficiency improve, raising the height of your step will raise the intensity of your workout. Supportive shoes are essential for any type of aerobic workout, and you may want to use an exercise mat or towel if you have to get on the floor.

FYI

"The Complete Guide to Exercise Videos" by Collage Video (1-800-433-6769)
Not only can you order from this catalog, but you also get the benefit of their video consultants who evaluate each tape for safety, effectiveness, difficulty, entertainment value, and instructor appeal.

Gymnastics

Pros

To be a gymnast, you need to be part acrobat, ballerina, and daredevil. Competitive gymnastics requires athletic ability and artistry to master all of the technically difficult stunts. Whether you practice gymnastics for fun and fitness, or to compete, the ultimate reward is pride and self-confidence that comes from mastering the flips, handsprings, and dismounts of your routine.

Cons

Gymnastics is a high-risk sport for injuries such as stress fractures, broken bones, sprained ankles and wrists, and pulled muscles. To prevent injuries like these, it's best to have a coach or trainer (which can get expensive), or at least a spotter. If you're considering gymnastics competition, you'll have to put in long hours of intense training sessions.

Body benefits

This sport works every muscle in the body and is great for developing coordination, flexibility, strength, and power. You'll also learn concentration and split-second timing. If you're into dance or cheerleading, gymnastics training can enhance your steps and movements.

Variations

You can try gymnastics for fun or get involved in local competitions once your coach determines that you're ready. There are four events in a women's gymnastics meet: the vault, the uneven bars, the balance beam, and the floor exercise. Athletes compete for medals in team and individual events. If your stomach does flip-flops at the mere thought of performing complicated moves on the balance beam or the uneven bars, you may be better suited to rhythmic gymnastics—a combination of gymnastics and dance. Using hand-held props like ropes, hoops, balls, or ribbons, you'll learn routines that incorporate precision, coordination, balance, and grace.

Equipment

If you're an aspiring gymnast, you'll need to find a well-equipped gym, training camp, or clinic, and get a qualified trainer or coach. Maybe your school offers gymnastics as part of the physical education department or even sponsors a team that you can try out for. If not, look in the Yellow Pages for a private gymnastics club and set up an appointment with the staff so you can get more information.

FYI

USA Gymnastics
United States Gymnastics Federation • Pan American Plaza • Suite 300, 201 South
Capitol Avenue • Indianapolis, IN 46225
www.usagymnastics.org
As the national governing body for the sport, USA Gymnastics selects and trains athletes for the Olympics and World Championships.

Hiking

Pros

Awaken your senses. Breathe in the fresh air. Listen to the sound of brush crackling under your feet. Get a natural high from Mother Nature's beauty. Blazing a mountain trail is a terrific way to get in shape while you enjoy the great outdoors. Exploring nature and ascending to the peak are experiences you won't soon forget.

Cons

Finding a place to hike might be a workout in itself. For information about trails in your area, contact your local Parks and Recreation Department or call a local outdoor specialty shop. Safety is a must for every hiker—never go on an outing by yourself. Bring a friend along and always let someone know where you're headed and when you'll return. Potential trail hazards do exist, so make your journey as enjoyable as possible by researching your route ahead of time. It's helpful to be aware of the vegetation (poison ivy and poison oak are no laughing matter), animal life, and terrain.

Body benefits

Uphill expeditions give your leg muscles a tougher workout than hiking on level ground and tend to be pretty gentle on the knees and ankles. Continuous walking on a long hike is also an aerobic activity that burns body fat. Always warm up and stretch before hiking to loosen up your calves, hamstrings, and shoulders. Once you head home from your uphill climb, get ready for a major quadriceps workout—the front of your thighs get a lot of exercise when you walk downhill. Just be sure to take it slow to minimize the stress on your knees.

Variations

Hikers can vary their workout by choosing different trails and terrain. The great outdoors offers so many different challenges that seasoned hikers as well as novice adventurers are bound to have a great time while getting in shape.

Equipment

Here's the list of what you'll need for a safe, comfortable, and eco-friendly hike:

Hiking boots: While rugged workout shoes will do for your first few outings, if you plan to hike regularly you'll need appropriate footwear. Shop for hiking boots with rounded toes, good traction, and weatherproof material.

Two pairs of socks: A thin sock liner and a thicker pair on top will help prevent blisters.

Day pack or waist pack: Carry your personal goodies like a camera, hair scrunchy, sunscreen, lip balm, and a flashlight.

Water bottle: You'll need to tote a quart of water for every 90 minutes of hiking.

Sunscreen: An SPF of 15 or above is best; if you've got fair skin, opt for an SPF of 30.

Bug repellent: You'll need this especially for summer hikes.

Toilet paper: You'll need it for those calls of nature.

Sunglasses: Choose a pair with strong UV protection and wear a hat, too.

Snacks: Fruit, raisins, and nuts taste great on a hike.

Lunch: One that's high in carbohydrates and protein (try a peanut butter and jelly sandwich) will provide the energy you need.

First-aid kit: Include adhesive bandages, antibiotic ointment, calamine lotion, gauze pads, first-aid tape, and identification for you and your trail-mate.

Trail map: You have to know where you're headed!

TIP: Respect the environment and don't litter the trails. Bring along baggies to stash your trash until you can recycle it or toss it in a dumpster.

FYI

Outward Bound
National Office, Dept. T • R2 Box 280 • Garrison, NY 10524
1-800-243-8520 • *www.outwardbound.org*
Outward Bound is dedicated to conducting safe, adventure-based programs while instilling a sense of appreciation for the environment and respect for oneself.

REI (Recreation Equipment, Inc.)
P.O. Box 1938 • Sumner, WA 98352
1-800-426-4840 • *www.rei.com*
REI sells gear for outdoor adventures through their retail stores and catalogs. They also hold free clinics on how to have a blast in the great outdoors.

Sierra Club
85 2nd Street, 2nd Floor • San Francisco, CA 94105
(415) 977-5500 • *www.sierraclub.org*
This organization is committed to the conservation of the national environment. Information on outings is available.

Horseback Riding

Pros

The best thing about horseback riding is that almost anyone can do it, and you don't have to be an experienced rider to have a great time. Many stables rent horses with gentle temperaments so even a greenhorn (inexperienced person) can saddle up for a pleasure ride. For those who want to learn more about equitation, lessons at a local stable or riding school are the best way to get started.

It's every rider's job to learn the fundamentals of horsemanship. Taking lessons from a qualified instructor will teach you everything you need to know about grooming, tacking up and untacking, how to use a pick to clean the horse's feet, and how to bandage the horse's legs. You can also learn basic skills such as mounting, dismounting, backing, turning, and stopping, as well as how to walk, trot, canter, and gallop. As you progress, you'll discover that riding is a lot more than sitting in a saddle. It's about you and your horse working together as a team.

Cons

The biggest hitch to horseback riding is the expense. Lessons, equipment, and owning or leasing a horse may be quite costly. Buying a horse is a major investment—definitely not something you shop for on the spur of the moment. Before you make a purchase, you need to be certain that you're serious about the time commitment and immense responsibility. Ownership requires an ability to meet other financial obligations as well. For starters, there's the bridle and saddle, blankets, board and care, vet fees, hay and feed, grooming supplies, and a blacksmith. Whoa! It is possible to cut stable costs by doing some of the work yourself, but be prepared—mucking out a stall, grooming and feeding the horse, and cleaning the equipment all require a lot of time on your part. You can't put off chores just because you're not in the mood to deal with them. You also have to be ready to handle the dirt and odor that come with caring for a horse.

Like any other sport, horseback riding can be dangerous if you're not properly trained. Use some horse sense and always obey the rules and regulations of the stable. The purpose of the rules is to ensure your safety. Although horses can bite, buck, or throw a rider, the more training you have, the better equipped you'll be to handle any situation and decrease your chances of getting hurt.

Body benefits

Horseback riding does wonders for the legs, particularly by toning the inner thighs and quads. It's also excellent for improving posture, endurance, and coordination.

Variations

Depending on your interest and riding ability, there's:

- Western: uses a roping saddle and reins, which cause the horse to respond to gentle pressure; includes roping, rodeo riding, barrel racing, and trail riding.

- English: uses a jumping saddle and snaffle bit and includes:

  Dressage: Horse and rider perform a series of dance-like movements to showcase the rider's proficiency and the horse's responsiveness.

  Jumping: You and your horse jump over fences, hedges, oil drums, poles, and water ditches.

  Three Day Eventing: The events include dressage, timed cross-country race, and stadium jumping.

Equipment

The first thing you'll need is a horse to match your riding goals and ability. Next you'll need equipment specific to the style of riding you choose. For

Western riding, you'll want a pair of boots with a heel, jeans or jodhpurs (tight riding pants), a Western saddle, and a cowboy hat, gloves, and chaps… if they suit your style. English riding is more formal and requires riding boots, jodhpurs, an English saddle, a crop, and a hunt or polo helmet for protection. For shows, you'll be required to wear a riding jacket, a ratcatcher shirt (specially made shirt with no collar), and a choker (tie). Before you make a mad dash to the saddle shop, ask your instructor for recommendations about riding apparel and equipment. This way, you'll be sure to buy the most appropriate items for your class and not waste money on unnecessary extras. Until you decide how committed you'll be to the sport, there's no need to purchase top-of-the-line riding attire. Just make sure any merchandise you buy is comfortable, fits properly, and meets safety requirements.

FYI

American Horse Shows Association
220 East 42nd Street • Suite 409 • New York, NY 10017-5876
(212) 972-2472
AHSA is the U.S. branch of the International Equestrian Federation, as well as the national governing body for equestrian sports. AHSA determines how riders qualify to compete in major national events.

Intercollegiate Horse Show Association
P.O. Box 741 • Stony Brook, NY 11790-0741
(516) 751-2803
The Intercollegiate Horse Show Association organizes regional equestrian events and national competitions between colleges.

United States Equestrian Team
Pottersville Road • Gladstone, NJ 07934
(908) 234-1251 • *www.uset.com*
USET represents the U.S. in all types of international competitions, including the Olympic games. Programs are also offered for young riders to help improve their equitation skills.

United States Pony Club
4071 Iron Works Pike • Lexington, KY 40511
(606) 254-76698 • *www.uspc.org*
USPC provides youth programs that teach young equestrians how to ride and care for their ponies.

Ice-Skating

Pros

Ice-skating can make you feel like you're dancing on clouds. Whether you're striving to perfect a double axel or leisurely skating around the rink, this sport is sure to satisfy an appetite for fun. Recreational skating builds strength, coordination, and confidence. Raise your fitness level and meet the challenge of the ice while skating solo or with a group of friends. It's also a great ice-breaker for a first date. You'll have a tough time keeping the smile off your face regardless of how proficient a skater you are.

If you're a beginner or would like to sharpen your skating skills, consider group lessons. Once you learn fundamentals like T-stops, crossovers, and three-turns, you'll be zipping in and out of crowded Saturday night sessions before you know it. For the more competitive spirit, the beauty, artistry, and athleticism of figure skating will take your breath away. Witness the drama unfold as professional figure skaters magically interpret a piece of music, and you'll be won over.

Cons

You'll need somewhere to skate. No rink in your neighborhood? Try in-line skating instead. You'll get a similar workout without sacrificing the fun. If it's your first time lacing up a pair of ice skates, falling on the cold, hard ice may leave you bruised and achy, but don't give up. With practice, you can learn to maneuver around the rink like a pro.

Be prepared for the expense if you have your heart set on competitive figure skating. Money spent on coaches, choreographers, costumes, ice time, equipment, competition fees, and travel expenses adds up quickly. Training also takes an amazing amount of dedication, drive, and passion, so you've got to be fully committed to succeed.

Body benefits

The side-to-side stroking movements of ice-skating work the legs, hips, rear, and thighs. The reward is strong, toned lower-body muscles. Skating is also good for developing coordination and balance, and does wonders for your heart (in more ways than one).

Variations

There's recreational skating if you just want to have fun, hockey skating if you're into team sports, speed skating if you love the thrill of high speed racing, and figure skating if you're drawn to spellbinding spins. Figure skaters can choose between singles skating, pairs, and ice-dancing. Some skaters turn professional once their competitive careers are over and make a living coaching, choreographing, or touring with ice shows.

Equipment

The most important thing you'll need is a pair of ice skates with good ankle support. If you don't own a pair, you can rent them inexpensively at the rink. Skating attire should be comfortable so you can move and bend with ease. Because most rinks are kept on the cold side, dress in layers and peel them off as your body warms up.

FYI

Ice Skating Institute of America
355 West Dundee • Buffalo Grove, IL 60089
(847) 808-7528 • *www.skateisi.com*
The ISIA oversees programs for hockey, freestyle, and figure skating for the beginner through advanced ice-skater. The Institute sponsors competitions, events, and exhibitions, and provides scholarship assistance, too.

United States Figure Skating Association
20 First Street • Colorado Springs, CO 80906
(719) 635-5200 • *www.usfsa.com*
The USFSA—the governing body for amateur figure skating in the U.S.—is dedicated to advancing competitive figure skating by providing financial assistance, skating camps, and scientific research to skaters.

In-Line Skating

Pros

Exhilarating and fun, in-line skating is a terrific workout and one of the hottest and fastest growing sports in the United States. "Blading" works your lower body, namely your legs, but you'll have so much fun skating the day away that the positive effects it will have on your figure are just a bonus. If you're new to the sport, sign up for a lesson at a roller rink, park, or other venue where in-line skates are rented—it's a good way to meet other enthusiasts excited about the sport and pick up fundamentals . . . like stopping. Because nasty collisions with the pavement are inevitable, classes on learning how to fall properly will help prevent injuries and may improve your confidence.

Cons

Minor mishaps, such as scrapes and bruises, and the more serious stuff like injuries to the wrists and forearms, are potential pitfalls of the sport. You can minimize the risk of injury by obeying the rules of the road:

1. Strap on wrist guards, elbow and knee pads, and a helmet.
2. Never blade where there's lots of traffic.
3. Always yield to pedestrians.
4. Skate on the right, pass on the left.
5. Remember your ABC's—Always Blade in Control.

For added safety, bladers should skate on smooth surfaces like paved trails and pathways. Watch out for hazards like broken glass, potholes, cracked pavement, oil, water, and gravel—they're accidents waiting to happen.

Body benefits

In-line skating works the cardiovascular system and the lower body. Side-to-side gliding strengthens and tones your inner and outer thighs, and gets your hips and buttocks in better shape. Blading is also a low-impact activity (unless you fall), so you don't put a lot of strain on your body. Who would have thought this much fun could actually burn calories, too?

Variations

There's an adrenaline rush for everyone. For fun junkies, there's recreational skating. Thrill seekers will be won over by speed skating. Street hockey is ideal for those who crave aggressive teamwork. And if outrageous stunts like flips, jumps, and spins are your thing, extreme blading may be calling your name.

Equipment

To get rolling, you'll need a pair of in-line skates and protective gear. The equipment necessary for safe skating isn't exactly high fashion, but it's an absolute must. No wrist guards, elbow pads, knee pads, or helmet—no skating. You may also want to check out crash pads, which are bike shorts with padding in the rear, to help take the sting out of falling on concrete. If you've never tried in-line skating, start by renting skates so you'll know if blading is for you. Once you're hooked, you may decide to buy your own set of wheels. Proper fit includes some stiffness for support but enough flexibility to move. Comfort is important, so try on lots of different brands and styles and ask questions to be sure you get the best fit. And don't forget the sunblock if you're skating outdoors.

FYI

Aggressive Skaters Association
171 Pier Avenue • Suite 247 • Santa Monica, CA 90405
(310) 399-3436 • *www.aggroskate.com*
The ASA fosters the growth of amateur and professional aggressive in-line skating by taking an active role in competitions, skate parks, events, and the newest gear.

International In-Line Skating Association
3720 Farragut Avenue • Suite 400 • Kensington, MD 20895
1-800-56-SKATE • *www.iisa.org*
IISA promotes the growth of competitive and recreational blading, and addresses safety standards for skaters through educational programs.

Rollerblade, Inc.
5101 Shady Oak Road • Minnetonka, MN 55343
(612) 930-7000 • *www.rollerblade.com*
Rollerblade, Inc., offers skaters tips on getting started, finding a safe place to blade, safety gear, and events.

United States Amateur Confederation of Roller Skating (USAC/RS)
4730 South Street • P.O. Box 65798 • Lincoln, NB 68506
(402) 483-7551 • *www.usacrs.com*
USAC/RS hosts skating events and clinics nationwide for speed, roller, and artistic skating.

USA Hockey In-Line, Inc.
4965 North 30th Street • Colorado Springs, CO 80919
(719) 599-5500 • *www.usahockey.com/inline/index.htm*
USA Hockey is the national governing body for ice hockey and in-line hockey in the U.S. This organization has lots of information on ice and in-line hockey for girls (and boys, too).

Martial Arts

Pros

The number of women getting a kick out of martial arts in the United States is growing by leaps and bounds. The rich ancestry of the martial arts emphasizes developing a healthy body, mind, and spirit as integral parts of personal growth. Students learn self-defense skills as well as discipline, respect, kindness, humility, awareness, and honor through physical grace and meditation. Most of the martial arts are based on philosophical concepts of high morals and ethics, which can be applied to everyday life. Many students of the martial arts develop a more positive state of mind and feel better about themselves, too.

Cons

Some of the movements taught in martial arts classes can put a lot of stress on muscles, tendons, and ligaments, especially in the knees and ankles. Getting punched or thrown by an opponent doesn't feel good at first, but learning how to fall without getting hurt is an essential part of the training.

Body benefits

Students develop strength, speed, power, control, endurance, agility, coordination, awareness, rhythm, and timing. Devotees also reap the rewards of mental training with improved self-esteem and confidence.

Variations

Men, women, and children of all ages can enjoy the martial arts. There's a wide variety of Asian arts and sports to choose from, and all are rewarding. Look in the Yellow Pages for a studio or youth center in your neighborhood. You may want to observe different classes or watch a tournament to see which style knocks you out. Some of the more popular forms include:

Aikido: Meaning "way of harmony," this discipline originates from Japan and focuses on teaching defense techniques without harming the attacker.

Judo: A nonviolent martial sport developed from jujitsu, judo requires students to focus on throwing their opponents to the mat and immobilizing them with choke holds and locks.

Jujitsu: This Japanese fighting art trains students to defend themselves against attackers using kicks, hand strikes, holds, chokes, and grabs.

Karate: This Japanese art teaches self-defense using hand strikes, chops, punches, and kicks. With perfect timing and focus, these blows are directed at vital parts of the opponent's body to render him or her defenseless.

Kick boxing: This sport originated in Thailand and is a combination of the more traditional martial arts and boxing. Since the goal is to knock the opponent out, kick boxers wear protective gear like gloves and headgear for sparring.

Kung fu: Many of the quick moves and fancy footwork of this ancient form of Chinese self-defense are based on animal movements, such as those of the tiger, snake, or crane.

Tae kwan do: This popular Korean art is known for its powerful high kicks. Hands, feet, elbows, and knees are used to strike the opponent. Students also learn how to break boards using their hands or head.

T'ai chi: T'ai chi is a classical Chinese art training students in techniques that use slow, graceful movements to relax the body; meditation plays a significant role.

Equipment

Here's one sport where shoes aren't necessary—martial artists train barefoot. Most dojos (a Japanese term for training hall) require students to wear the traditional martial arts uniform, which consists of white or black drawstring pants and a wrap-around jacket. If you're a beginner, you'll wear a white belt and earn darker colors as you increase your rank. Depending on the instructor and the art, head gear, elbow pads, shin pads, and/or hand and foot gloves may be necessary.

FYI

If you're interested in the martial arts but aren't sure which one would be best for you, visit the library or bookstore. There are lots of books and magazines to help you learn about the different histories and philosophies of various martial arts.

Aikido Association of America

5838 Henry Avenue • Philadelphia, PA 19128

(215) 483-3000 • *www.aaa-aikido.com/*

This national organization furthers the advancement of aikido through rank certification, workshops, and demonstrations.

American Amateur Karate Federation

1930 Wilshire Boulevard • Suite 1208 • Los Angeles, CA 90057

(213) 483-8262

The American Amateur Karate Federation is the national federation for karate, sanctioning events for members and providing referrals to schools.

USA Karate Federation, Inc.

1300 Kenmore Boulevard • Akron, OH 44314

(330) 753-3114 • *www.usakarate.org/*

USA Karate supports the art of karate through educational and research programs, scholarships, clinics, and tournaments.

U.S. Aikido Federation

142 West 18th Street • New York, NY 10011

(413) 586-7122 • *www.usaikifed.org/usaf/home.html*

USAF gives members access to information about schools that belong to the Aikido Federation.

U.S. Judo Association

21 North Union Boulevard • Colorado Springs, CO 80909

(719) 633-7750 • *www.csprings.com/usja*

As the national governing body for judo, USJA provides information about clubs across the country, sanctions competitive events, and encourages participation in the martial arts.

U.S. Tae Kwan Do Union

One Olympic Plaza • Colorado Springs, CO 80909

(719) 578-4632 • *www.ustu.com/taekwondo/*

The USTU sponsors competitions, state championships, and the Junior Olympics and is the national governing body for the sport.

Playing

Pros

No scores to keep, no finish line to race for, no timer ticking away the milliseconds you spend sweating. Just you (and maybe a friend or two) and your childlike enthusiasm. Playing around may not win you a spot on the team or give you the stamina to go the distance in a marathon, but what it will give you is the main benefit necessary to sticking with an exercise program—fun. There's no rule saying that whatever you decide to try in your pursuit of fitness must be a definable, measurable activity. Let your imagination run free, and your body will follow. Simple, playful (and even goofy) pastimes can all be considered fitness activities as long as they get your body moving.

Cons

What could be bad about giving in to your playful side?

Body benefits

Your body will benefit from anything you get it to do. Run around chasing a Frisbee, hold onto your kite string and stand firm against the wind, bend down and sink your gardening tools into the earth—the potential health benefits of activities like these begin when you get off the couch and start moving. Improved flexibility, strength, and muscle tone in your arms and legs, increased aerobic fitness, relaxation, and peace of mind are all perks. What you really gain is enjoyment, and that's what life is about.

Variations

The opportunities are endless and only limited by how much energy you've got to stay moving. Combine fun and fitness and give these classics a try:

- hide and seek
- climbing trees
- badminton
- flying a kite
- playing with your pet
- bowling
- jump rope
- Frisbee
- Ping-Pong
- hopscotch
- boogie-boarding
- yard work/gardening

Equipment

All you really need is yourself (unless you try one of the variations listed above).

FYI

Explore your imagination to find what you need.

Racquet Sports

Pros

Racquet sports are a great way to have fun, get fit, and meet people. A regularly scheduled match gives you an incentive to exercise, plus the opportunity to catch up with friends. Playing in tournaments, taking group lessons, or joining a racquet club will no doubt heat up a ho-hum social life. Here's your chance to meet new people and ace the fitness game at the same time. If you can't round up a partner for a rally, use an enclosed court to practice your skills and power moves on your own.

Cons

A major drawback to an outdoor sport like tennis is the weather. If it rains or snows, you'll probably have to opt for an alternative activity, unless you can play indoors at a health and fitness club with indoor courts. If you're a racquetball or squash fan, finding a place to play may be difficult, unless you belong to a health club or gym with court facilities. If you don't have access to the courts, work at improving your game by jumping rope, jogging, and practicing strokes in front of a mirror.

The cost of reserving facilities at a club or gym is a general drawback to racquet sports. Many public parks have courts available on a first-come, first-served basis. Perhaps your school has a court. You can avoid injuries like tennis elbow, rotator cuff tendinitis, shin splints, pulled muscles, and sprained ankles with proper conditioning, good technique, and use of the proper equipment for your size, ability, and strength. Always warm up and stretch before you begin a match so you don't have sore muscles later.

Body benefits

Your overall fitness level is bound to improve when you play these fast-paced games. The more intense the match, the more your body gets out of it. Novice players benefit from toning and strengthening their arms, hips, thighs, and calf muscles. Advanced players will develop arm and shoulder strength, speed, agility, and power. Racquet sports challenge the mind as well as the body. Reflexes, coordination, and concentration are put to the test as you learn to read your opponent, anticipate shots, and plan your return strategy.

Variations

Singles tennis tends to be more physically taxing than doubles, since you've got to cover the entire court by yourself. This requires lots of side-to-side running, sprinting from the baseline (the far end of the court), and using powerful strokes to send the ball whizzing over the net. Racquetball matches can be played as singles, doubles, or cutthroat, which is when three players compete against each other. Like racquetball, squash is played with a hollow rubber ball in an enclosed court. The specially designed squash ball comes in four different densities, which determine how fast it will move on the court. Because the ball "squashes" when you hit it, whacking it as hard as possible doesn't result in the speedy zing you get with other racquet sports; players learn to strategically "press" the ball where their opponent can't reach it in order to score.

Equipment

A racquet, a few balls, and a pair of court shoes are the tools of the trade. Racquets for tennis, racquetball, and squash come in many weights, materials, and price ranges, but beginners don't have to spend a fortune. The most important factor when selecting a racquet is the size of the grip and how it feels when you swing. Selecting the wrong equipment may lead to injuries due to overworking muscles in the forearm or shoulder. Ask a pro for some expert advice before making a purchase.

Shoes for racquet sports should provide ankle support, good traction, and lateral stability for pivoting moves and quick changes of direction. Clothing that allows you to move freely, like shorts and a bra top or T-shirt, make for comfy court attire. Since the balls ricochet off the walls so unpredictably, racquetball and squash players are strongly advised to wear goggles for eye protection. To improve your grip and help prevent blisters, a glove is a good idea, too.

FYI

Intercollegiate Tennis Association
P.O. Box 71 • Princeton University • Princeton, NJ 08544
(609) 258-1686 • *www.tennisonline.com/ita*
The ITA is an organization for college tennis coaches whose goal is to improve the popularity of this sport at the collegiate level.

United States Racquetball Association

1685 West Uintah • Colorado Springs, CO 80904

(719) 635-5396 • *www.racquetball.org/*

The USRA is the national governing body for amateur racquetball and provides information on rules and tournaments, and also publishes a racquetball magazine.

United States Tennis Association

70 West Red Oak Lane • White Plains, NY 10604

(914) 696-7000 • *www.usopen.org*

As the national governing body for tennis, the USTA promotes fitness through playing tennis, as well as organizes tournaments and youth tennis programs.

U.S. Squash Racquets Association

Box 1216 • Bala Cynwyd, PA 19004

(610) 667-4006 • *www.us-squash.org/squash/*

The USSRA, the national governing body for the sport, sanctions squash racquet events and tournaments from the local to the international level.

Running/Jogging

Pros

If your body craves the adrenaline rush of pure physical exertion, running may be the answer. Lace up a pair of shock-absorbing workout shoes, find a safe path and a jogging partner, and you're off to a running start. A vigorous run/jog (interchangeable words that basically describe the speed and distance at which you train—"running" refers to longer, faster workouts, and "jogging" implies a more leisurely pace) can be a great outlet to help work off steam, let go of the day, and propel yourself to greater levels of achievement.

Cons

Running/jogging can be very jarring, and not every body is built to withstand this type of high-impact activity; the continual pounding and stress can contribute to injuries. The easiest way to reduce your risk of hurting yourself is to select a good running surface. Here are a few to consider:

Asphalt: Most roads are covered with asphalt, and this surface makes a pretty good running path. It offers some cushioning, is easily accessible, and provides a fairly even running surface.

Concrete: Although jogging on concrete or cement (like sidewalks) will help you avoid problems like traffic and unforeseen potholes, this unyielding surface is hard on the shins, knees, and back.

Dirt and grass: Paths and trails made of these natural substances will bring your legs relief. Not only are dirt and grass softer than concrete, they're also usually found in more shady and wide-open places, making for a pleasurable running experience. The downside may be uneven or rocky terrain, which can overwork your legs and alter your stride, or become slippery and muddy when wet.

Sand: Jogging on soft sand or the hard-packed sand at the water's edge provides a resistance workout, increasing your leg power. But beware: It's easy to overstress your tendons (particularly your Achilles tendon) when you're doing a lot of sand training.

Like lap swimming and walking, jogging can be a bit boring for some people. Others can't get enough of the solitude and opportunity for introspection. Long, slow distance runs are a great time to blow off steam, daydream, or get in tune with the rhythm of your body.

Body benefits

Running is an outstanding aerobic workout for burning fat and building stamina. It's also a great way to shape and develop strong, sleek legs.

Variations

You can spend part of your workout jogging on the grass, then run on asphalt; you can head to the beach one day and stick to the park the next. You can also alternate intervals of walking with sprinting and jogging for a challenging variation. Another option is to change your training distance each time you run, going for a long, leisurely jog one day followed by a speed session the next, covering a shorter route at a faster pace. Adding hills or inclines to your workout increases the intensity. If you have access to a motorized treadmill, you'll have a good workout option for bad-weather days.

Running clubs can be a fun way to meet fellow athletes, pick up training tips, and provide structure to your routine by offering workout buddies. Make the most of your competitive spirit by looking into one of the many competitions listed in a local newspaper or a running magazine—5K, 10K, half-marathons, marathons, and cross-country races are held all the time.

Equipment

Get a pair of shock-absorbing athletic shoes, and you're set. Aside from a supportive exercise bra, your running attire need only be comfortable—shorts, leggings, a sweatshirt, or a loose-fitting T-shirt. If you're running near traffic, wear reflective clothing so you'll be seen by drivers and bikers. Always carry identification and a whistle or other protective device for safety.

FYI

American Running and Fitness Association
4405 East West Highway • Suite 405 • Bethesda, MD 20814
(301) 913-9517 • *www.arfa.org*
The mission of this educational organization is to keep people fit through aerobic activity. The AR&FA offers advice on starting a fitness program, nutrition, injury prevention, and shoe selection.

Road Runners Club of America
1150 South Washington Street • Suite 250 • Alexandria, VA 22314
(703) 836-0558 • *www.rrca.org*
The RRCA is a running organization that promotes the benefits of running. The organization sponsors community clubs, programs, and races.

Skiing

Pros

Who can resist the feeling of freedom that comes from soaring down a mountain blanketed in snow, wind whipping against tingling cheeks? Or what about the intense workout of cross-country skiing along wooded trails on a wintry day? Whether leisurely snow-plowing your way down a cruiser run, carving deep edges in challenging terrain, or putting your endurance to the test on a cross-country course, you get to decide how much of a challenge you want. From groomed bunny slopes for beginners to double-black diamond runs, there are trails to accommodate every ability level. If the weather turns nasty, sipping a cup of hot chocolate next to the fireplace is sure to make you warm and toasty.

Cons

Staring down the face of a steep run can be pretty scary if you don't know what you're doing. And putting on a pair of cross-country skis without knowing how to use them properly will make a day on the trails an exercise in frustration. Solve these problems by attending a fun ski clinic or taking a group lesson from a resort pro. Specialty programs can fine-tune your skill regardless of how experienced (or inexperienced) you are. Taking lessons is a great way to improve your technique and meet other skiers, too.

Accidents do happen, but you can reduce your risk of injury by following a few rules:

1. Take lessons, especially if you're a beginner or you haven't skied for a while.

2. Make sure your equipment is up-to-date and in good condition, and that it matches your skiing ability. Wearing the right gear is essential, too. For tips on your equipment/clothing needs, see "Equipment," p. 234.

3. Have a qualified professional adjust your bindings.

4. Ski in control and at moderate speeds. You must be able to stop or avoid obstacles (such as trees, rocks, and people), or you could get seriously hurt.

5. Watch out for fellow skiers on the trail and, if you stop, be sure that you're visible to skiers coming from above you.

6. Never ski out of bounds.

7. Stop when you feel tired.

Like most winter sports, skiing is seasonal. Unless you live near a resort, it's difficult to hit the slopes on a regular basis. Prices for lift tickets can range anywhere from $12 to $60 per day (brrr!). Many resorts offer seasonal passes and discounts if you're under 18 or if you ski multiple days. Ski gear is pretty expensive, too. Paying for new equipment and clothing can drain your allowance for the next decade. A good option is to look into season-long leasing plans, which are offered by some ski shops at cut-rate prices. You may also get a deal by "demo-ing" the latest technically advanced equipment at a resort. If you decide to purchase ski gear, buying off-season or at ski swaps might save you a mountain of cash.

Body benefits

Downhill skiing works all the major muscle groups including the thighs, buttocks, calves, arms, shoulders, and abdominals. It's also great for improving endurance, balance, and coordination. Cross-country skiing involves continuously moving your arms and legs, which really gets your heart pumping and provides an aerobic workout. This strenuous sport requires skill, balance, coordination, and lots of energy.

Variations

There's a skiing technique to suit every style. Slalom skiers carve sharp turns and weave their way between gates, while speed skiers careen down steep runs at breakneck speeds. To satisfy a need for speed, Alpine (downhill) is the way to go; you can tackle all types of terrain (depending on your skill level) for fun. Beyond the slopes, there's cross-country skiing (a.k.a. Nordic skiing) and telemarking, where skiers using Nordic equipment tackle downhill runs. For off-season conditioning, a Nordic Track (or similar ski machine), slide-board (a board with bumpers on each end for sliding on), or Pro-Fitter (sim-ulates ski turns) are great substitutes for the slopes.

Equipment

First, you'll need a snow-covered mountain or trail; next, you'll need boots, bindings, skis, and poles. If you don't own equipment, you can rent or lease gear at a ski resort or sporting goods store, or look into demo equipment. Beware of buying skis and bindings at garage sales or from the newspaper classifieds—outdated equipment may pose safety problems. When renting skis, make sure the bindings are adjusted according to your height, weight, and skiing ability.

Think "layers" when dressing for winter sports. Start with thermal underwear (polypropylene is a good choice) and build from there. Most skiers wear a turtleneck underneath a sweater or fleece pullover. For the outer layer, check garment tags and look for wind-resistant and waterproof fabrics to keep you warm and dry. Pick up a pair of disposable heat packs and tuck them into your gloves and boots for extra warm fingers and toes. Top off your ensemble with a hat and warm gloves, and you're ready to go. To reduce glare from blinding snow and help you see in poor weather con-ditions, you'll need anti-fog goggles. On sunny days, sunglasses with 100% UV protection are a must to protect your eyes from harmful ultraviolet rays. And finally, don't forget plenty of sunscreen for exposed cheeks, ears, nose, and lips. Lip balm is essential, too.

FYI

International Ski Federation of North America

P.O. Box 477 • Vail, CO 81658

(970) 926-SNOW

This organization is the international governing body for Alpine, freestyle, cross-country, and Nordic skiing, as well as ski jumping and snowboarding.

Nordic Track, Inc.

104 Peavey Road • Chaska, MN 55318

1-800-358-3636 • *www.nordictrack.com*

Nordic Track makes home-exercise equipment that can be purchased through their catalog or retail stores.

U.S. Ski and Snowboard Association

P.O. Box 1001500 • Kearns Boulevard • Park City, UT 84060

(801) 649-9090 • *www.usskiteam.com*

USSA is the national governing body for Olympic skiing and snowboarding. The association develops programs and competitions for Alpine skiing, cross-country, disabled Alpine and cross-country, freestyle, ski jumping and Nordic combined, and snowboarding.

Snowboarding

Pros

Snowboarding is the fastest growing winter sport in the United States. Once you learn the technique of snowboarding, you'll probably discover it's so much fun that you'll never want winter to end. With lots of practice (not to mention courage), it's possible to express yourself creatively on the mountain. Freestyle boarders jump, fly, and twist in the snow. Or stated in their own lingo, they "shred," "bone," "jib," "grab," and "grind." Unlike downhill skiing, snowboarding doesn't require perfect conditions to make it a worthwhile venture (although icy snow isn't recommended for beginners). Boarders can carve ice, moguls, or even dirt patches with their boards, or "go off" the halfpipe, which is a long U-shaped valley packed with snow.

Cons

Snowboarding is tricky to learn, and lessons are very important for the beginner. You're better off learning from a pro than trying to just pick it up on your own. Without qualified instruction, you'll be likely to get frustrated and learn a lot more slowly. Plus snowboarding is a seasonal sport—if you live near ski runs, you're in luck, but lift tickets are sure to be expensive. Fortunately, many ski resorts offer substantial discounts if you're under 18. When snowboarding, the risk of knee and wrist injuries is high, so use caution on the slopes. Learning from a skilled expert will help you reduce your chance of blowing out a knee or breaking a bone.

Body benefits

Snowboarding offers a great lower-body workout—you'll really feel it in your thighs, legs, and rear end. This radical sport is also great for improving balance, coordination, and endurance.

Variations

Recreational boarding is for anyone looking for a little excitement on the slopes. Daredevils may crave the thrill of slalom racing or freestyle boarding, which includes performing high-altitude tricks and stunts while airborne (a.k.a. "catching air").

Equipment

All you "Shred Betties" (that's snowboarding jargon for girl snowboarders) will need a board to surf the powder. You can buy or rent one from a local sporting goods store or at a ski resort. Whichever board you choose, make sure it's right for your height, weight, and snowboarding ability.

You'll need warm clothes for protection against cold and wind, and designers are creating great girl-gear for the slopes. Just be sure to dress in layers—add garments to keep warm and peel them off to cool down. Polypropylene underwear is best for the base layer because the fabric repels moisture so your skin stays dry. Wear a snow hat (anything from a baseball cap to a colorful wool beanie) to keep your body heat from escaping, and don't neglect your fingers and toes—warm gloves and socks are a must for the snow scene. Be sure to apply sunscreen and strap on a pair of wrist guards before setting off.

FYI

U.S. Amateur Snowboarding Association
18 Corporate Plaza • Newport Beach, CA 92660
(714) 644-8769 • *www.usasa.org*

USASA is the sanctioning body for the International Snowboarding Association, sponsoring grassroots-level to professional events.

U.S. Ski and Snowboard Association See p. 235.

Strength Training

Pros

Like a sculptor seated before a lump of clay, when you're strength training, you're actually shaping your body into its most glorious form. Whether you have an assortment of tools—free weights (dumbbells and barbells), machines, gadgets such as inflatable exercise balls and/or resistance tubes and rubber bands—or you're simply using your own body weight for resistance, you'll have no problem chiseling a unique physique. It's a myth that pumping iron makes you bulky. If you've been hesitant to try working with weights for fear of looking like Conan the Barbarian, don't worry—most women's bodies lack the hormones necessary for the muscle mass guys are capable of developing. In reality, the more muscle tissue you have, the more efficiently your body uses fat for energy.

Cons

For any novice, safety is the biggest concern. If you're clueless when it comes to weights or other resistance equipment, and you work out anyway, you're running the risk of injury. It's dangerous to lift too much too soon or use improper form, so it's a good idea to learn from a coach or certified trainer who can teach you the correct techniques and supervise your workout. Qualified personal trainers should be certified through a health club program, a college or university, or one of these reputable organizations: Aerobics and Fitness Association of America (AFAA), American College of Sports Medicine (ACSM), American Council on Exercise (ACE), The International Association of Fitness Professionals (IDEA), National Athletic Trainers Association (NATA), and National Strength and Conditioning Association (NSCA).

Gym memberships or large weight equipment can be quite costly, but there's no need to consider such a hefty investment. If your school has a weight room, take advantage of it. Another inexpensive option is a home workout program incorporating free weights and resistance exercises that use your own body weight (squats and lunges, for example). Strength training can give you a lean, hard body; what it can't do is give you an aerobic workout or make you limber. For total fitness, don't neglect cardiovascular exercise to burn body fat and strengthen your heart and lungs, and stretching exercises to increase your flexibility.

Body benefits

For a strong, defined body, strength training is the way to go. Stronger muscles burn fat more efficiently and contribute to improved posture, reduced risk of injury, and increased body awareness. Strength training gives you the freedom to be creative with your routine and focus on the areas you really want to improve. You can work on a single body part by doing bicep curls to tone your upper arms, for example, or train several muscle groups at once by doing lunges to work your thighs, buttocks, hips, abdominals, and lower back. Working out with weights is also an excellent way to condition your body for team sports like basketball, field hockey, soccer, or softball, and seasonal activities like water skiing, swimming, snow skiing, and snowboarding.

Variations

You can use light, hand-held or strap-on weights, rubber bands, weighted balls, dumbbells, barbells, or a variety of weight machines to carve a well-toned body. If you venture into the school weight room or join a gym, don't be intimidated by the equipment. Simply ask a coach or qualified instructor to show you around and help create a safe, effective program to strengthen and tone each of your major muscle groups. Using your own body as resistance is another form of strength training. Exercises such as squats, lunges, push-ups, pull-ups, and tummy crunches all tone and tighten your muscles as well as any fancy weight machine can.

When you start training, make sure that you can comfortably complete a set of 10–15 repetitions using proper form. If that gets too easy, try using a little more resistance, doing additional sets, or taking shorter rest periods. Should you find yourself struggling, losing your form, or feeling pain, decrease the resistance so you don't run the risk of injuring your developing body. Work with weights every other day, at most, to give your muscles time to recover and get stronger.

Equipment

If you're going to spend money on a set of free weights, purchasing a few pairs of light dumbbells ranging in weight is a good way to get started. This way, you can begin with the lightest weight and work up to heavier weights as you get stronger. Check out a sporting goods store for soft, vinyl-coated cast-iron dumbbells. They provide a comfortable grip, and many come in a range of colors to give your motivation a lift. You may also want to buy weight-lifting gloves to help prevent calluses from forming on your hands. Gloves range in price and come in loads of styles.

For a truly cost-effective strength-training workout, be inventive and make your own weights by using things that you have around the house. Cans of soup, plastic bottles of water, or rolls of coins stuffed into a sock make cheap and easy props. If you're ready to flex some muscle, there are many great books and videos available to provide the guidance every beginner needs.

FYI

Aerobics and Fitness Association of America See p. 203.

American College of Sports Medicine
P.O. Box 1440 • Indianapolis, IN 46206-1440
(317) 637-9200 • *www.acsm.org/sportsmed*
The ACSM promotes health and physical fitness through research and educational programs, and also offers certification for personal trainers and exercise instructors.

American Council on Exercise
5820 Oberlin Drive • San Diego, CA 92191
(619) 535-8227 • *www.acefitness.com*
ACE provides a certification program for fitness instructors and personal trainers. Exercise enthusiasts can also join and receive training tips and information on nutrition and fitness products.

International Association of Fitness Professionals See p. 203.

National Athletic Trainers Association
2952 Stemmons Freeway • Dallas, TX 75247
1-800-879-6282 • *www.nata.org*
NATA is the professional association for Certified Athletic Trainers, whose goal is to improve the quality of care for athletes.

National Strength and Conditioning Association
P.O. Box 38909 • Colorado Springs, CO 80937-8909
(719) 632-6722 • *www.colosoft.com/nsca*

This organization is the authority on strength and conditioning for improving athletic performance. Personal trainers and strength coaches can become certified by the NSCA.

Swimming

Pros

Are you ready to make a splash? Swimming laps and doing water aerobics are great ways to get in shape without placing a lot of stress on your bones and joints because the water makes your body practically weightless. Your body isn't the only thing to benefit from a pool workout—swimming can have a soothing effect on your spirit as well. As you glide through the water, your mind feels connected to your body, and your thoughts are free to flow in and out of your head as your arms and legs move in unison. If you prefer camaraderie in the pool, you and a friend can grab some kickboards and paddle your legs for a great lower body workout. Aspiring "mermaids" should inquire about lessons or water aerobics classes at school, the YWCA, or a health club or recreation center.

Cons

Unless you have easy access to a pool, swimming isn't very convenient, and convenience is crucial to sticking with any fitness program. On cold and rainy days, who can blame you for skipping a workout if there isn't a heated indoor pool available? But this is no excuse to become one with the couch. Like running and walking, lap swimming can be a bit monotonous, which is why it's a good idea to vary your routine. Beat the boredom by using this quiet time to work out problems or come up with a strategy for your upcoming history test or other schoolwork. One other drawback is all the chlorine that's added to pool water. Chlorine can be rough on your hair and eyes, but you can easily combat these irritants with a swim cap, hair conditioner, and a pair of goggles.

Body benefits

If you have a minor injury or aren't keen on impact activities like jogging or plain old jumping jacks, swimming is great exercise. The water's natural buoyancy makes working out stress-free. Incorporating different strokes is a good way to condition all the major muscle groups, including your shoulders, back, arms, legs, buttocks, and stomach. Keep your body moving vigorously for at least 15–20 minutes and you've got a good aerobic workout. Vary the strokes and intensity to suit your style.

Variations

Swim laps using the five basic strokes: freestyle, breaststroke, backstroke, butterfly, and sidestroke. Any movements you do on land, like jogging and calisthenics, can be simulated in the water, adding variety to your routine. If team sports are your thing, consider joining a swim team. If your school doesn't sponsor one, contact a local swim school or the YWCA for more information. Synchronized swimming is another option. Solo, duet, or group swimmers perform ballet-like routines in time to music. Synchronized swimming requires tremendous strength, skill, and artistry and is perfect for those who love poetry in motion. Don't overlook playful splashing or friendly pool games like water volleyball or tag as fun recreational activities.

Equipment

For starters, you'll need a pool, goggles, and a bathing suit. A one-piece or racing suit is a good choice for lap swimming (you'll avoid potentially embarrassing moments should your bikini top come off while perfecting flip-turns). If getting into a swimsuit for an aqua aerobics class doesn't thrill you, suit up with workout apparel designed especially for the water. Choose from tights, shorts, leotards, bodysuits, and shirts made of special chlorine-resistant fabrics such as lycra or neoprene. They keep you warm in the water and offer lots of support, too.

To add resistance to lap swimming, try wearing swim mitts, which come with or without weights. If you want to get more inventive with your routine, make waves with funky pool toys, such as wet vests, hydrotones (styrofoam dumbbells), pull-buoys (floats to put between your ankles), hand paddles, fins, and wave webs (gloves with webbing between the fingers), all of which are designed to add a challenge to your workout. You can find these products at sporting goods stores and aquatic centers.

FYI

Amateur Athletic Union

c/o Walt Disney World Resort • P.O. Box 1000 • Lake Buena Vista, FL 32830-1000

(407) 363-6170 • *www.aausports.org*

AAU is the largest multisport youth association in the U.S., offering free brochures on individual sports and sponsoring tournaments from local to national championships, including the Junior Olympics.

Aquatic Exercise Association

P.O. Box 1609 • Nokomis, FL 34274

(888) 232-9283 • *www.aeawave.com*

The goal of the AEA is to promote the benefits of aquatic exercise. The association provides Instructor Certification programs as well as educational information for the general public.

United States Swimming/United States Olympic Committee on Swimming

One Olympic Plaza • Colorado Springs, CO 80909-5770

(719) 578-4578 • *www.usswim.org*

This organization is the national governing body for competitive swimming. Members may receive information on fundraising, video resources, and educational programs.

United States Water Fitness Association, Inc.

200 Knutch Road • Suite 224-D • Boynton Beach, FL 33424-3279

(561) 732-9908 • *www.emi.net/~uswfa/*

USWFA is dedicated to increasing awareness of the positive aspects of aquatic exercise and offers educational materials covering a range of topics.

U.S. Diving

Pan American Plaza • 201 South Capitol Avenue • Suite 430 • Indianapolis, IN 46225

(317) 237-5252

As the national governing body for the sport, U.S. Diving provides resources and programs to help athletes become the best divers they can be.

U.S. Synchronized Swimming

Pan American Plaza • 201 South Capitol Avenue • Suite 901 • Indianapolis, IN 46225

(317) 237-5700 • *www.usasynchro.org*

Synchro Swimming USA, the national governing body for the sport, promotes all levels of competition, from the local level to the Olympic games.

Team Sports

Pros

There's no denying that participants of team sports score big in more ways than one. Working together to play sports like basketball or soccer fosters a great sense of teamwork. To score points, players learn to depend on their teammates and trust one another. Uniting as a group to achieve a common goal and learning to get along with others are also huge assets for succeeding in the "real" world once you graduate from school. The social aspect of team sports may be the best part. Meeting others who share your passion for the game, celebrating after competitions, "pumping up" fellow players with friendly shouts of encouragement, and the feeling of belonging all nurture camaraderie among team members.

Cons

Overly competitive teams with the motto "Winning isn't everything, it's the only thing" can be a bit intimidating and take the fun out of team sports. Nevertheless, being involved in team play is a great opportunity for young women to learn that being aggressive (in sports and in life) doesn't compromise femininity. The best team sport scenario is one where everybody gets a chance to play and the pressure to win isn't at the expense of fun or good sportsmanship. But some coaches rely solely on the skills of their top athletes while everybody else warms the bench. If you find yourself in a situation where the negatives outweigh the positives of the experience, consider playing for another team or trying a different sport.

Body benefits

Team sports require teamwork, physical skill, and fitness. Basketball, soccer, field hockey, ice hockey, and roller hockey involve constant movement, making them great aerobic workouts. Softball and volleyball are physically demanding and really put your agility, power, and strength to the test. Training with weights, running or jogging, and jumping rope are all super pre-season conditioners. To fine-tune your sport-specific skills, ask your coach or gym teacher for pointers on how to strengthen your game so you'll shine on the court, field, or ice.

Variations

When you can't practice with the entire squad, don't sweat it. You can still work on skills and strategies such as specific plays, ball handling, dribbling, and shooting on your own or with another player.

There's a sport for every season. Popular options include:

Basketball: Hands down, basketball is the most popular sport played in U.S. high schools and colleges, and it's also played by millions of people in more than 130 countries worldwide. There are four 8-minute quarters in high school ball, two 20-minute halves at the college level, and four 12-minute quarters in pro basketball. Basketball isn't exclusive to indoor venues with highly polished wood floors; people can be found shooting hoops on playgrounds and driveways, too. Women can go on to play college basketball, compete in the Olympics, or shoot for a pro career.

Field hockey: Field hockey is played on a grass field or "pitch," with players running while dribbling, passing, pushing, and flicking the ball with a field hockey stick. The game has two halves, 35 minutes each. In the United States, girls play field hockey in high school and college, and at the Olympic level.

Ice hockey: Action-packed, rough and rowdy, ice hockey is a fast-moving sport played on the ice in three 20-minute periods. Players skate at breakneck speeds (sometimes up to 35 miles per hour!), maneuvering to gain possession of the puck, dribble, pass, and shoot. The game requires excellent skating skills, including the ability to execute sharp turns, strong crossovers, powerful starts, and quick stops. The aggressive nature of hockey and the fast-moving puck makes it essential for players to protect themselves by wearing lots of padding, gloves, and a helmet with a face mask.

Roller hockey: Whether you're in a competitive league or just playing a pickup game after school, a lightning-fast game of roller hockey is sure to get your adrenaline pumping. Wearing in-line skates, players "shush" the puck with the tip of their blade, shovel it off to a teammate, break away, and score. There are four or five skaters on a team and sometimes a goalie. While this sport is loads of fun, it can get down and dirty, so you'll need to wear full protective gear, including head-to-toe padding and a helmet with a face guard.

Soccer: Talk about nonstop action! Soccer is an incredibly fast-moving game played by two teams of eleven players each. The game generally consists of two 45-minute halves, though some youth soccer leagues play shorter matches. Players run constantly and use their head, chest, thighs, and feet to dribble, trap, pass, head, tackle, move the ball down the field, and shoot for a goal. While each team member has a specific position and responsibility, ranging from helping defend the goal to being the main shooter, all but the goalie can roam the field to lend a hand (or, in this case, a foot). In the United States, about 12 million kids and teens play youth soccer, and most youth soccer leagues follow a strict philosophy of positive coaching and sportsmanship, where everyone plays and anyone can sign up. Women's soccer is played in the Olympics, too.

Softball: Enjoyed by millions of people in little leagues, high school teams, city leagues, the park, and at fun, informal get-togethers, softball is the #1 sport among high school girls, with over 200,000 participants. The game is played with nine or ten players on the field and is similar to baseball, except that in softball there are seven innings instead of nine, the pitchers throw underhand, the pitching area is flat, the infield is dirt (not grass), and softballs are bigger and softer than baseballs. Take a swing at slow pitch (where the ball is tossed to the batter in a high, sweeping arc) or fast pitch (pitches can whiz by at speeds up to 75 miles per hour). This sport demands quick reactions for fielding and sliding, power for hitting and throwing, and speed for base running. Women's fast-pitch softball is a medal sport at the summer Olympic games.

Volleyball: The six members of a volleyball team can use any part of their body above the waist to prevent the ball from hitting the floor, set it for an attacker, and send it hurtling over the net. Volleyball is a pure team sport, meaning a single player can't dominate the game and each team member's contribution is a critical part of the overall effort. Skills required include quickness, jumping ability, body control, and balance. After executing or receiving a serve, the ball is moved between passers, setters, and hitters, who dig, dive, block, and spike until a point is scored. Volleyball can be played indoors or outdoors, on wooden floors, grass, concrete, or sand. Beach volleyball is a variation of regular volleyball and is one of the fastest growing sports in the world. Two-person pro beach volleyball teams tour all over the world and compete in the summer Olympics.

Equipment

The equipment needed for team sports depends on which game you play. When you play sports in school, equipment and uniforms are usually provided. If you're playing on a city league, a local community team, or a team sponsored by a business, the sponsor may pick up the tab for uniforms and equipment. Each player may have to shell out some money toward the cost of gear, though. Fundraisers like car washes and bake sales are some ways teams raise money for jerseys and other equipment.

FYI

Amateur Athletic Union See p. 242.

Amateur Softball Association
2801 Northeast 50th Street • Oklahoma City, OK 73111
(405) 424-5266 • *www.softball.org*
The ASA is the national governing body for amateur softball in the U.S. They offer information on schools, softball clinics, and educational materials like rule books and videos.

American Youth Soccer Organization
5403 West 138th Street • Hawthorne, CA 90250
(310) 643-6455 • *www.ayso.org*
"Everyone plays!" is the motto of AYSO. Programs sponsored by this organization promote fun, education, good sportsmanship, and a positive experience for all players.

National Association for Sport and Physical Education
1900 Association Drive • Reston, VA 20191
(703) 476-3410 • *www.aahperd.org*
As a resource for P.E. teachers, coaches, athletic directors, and athletic trainers, this organization is dedicated to promoting and supporting quality physical education programs in schools.

National Association of Intercollegiate Athletics
6120 South Yale • Suite 1450 • Tulsa, OK 74136
(918) 494-8828 • *www.naia.org*
NAIA is a resource for college-bound students to find out eligibility requirements for athletic participation. This organization can also give students a listing of schools who are NAIA members.

National Collegiate Athletic Association
6201 College Boulevard • Overland Park, KS 66211
(913) 339-1906 • *www.NCAA.org*
The NCAA encourages sports participation for college students, establishes rules and eligibility standards for intercollegiate athletics, maintains performance records, and monitors college and university athletic programs.

USA Basketball
5465 Mark Dabling Boulevard • Colorado Springs, CO 80918-3842
(719) 590-4800 • *www.usabasketball.com*
USA Basketball is the national governing body for men's and women's basketball. Teams representing USA Basketball compete in the Junior Nationals, the Pan American Games, and the Olympics.

USA Hockey In-Line, Inc. See p. 223.

U.S. Field Hockey Association
One Olympic Plaza • Colorado Springs, CO 80809
(719) 578-4567
Membership in the U.S. Field Hockey Association qualifies athletes to participate in events and receive a newsletter including information on camps for players, rule books, and youth leagues.

U.S. Soccer Federation
1801-1811 South Prairie Avenue • Chicago, IL 60616
(312) 808-1300 • *www.us-soccer.com*
The U.S. Soccer Federation is the national governing body for soccer, and its goal is to increase the popularity of soccer in the U.S. by encouraging participation in sanctioned events.

U.S.A. Volleyball
3595 East Fountain Boulevard • Suite I–2 • Colorado Springs, CO 80910
(719) 637-8300 • *Volleyball.org/usav/*
USA Volleyball, the national governing body for the sport, is dedicated to increasing interest for players and fans, and providing information on camps, clubs, and programs like beach volleyball and the Junior Olympics.

Youth Basketball of America
P.O. Box 36108 • Orlando, FL 32823
(407) 363-0599
This organization is dedicated to the development of youth basketball in the U.S. Services include fundraising ideas, uniform discounts, and tournament sponsorship.

Thrill (or Extreme) Sports

Pros

Thrill sports, also known as extreme sports, are guaranteed to deliver excitement. They get your pulse racing and your heart pumping, and challenge your mind as well as your body. If you live by the motto "No guts, no glory," the need to participate in thrill sports may be in your blood. Rock climbing, windsurfing, or kayaking have no finish line and nobody keeps score, but the rush of pitting athleticism and sheer nerve against the challenges of Mother Nature is sure to elevate your spirit. Tackling and overcoming obstacles like rocky cliffs, raging rapids, or icy terrain may provide you with a whole new outlook on life.

Cons

This stuff isn't called extreme for nothing! Thrill sports can be dangerous and should only be attempted by well-trained athletes. Working with a certified guide and instructor is top priority, but this expert training can be costly. So can all the equipment required for adventure sports. While the costs of training and getting properly outfitted can add up quickly, consider it an investment in your safety—and you're worth every penny.

Body benefits

If you're new to the workout scene, you don't want to choose adventure activities like technical climbing as a way to get in shape. You have to be fit before ever attempting activities like these. Strength, stamina, agility, flexibility, and athleticism—plus the ability to use all these components to perform challenging athletic maneuvers—are required for thrill sports. If you're fit to give them a try, are properly trained, and have the guidance of a qualified instructor, put your fear aside and take your workout to the extreme.

Variations

Contacting an organization in your area of interest, a large adventure outfitting store (such as REI or Adventure 16), or a wilderness club is a good way to find a qualified instructor (see "FYI" below for a list of organizations). You can also get information on what equipment to buy. Be sure to ask potential guides or instructors for their credentials, and only embark on outings that are within your ability.

Kayaking and whitewater rafting: Rapids (nature's obstacles) are the turbulence created as water rushes over submerged boulders. Kayaks—narrow boats designed to hold one or two people—and rafts are the crafts that thrill-seekers use to tackle rapids. Using double-bladed paddles, kayakers work to keep their small craft afloat as they ride the rapids. Whitewater rafts, by comparison, are larger and may accommodate seven to ten people, as well as camping gear and food. Whitewater rafting tests your wits and promotes teamwork as enthusiasts work together to navigate the surging river. Maneuvering with oars or paddles takes upper body strength and tenacity, and all rafters need to be alert and ready to pitch in.

Knowledge and experience are the primary qualifications for white-water sports. Rafters must be able to spot hazards, read the river, and find the best chute (a clear channel between obstacles) to go for. Thorough research before embarking on an adventure means knowing the class or scale rating (level of difficulty) of the river, as well as your own ability. A flotation vest is a necessity, and you need to know how to swim. Potential rafting hazards include flipping the raft and colliding with rocks and boulders. If you're a beginner, rafting with an organized tour, complete with experienced guide, may be the perfect way to "wet" your appetite.

Rock climbing: Inch by precarious inch, rock climbers methodically work their way up the rugged peak. New technology and expert instruction have made this sport safer than it may seem, but it does require proper technique, focus, and a good measure of arm and leg strength. Climbers use foot- and hand-holds found in the rocky terrain or create their own with rock-climbing equipment such as "nuts" and "camming devices." Pushing and pulling their way ever upward, these athletes are on a quest for the ultimate high. Indoor climbing on a rock wall is an alternative to outdoor climbing. Using treadwalls (vertical climbing tracks with built-in hand- and foot-holds that move continuously at pre-set speeds), thrill-seekers can get a taste of climbing in the safety of a gym. Indoor climbing also gives serious climbers a way to train between outings.

Surfing: Using strength, agility, balance, and controlled precision, surfers ride their boards toward shore across the face of the most excellent waves. Surfboards come in many shapes and sizes (colors, too), so even surf punks (beginning surfers) are sure to find one they can handle. A foam and fiberglass board, plus a wet suit for protection against cold waters, is the equipment you'll need. Be sure to take a lesson so you don't look like a total "Fred" (nonsurfer trying to act like she knows what she's doing). Ask for an instructor referral at a surf shop. Even if you're "cooking," which is surf lingo for surfing aggressively, "getting drilled" (meaning you're having a bad experience with a rough wave) is inevitable because the ocean is so unpredictable. It's also possible to get pounded onto rocks or coral, or be held under the water after a wipeout. Risks are part of the ride.

If the thought of standing up on a board starts your stomach churning, consider boogie boarding. It can be just as fun and a lot less intimidating. No matter how you decide to ride the waves, always surf with caution, make sure there's a lifeguard on duty, be aware of weather conditions, and never surf alone.

Technical climbing: This sport, which includes bouldering and ice climbing, takes the fundamental challenge of rock climbing over the top. Powerful acrobatic maneuvers, balance, and tons of muscular control are needed to scale smooth-sided boulders, horizontal overhangs, and icy glaciers. The goal: to overcome gravity, the elements, and your own physical limits to propel your body onward and upward. Teamwork with fellow climbers, appropriate use of climbing gear such as ropes, a harness, and—you guessed it— nerves of steel, are mandatory to excel as a technical climber.

Windsurfing: Wherever there's a water resort, the popular sport of windsurfing thrives. To sail their course, windsurfers stand on their board, using balance and upper body strength to jibe and tack (windsurf-speak for maneuvering in the water). The challenges are as numerous as the multitudes of boards and colorful sails, and as unlimited as the weather conditions. Variations include wave sailing, wave jumping, speed sailing, and freestyle surfing. A wet suit to protect your body from chilly water, boots or shoes with good traction, and a flotation vest are standard attire for this thrill sport.

While a reasonable level of fitness and balance will help, it's important to remember that windsurfing can be dangerous. Learn how to handle potential pitfalls like strong winds, tides, cold water, equipment failure, and gnarly wipeouts. Take a lesson, catch some fair wind (sailing lingo for "a breeze that suits you"), and you'll be skimming the water in no time.

Equipment

Each thrill sport needs its own specialized equipment. Check with a certified instructor or an adventure outfitting store for the equipment needed to perform these activities safely.

FYI

American Alpine Club
710 10th Street • Suite 100 • Golden, CO 80401
(303) 384-0110 • *www.americanalpineclub.org*
The American Alpine Club provides information and resources for rock climbing and mountaineering athletes.

American Alpine Institute
1515 12th Street • Bellingham, WA 98225
(360) 671-1570 • *www.mtnguide.com*
AAI is a climbing school that offers all levels of training courses and expeditions in snow, rock, and ice climbing.

American Canoe Association
7432 Alban Station Boulevard • Suite B-226 • Springfield, VA 22150
(703) 451-0141 • *www.aca-paddler.org*
This association certifies instructors, sanctions events and courses, and provides educational materials such as books, videos, and newsletters.

American Whitewater Affiliation
P.O. Box 636 • Margaretteville, NY 12455
(914) 586-2355 • *www.awa.org*
Dedicated to conserving America's whitewaters, AWA provides safety information on white-water sports and sponsors events and contests.

National Outdoor Leadership School
288 Main Street • Lander, WY 82520
(307) 332-6973 • *www.nols.edu*
NOLS is a school that teaches beginning to advanced students outdoor courses, wilderness education, and leadership skills. NOLS also offers a catalog with course descriptions.

National Scholastic Surfing Association
P.O. Box 495 • Huntington Beach, CA 92648
(714) 536-0445 • *www.nssa.org*
The NSSA is a surfing association for amateurs interested in competitive surfing.

REI (Recreation Equipment, Inc.) see p. 217.

Sierra Club
85 2nd Street • 2nd Floor • San Francisco, CA 94105
(415) 977-5500 • *www.sierraclub.org*
The Sierra Club is dedicated to conserving the national environment as well as providing information on outdoor activities.

U.S. Windsurfing Association
P.O. Box 978 • Hood River, OR 97031
(541) 386-8708
The U.S. Windsurfing Association is the national governing body of the sport and provides information on how and where to windsurf, as well as competition news.

Track and Field

Pros

If you can put one foot in front of the other, you're a candidate for the sport of track and field. The exhilaration of pushing your body to the limit, the discipline of perfecting your skill and technique, and the excitement of cheering a teammate to the finish line are all elements of track and field. With events to fit almost anybody's size, shape, and talent, variety is a big benefit of participating in track and field. There's bound to be an event just for you. The question is, what do you excel at? For those who crave the wind in their face and possess a natural gift for speed, sprinting or hurdling are ideal challenges. On the other hand, distance running suits those athletes who prefer more lengthy, and sometimes solitary, endeavors. The field events, which include jumping and throwing, demand concentration, athleticism, and a body built for power.

Track and field is about pushing your body farther and faster, and being convinced that you can do it. The events require a willing mind, the ability to focus, dedication to hours of practice, and unshakable determination. But for all their excitement and flash, track meets aren't just about winning medals—they're about inner victories, too. The entire experience counts . . . everything from having a great time to striving toward your personal best. As a member of the track team, you'll be an integral part of each meet, whether you're the team's voice of encouragement or the one who delivers a record-setting performance.

Cons

To get the most from this sport, you have to put a lot into it. This means lots of training, so if you're not into running and jogging, steer clear of the track. Perfecting the ancient art of throwing the discus or javelin also requires coaching, concentration, and practice. But imagine the beauty and grace of your finely trained body mastering a new challenge and sending that javelin soaring. Not everyone can be a champion, and it's important to remember that you don't have to come in first to be a winner. Set realistic goals so you can achieve them. Focus on making personal gains, doing your best, and experiencing the excitement and camaraderie that comes from being part of the team.

Body benefits

Lean arms and sleek, toned legs define the physique of a track athlete. The physical demands of each event help sculpt a trim, muscular body, and the training itself will definitely get you fit. Endurance events, such as the 5,000 and 10,000 meter race, burn body fat for fuel and require strength to go the distance. Sprinting, on the other hand, demands quickness for exploding out of the starting blocks coupled with power to fly across the finish line. For the throwing events, including the javelin, discus, and shot put, you need strength, power, and agility to sprint, spin, or slide, and then to throw each object. All in all, track and field benefits your whole body as it brings out the athlete inside you.

Variations

You can run, jump, throw, or do all three as an all-around athlete in the seven-event heptathlon. Check out all of these variations:

Heptathlon: In this competition, athletes earn points based on their performance in each of seven events. Over two days, heptathletes compete in the 100 meter hurdles, the high jump, the shot put, the 200 meters, the long jump, the javelin, and the 800 meters. Jackie Joyner-Kersee, considered by some to be the greatest female athlete ever, put the heptathlon on the map. She won the gold medal in the '88 and '92 Olympic games.

Jumping: Women compete in the high jump, long jump, and triple jump. Grace under fire is a fitting description of these awesome athletes in motion. After taking a running start, the high jumper's goal is to launch herself over a bar without knocking it down, and land in the pit (which is a giant mat). Long jumpers, on the other hand, sprint at top speed down a 40–50 meter runway, hit a board (marking their take-off point), and leap for distance into a pit of sand. Triple jumpers add a hop and step before the jump. Powerful arm and leg motions, good body control, and excellent leaping ability contribute to the height and distance jumpers attain.

Running: The running events are divided into sprinting, middle distance races, and long distance races. Sprints are short and quick, and include events of 100, 200, and 400 meters. Hurdlers race down the track and glide over obstacles (hurdles) as they go for the finish line. In sprinting relays, four runners each cover equal distances (called legs) and pass a small stick (baton) to one another. The two relay events are the 400 (4 x 100) or 1,600 (4 x 400) meters.

Speed and endurance combine to provide the necessary tools for a middle distance runner. Since middle distance races are too long to sprint all out and too short to hold back, these running events require strategy, speed, and excellent conditioning. The races include the 400 and 800 meters. Long distance events are just that—long. Stamina is key as runners compete at distances of 1 or 2 miles (1,500 or 3,000 meters), 10,000 meters (6 miles), or 26.2 miles, also known as the marathon.

Throwing: In ancient Greece, basic sprinting events and the throwing sports constituted the first Olympic games. A specific technique is associated with each throwing event, and the effort required to execute the moves is tremendous. Women compete in the shot put, the discus, and the javelin. The shot is a round steel ball that's 4 inches in diameter and weighs around 9 pounds. Competitors—bent forward and balanced on one leg, with the shot held under their chin—slide across a 7-foot circle, turn, and hurl the ball with all their might. Throwing the discus, by comparison, involves several spins across an 8-foot circle followed by a sidearm sling of the 7-inch, 2-pound disc. The javelin looks kind of like a spear. Holding it with one hand, throwers sprint down a runway, cock their arm, and let the 7-and-a-half foot javelin fly as far as possible.

Equipment

Since the majority of your training will involve running, what you'll need is a pair of running shoes with excellent support and cushioning. Some track events call for spikes, special lightweight shoes with four to six sharp metal pieces (spikes) in the sole for traction. Ask your coach which type of shoes or spikes are recommended for your event and the type of surface that you'll be training and racing on. For track and field, just put on comfortable attire and you're ready to go. Your team may require you to wear a uniform for meets, with a number pinned to your shirt. If your school doesn't have a team, check with your local parks department or ask a coach to recommend a club team.

FYI

Amateur Athletic Union See p. 242.

National Association for Sport and Physical Education See p. 246.

National Association of Intercollegiate Athletics See p. 246.

National Collegiate Athletic Association See p. 246.

USA Track and Field
P.O. Box 120 • Indianapolis, IN 46206-0120
(317) 261-0500 • *www.usatf.org*
USA Track and Field, the national governing body for track and field and long distance running, sanctions events at all levels of competition.

Walking

Pros

Hang up the phone, turn off the TV, and take a walk on the wild side. You can do it almost anywhere. Walking takes no equipment other than a decent pair of shoes and can be a relaxing, peaceful experience. All it requires is placing one foot in front of the other. Walking your dog, picking up the pace as you trek from class to class, or doing a few brisk laps around the mall are simple ways to give your cardiovascular system a boost.

Turn walks into a special time for quiet reflection or make walking a social event. Invite a friend (or a special someone) on a power walk around your neighborhood or local park. Think about the fun you'll have getting a group of friends together and starting your own walking club. The gentle nature of this low-impact sport allows for easy chitchat. Rev up your heart rate and visit at the same time.

Cons

Unless you own a treadmill, this sport often depends on weather conditions. When the weather is cold or wet, you may be tempted to skip working out. Walking at night isn't a safe idea either, so be sure to schedule a walk before the sun goes down. While some people may find long strolls boring, many consider it a great opportunity to clear their head and put some distance between themselves and the pressures of the day.

Body benefits

Brisk walking elevates your heart rate, burns body fat, and improves your cardiovascular fitness. If you keep up a moderate to fast pace, you'll actually exert more effort than you would if you broke into a run. Slow walks, on the other hand, are a great way to recover if you're stiff or sore from a grueling workout the day before. You can even vary your pace along the way by speeding up and slowing down every 5 or 10 minutes, which is called interval training. Maintaining good posture while walking and taking quicker, rather than longer, strides will tone and strengthen your thighs, calves, hips, rear, back, and abdominals. Pumping your arms as you walk gives you a good upper body workout, too.

Variations

Warm up on level ground, then head for the hills. Walking up and down elevated areas, or inclines like hills or sloped driveways, is a great way to intensify your workout. Hills and slopes make your thighs work harder and help develop sleek, strong legs, as well as improve your endurance. Vigorously pumping your arms while striding uphill also tones your shoulders and waist. Varying your walking terrain boosts the benefit of your workout, too. Surfaces like grass, gravel, and sand offer resistance to your stride that you won't find on asphalt or concrete. You may laugh, but walking backwards (also called "retro walking") is a challenging approach to a basic activity. As long as you pick your route carefully and avoid hazards, the perks of retro walking include an added workout for the abdominals, lower back, quadriceps, and hamstrings.

Equipment

A supportive pair of shoes designed to absorb shock is all you need. Canvas slip-ons are cute, but they provide little or no cushioning or arch support. Wear them on a power walk, and you're likely to end up with achy feet and sore lower legs. Walking shoes are available in just about every price range, so take your pick. A running shoe will also provide adequate shock absorption for this low-impact activity. For indoor workouts, give a treadmill a try. Some treadmills allow you to adjust the incline for a more vigorous workout.

FYI

American Volkssport Association
1001 Pat Booker Road • Suite 101 • Universal City, TX 78148
1-800-830-9255 • *www.ava.org*
Walking for fun and fitness is what AVA is all about. The noncompetitive events sponsored by this organization promote the health and social benefits of walking.

American Walking Association
P.O. Box 18323 • Boulder, CO 80308-1323
(970) 527-4557
The American Walking Association offers how-to videos and training camps for walking enthusiasts.

North American Racewalking Foundation
P.O. Box 50312 • Pasadena, CA 91115-0132
(818) 577-2264
Members of this organization have access to the latest information on racewalking clubs, equipment, and national races. Aspiring racewalkers can receive publications, videos, personalized training programs, and analyses of their technique.

Yoga

Pros

If you rush through your days feeling crazed, what you need is a little peace of mind to help you chill out. Yoga is a gentle, noncompetitive form of exercise and a super way to de-stress. Practicing yoga can help you relax and get centered. The word "yoga" means union and refers to the joining of the physical, emotional, and spiritual elements of life. This discipline promotes a philosophy of high moral conduct, well-being, learning, and balance. Yoga is all about doing what's right for your body, mind, and soul. Yogis (people who practice yoga) perform poses with slow, rhythmic grace and concentration. Don't be fooled by the nonaggressive movements of this ancient art—many of the poses are harder than they look.

Yoga is an excellent way to keep fit, it's easy to learn, and it allows you to work out at your own pace. But the best thing about yoga is that it helps you feel recharged both physically and mentally. Students can journey on the path to self-discovery and acquire a better understanding of who they are.

Cons

It's possible to strain your muscles, ligaments, and/or tendons if you stretch too far, too soon. To avoid injury, don't shock your muscles by knotting yourself up like a pretzel before you warm up your body. Move into the poses slowly and very gently. Never bounce or force yourself into extreme positions, either. Stretch only as far as it feels comfortable, and if you feel pain or strain doing any of the poses, STOP.

Body benefits

Here's what yoga enthusiasts can look forward to:

- stronger, more flexible muscles and spine

- improved posture and body alignment

- better coordination and balance

- reduced stress

- improved circulation

- ability to concentrate and relax more fully

Variations

There are many different positions to practice. Yoga students can master such poses as the Sun Salutation, the Hero, and the Wheel and the Bow. Once you learn the basic poses, you can make up your own routine to a piece of music that moves you. Many devotees enjoy meditation or prayer with their yoga session for a more spiritual experience. In the western world, hatha yoga is the most commonly practiced form of yoga, and it focuses on control of the body as well as the balance of body, mind, and spirit. Many physical therapists and health practitioners use hatha yoga in rehabilitation to help people stretch their muscles and strengthen their bodies.

Equipment

To get started at home, you'll need a yoga book with clear illustrations or a video with a motivating teacher (guru), and a pleasant, quiet space where you won't be disturbed. Yogis wear loose, comfortable clothing and practice poses in bare feet on nonslip surfaces such as a mat, folded blanket, towel, or carpet. To create a serene mood, dim the lights and play your favorite soothing tunes or nature CDs in the background. If you're interested in taking classes, you might find a teacher at a yoga center, health club, the YWCA, a hospital, a community college, or even a church or Jewish community center.

FYI

Ali MacGraw's "Yoga Mind and Body" by Warner Home Video
Led by yoga master Erich Schiffman, this award-winning video guides students through a beginning workout that's physically and visually dynamic.

Kathy Smith's "New Yoga Basics" by Body Vision
This video provides beginners with a thorough workout, including basic poses, breathing techniques, and guided relaxation.

Lilias! Yoga Workout for Beginners by PBS (Public Broadcasting System)
Lilias Folen has a PBS series on yoga. Her set of two videos for beginners explains the principles of yoga, basic breathing, stretching techniques, and how to make the most of each move.

Yoga Journal's "Yoga Practice for Beginners" by Healing Arts
The first in a series of videos by the *Yoga Journal*, this beginner's workout includes step-by-step instructions and a 52-page book to help students learn basic yoga poses and principles.

More Resources for Girls

Many other organizations and Web sites can give you more information on health and fitness, self-esteem, athletics, and other topics you may be interested in. Check out the following ones:

BodyPRIDE
www.bodyPRIDE.com
Based on the book *BodyPRIDE: An Action Plan for Teens Seeking Self-Esteem & Building Better Bodies*, this Web site features a chat room where you can get in touch with other teens, plus a Web pals connection. You can read stories about teens like you and post messages on bulletin boards. There are links to other sites with health information, but the emphasis is more on linking young people together.

Girl Scouts of the U.S.A.
420 Fifth Avenue • New York, NY 10018-2702
(212) 852-8000 • *www.girlscouts.org*

The Girls Scouts organization has always emphasized self-esteem, values, leadership, decision-making, and the importance of reaching your highest potential. Becoming a Scout (programs are designed for all ages, from 5 to 17) is a great way to pursue interests, meet other girls, and learn to make the most of who you are. GirlSports is a new Girls Scouts program that emphasizes sports and fitness activities. The focus is on developing a healthy lifestyle by learning to eat right, exercise, and cope with stress. According to the Scouts, "A healthy lifestyle is a personal choice. Making that choice and sticking to it can give you a wonderful sense of empowerment."

Ms. Foundation

120 Wall Street • 33rd Floor • New York, NY 10005
(212) 742-2300 • *www.ms.foundation.org*
The Ms. Foundation supports the efforts of women and girls to govern their own lives and influence the world around them. The Foundation is involved in female health issues (physical and mental) and developed the Girls, Young Women and Leadership program to specifically address the needs and concerns of girls. One of their many successful public programs includes Take Our Daughters to Work Day, which encourages girls to spend a day on the job with a parent or other adult they're close to.

Participating in the Lives of America's Youth (PLAY)

NIKE, Inc. • One Bowerman Drive • Beaverton, OR 97005
1-800-929-PLAY (Touch-Tone users only) • *www.nike.com*
Sponsored by NIKE, this organization is committing to making sure that kids have the opportunity to participate in sports and recreational programs. PLAY organizes sports clinics, promotes access to safe playgrounds, organizes community volunteer events, and works to provide young people with quality sports programs. PLAY also sponsors "Play Corps," a program in which college students volunteer as coaches for kids' athletics.

President's Council on Physical Fitness and Sports

Room 738H, Humphrey Building • 200 Independence Avenue SW • Washington, D.C. 20201
(202) 690-9000
Dedicated to encouraging Americans of all ages to participate in physical activities and sports, the Council strongly believes that regular exercise can improve an individual's character development, confidence, discipline, self-esteem, and well-being. The Council has a special focus on the nation's youth and works directly with schools to motivate kids to lay the foundation for an active, healthy adult life.

Women's Sports Foundation

Eisenhower Park • East Meadow, NY 11554
1-800-227-3988 (information line) • *www.lifetimetv.com/WoSport/index.htm*
Founded in 1974 by tennis star Billie Jean King and Olympic swimmer Donna DeVerona, this nonprofit foundation encourages girls and women to participate in sports, advocates on behalf of women in sports, sponsors research, and provides grants and scholarships.

Check out the Web site for scholarship information, the latest legal news, information on a wide variety of sports, listings for lots of other sports-related organizations, and brief biographies of women athletes.

YWCA of the U.S.A.
Empire State Building • Suite 301 • 350 Fifth Avenue • New York, NY 10118
(212) 273-7800 • *www.ywca.org*
The mission of the YWCA is to empower girls and women to work to eliminate racism. YWCAs across the nation not only offer physical and mental health services and sports and fitness programs but also employment services, crisis intervention, volunteer opportunities, and much more.

The Last Word

There's no "perfect" time to go for it. If you put things off or give in to your doubts, you're probably going to remain right where you are, feet plastered in place, wondering what you could have accomplished. No one ever succeeded by saying "I can't." Believe in yourself. After all, great things are possible as long as you're willing to try.

As you work toward your health and fitness goals, make these your words to live by (hang this message where you'll see it each day):

1. Live in the moment.

2. Set goals for your future.

3. No more excuses. No more saying, "I'll do it tomorrow."

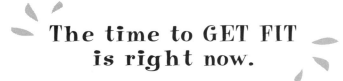

The time to GET FIT is right now.

Bibliography

Books

Abner, Allison, and Linda Villarosa. *Finding Our Way: The Teen Girls' Survival Guide.* NY: HarperCollins, 1995.

Bauer, Joy, M.S., R.D. *The Complete Idiot's Guide to Eating Smart.* NY: Alpha Books, 1996.

Bode, Janet. *Food Fight: A Guide to Eating Disorders for Preteens and Their Parents.* NY: Simon & Schuster Books for Young Readers, 1997.

Brumberg, Joan Jacobs. *The Body Project: An Intimate History of American Girls.* NY: Random House, 1997.

Cohen, Neil, ed. *The Everything You Want to Know About Sports Encyclopedia: A Sports Illustrated for Kids Book.* NY: Bantam Books, 1994.

Cooke, Kaz. *Real Gorgeous: The Truth About Body and Beauty.* NY: W. W. Norton & Company, 1996.

Covert, Baily. *Smart Exercise: Burning Fat, Getting Fit.* NY: Houghton Mifflin, 1994.

Duyff, Roberta Larson, M.S., R.D., C.F.C.S. *The American Dietetic Association's Complete Food & Nutrition Guide.* Minneapolis, MN: Chronimed Publishing, 1996.

Everest, James. *Name Your Adventure: Sports.* NY: Aladdin Paperbacks, 1995.

Folkers, Gladys, M.A., and Jeanne Engelmann. *Taking Charge of My Mind and Body: A Girls' Guide to Outsmarting Alcohol, Drug, Smoking, and Eating Problems.* Minneapolis, MN: Free Spirit Publishing Inc., 1997.

Graff, Cynthia Stamper, Janet Eastman, and Mark C. Smith. *BodyPRIDE: An Action Plan for Teens Seeking Self-Esteem & Building Better Bodies.* Glendale, CA: Griffin Publishing Group, 1997.

Jacobson, Michael F., and Bruce Maxwell. *What Are We Feeding Our Kids?* NY: Workman Publishing, 1994.

Parker, Steve. *How the Body Works.* NY: Readers' Digest Books, 1994.

Pipher, Mary, Ph.D. *Reviving Ophelia: Saving the Selves of Adolescent Girls.* NY: Ballantine Books, 1994.

Wolf, Naomi. *The Beauty Myth: How Images of Beauty Are Used Against Women.* NY: William Morrow and Company, Inc., 1991.

Journal

Havala, Suzanne, M.S., R.D., and Johanna Dwyer, D.Sc., R.D. "Position of The American Dietetic Association: Vegetarian Diets." *Journal of the American Dietetic Association* 93: 11 (1993), 1317–1319.

Pamphlets/Reports

American Association of University Women, "Shortchanging Girls, Shortchanging America, Executive Summary," 1994.

Centers for Disease Control, "Youth Risk Behavior Surveillance System," 1995.
——— . "Physical Activity and Health: A Report of the Surgeon General," 1996.
——— . "Physical Activity and Health At-a-Glance," 1996.

Food and Drug Administration/Food Safety and Inspection Service, "An Introduction to the New Food Label," 1993.

National Institutes of Health, "Consensus Development Conference Statement, Physical Activity and Cardiovascular Health," 1995.

U.S. Department of Agriculture/U.S. Department of Health and Human Services, "Choose a Diet Low in Fat, Saturated Fat, and Cholesterol," 1993.
——— . "Choose a Diet with Plenty of Vegetables, Fruits, and Grain Products," 1993.
——— . "Continuing Survey of Food Intakes by Individuals," 1994–95.
——— . "Dietary Guidelines for Americans," 1995.
——— . "Eat a Variety of Foods," 1993.
——— . "Eating Better When Eating Out Using the Dietary Guidelines," 1993.
——— . "If You Drink Alcoholic Beverages, Do So in Moderation," 1993.
——— . "Maintain a Healthy Weight," 1993.
——— . "Shopping for Food and Making Meals in Minutes Using the Dietary Guidelines," 1993.
——— . "The Food Guide Pyramid," 1993.
——— . "Use Salt and Sodium Only in Moderation," 1993.
——— . "Use Sugars Only in Moderation," 1993.

Index

Web Site Index

About the Authors

Tina Schwager is a Certified Athletic Trainer (A.T.,C.) and licensed Physical Therapy Assistant (P.T.A.). She earned a B.A. in Athletic Training from California State University. During her ten years of athletic training, she has worked at the clinical, Olympic, high school, and university levels. Currently, she works for a physical rehabilitation center, developing programs for athletes and celebrities. Tina is committed to a lifestyle of health and fitness, and to helping others achieve their fitness goals. She has 13 years' experience as an aerobics instructor, and her "Back In Action" exercise video—which she wrote, produced, and appeared in—is designed to help people strengthen their lower back muscles. Tina is also a public speaker who has toured universities, high schools, and corporations to lecture on topics such as fitness and injury prevention/rehabilitation.

Michele Schuerger holds a B.A. in Communication Studies from the University of California Los Angeles (UCLA). She has worked in the entertainment industry for the past 12 years and is currently employed at an advertising agency. She helped Tina write and produce the "Back In Action" video, and co-starred in the production. Michele's athletic career included eight years of competitive figure skating, and she continues to enjoy noncompetitive skating and many other types of exercise. She believes that her involvement in sports encouraged her positive attitude, increased her confidence, and helped her find the courage to pursue her dream of writing books.

Other Great Books from Free Spirit

Totally Private & Personal
Journaling Ideas for Girls and Young Women
by young author Jessica Wilber

Written by a fourteen-year-old, this book offers personal insights and guidance, journaling tips and suggestions, advice about being a girl, and more. Ages 11–16.
ISBN 1-57542-005-8; $8.95; 168 pp.; softcover; 5⅛" x 7⅜"

Taking Charge of My Mind & Body
A Girls' Guide to Outsmarting Alcohol, Drug, Smoking, and Eating Problems
by Gladys Folkers, M.A., and Jeanne Engelmann

First-person stories, current research, and clear advice empowers and encourages girls and young women to make responsible decisions about how to treat their minds and bodies. Ages 11–18.
ISBN 1-57542-015-5; $13.95; 208 pp.; softcover; 6" x 9"

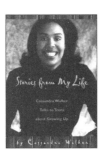

Stories From My Life
Cassandra Walker Talks to Teens about Growing Up
by Cassandra Walker

In true stories from her life and heartfelt letters to her readers and fans, a syndicated columnist and popular speaker encourages young people to believe in themselves, make good choices, and be winners.
ISBN 1-57542-016-3; $6.95; 160 pp.; softcover; 5⅛" x 7⅜"

Girls and Young Women Entrepreneurs
True Stories About Starting and Running a Business *Plus* How You Can Do It Yourself
by Frances A. Karnes, Ph.D., and Suzanne M. Bean, Ph.D.

This book teaches girls (and boys) how to think like entrepreneurs, take positive risks, and strengthen their talents. Ages 11 and up.
ISBN 1-57542-022-8; $12.95; 200 pp.; softcover; B&W photos; 6" x 9"

Girls and Young Women Inventing
20 True Stories about Inventors *Plus* How You Can Be One Yourself
by Frances A. Karnes, Ph.D., and Suzanne M. Bean, Ph.D.

This book will inspire and motivate all young inventors. Includes stories by successful young inventors, instructions on how to be an inventor, information about inventors' organizations, and more. Ages 11 and up.
ISBN 0-915793-89-X; $12.95; 176 pp.; B&W photos; softcover; 6" x 9"

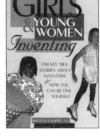

Girls and Young Women Leading the Way
20 True Stories About Leadership
by Frances A. Karnes, Ph.D., and Suzanne M. Bean, Ph.D.

First-person stories by girls and young women prove that anyone can be a leader, regardless of gender or age. Ages 11 and up.
ISBN 0-915793-52-0; $11.95; 168 pp.; softcover; B&W photos; 6" x 9"

Find these books in your favorite bookstore, or contact:
Free Spirit Publishing Inc.
400 First Avenue North • Suite 616 • Minneapolis, MN 55401-1724
toll-free (800) 735-7323 • local (612) 338-2068 • fax (612) 337-5050
www.freespirit.com • help4kids@freespirit.com